TAKE ME TO YOUR PARADISE

A HISTORY OF CELTIC RELATED INCIDENTS & EVENTS

LIAM KELLY

Dedicated to the late Brian Duffy, a dear friend and a gentleman. May he rest in peace.

CONTENTS

INTRODUCTION

Celtic can be said to shape one's culture, identity, ethics and even politics. For many, supporting the club is about more than watching the team for an hour and a half each weekend. It is part of the fabric of our social lives. We congregate on supporter's buses, sing songs of our heritage, read the latest news from Parkhead and like other Celtic authors, I personally write about the club too.

Following the success of my first book, Our Stories & Our Songs: The Celtic Support, I decided that I wanted to write something with a greater focus on the history of the club. My aim was to write with a similarly unique approach, looking at the Celtic story from an unusual angle. With that in mind, I began to draft up a few ideas in early 2016 and finally decided that I would focus on a combination of individual incidents and organised events throughout every decade of the club's unbroken existence.

Recent matches and trophy laden achievements are never far from the conversations heard in popular Celtic haunts. Yet beyond that, we converse about incidents such as freak red cards, ineligible players and chaotic trips to the continent. We discuss events like the Baird's Bar press conference, The Jungle's Last Stand and our stadium being used to host historic occasions. Fans relay tales of the incidents and events from yesteryear, sharing stories that have been passed down the generations like family heirlooms. The tragedy of John Thompson, Jock Stein jumping into the crowd at Sterling Albion or a supporter's function being held in dedication to James McGrory. Every Celt has grown up hearing a story of this nature.

The purpose of this book is to bring a selection of those Celtic related controversies, incidents and organised events together in one place. I hope it is an enjoyable read, which leaves you cherishing our lesser known history. After all, it is what makes us one of the most extraordinary football clubs in the world.

PAT 'TAILOR' WELSH

The story of Patrick Welsh is one of both intrigue and importance in terms of the history of Celtic. Welsh was born in the town of Killargue, County Leitrim, in 1848. He grew up to become a Fenian activist and it was his political action that eventually entwined him with the club.

The tale has its beginnings in the 1867 Fenian Uprising. The Fenian Brotherhood had been founded by Irish immigrants in the USA, less than a decade after the great famine. Its ranks were bolstered by the emergence of the American Civil War, in which thousands of Irishmen had taken part, fighting on both sides of the Union/Confederate divide. The experiences that had been gained in the battlefield encouraged a swell of volunteers to enlist with the Fenian movement; the organisation's name deriving from the 'Fianna' – a legendary band of warriors in the realm of Gaelic mythology. The Brotherhood's leadership wasted no time in attempting to strike a blow for Irish freedom when, in 1866, they carried out a series of unsuccessful raids in Canada (then under British rule). The aim of the raids was to seize the transportation network of the country, with the ambition that this would force the British to exchange Ireland's independence for possession of their Province of Canada.

The Irish Republican Brotherhood (Irish based counterpart of the Fenian Brotherhood, known as the IRB) soon decided to mount a militant insurrection of their own. The decision was taken following considerable unrest within the Nationalist community, which had largely been instigated by the suppression of The Irish People newspaper: the voice of the IRB.

The Rising of early 1867 was initially stifled due to a combination of poor planning and British infiltration. However, the latter stages of the year saw resurgent efforts in the form of a dynamite campaign and a series of raids.

A youthful Patrick Welsh participated in this effort, which, although ultimately unsuccessful in a military sense, led to the establishment of the Amnesty Association to which he later became Vice-President. The Association was a group set up by Isaac Butt, with the aim of gaining the men of the Fenian Rising release from prison.

For his part in the rebellion, Welsh found himself on the run from the authorities in the latter stages of the year. One evening he hid from security forces in Dublin at the docks in the vicinity of Pigeon House Fort, on the banks of the River Liffey. Welsh was hiding with the hope of boarding a ship bound for Scotland. However, he looked to his horror as he found himself being confronted by a British soldier wielding a rifle.

The soldier, who was on patrol with the North British Fusiliers Regiment, barked at Welsh: "Halt he who goes there?" Welsh instantly detected an Irish accent and pleaded, Irishman to Irishman, that he had no sinister intentions and only longed for a life of peace in Glasgow. The soldier, a County Clare man from Ennis, understood the plea as he himself had previously left home to join the army in England. Thus, at considerable risk to himself, he led Welsh to the appropriate ship. Before parting, the pair exchanged names. The name of the soldier: Thomas Maley.

Once in Glasgow, Pat Welsh served an apprenticeship as a tailor before becoming a master in the trade, owning a renowned business on Buchanan Street. The Irishman immersed himself in the local community and built some sound relationships within his local parish of St Mary's.

Enjoying his fruitful new life, the runaway Fenian maintained appreciation for the soldier who had granted his freedom. Indeed, the pair always kept in touch and after Thomas Maley had completed 21 years of active service with the British Army, he informed Welsh that he had started to view the prospect of life in Glasgow as a notion much more appealing than attempting to raise a young family where he had been stationed, in an Ireland that was still suffering from the effects of the famine.

Approaching his discharge from the army in 1869, on the invitation of Welsh, Thomas Maley and his young family headed to Glasgow, where his Canadian born wife's parents hailed from. Welsh was glad to be of assistance to the Maley clan and agreed to see to their housing in St Mary's parish until such a time that Thomas found employment. Thomas soon found a job when he was appointed Drill Instructor of the 3rd Renfrewshire Rifle Volunteers at Thornliebank.

The former Sargant's sons, Tom and Willie, (the latter being born in an army barracks in Newry prior to their move) embedded themselves into city life. Both had a keen interest in sport, becoming respected footballers; whilst Willie also earned the title of the 100 Yard Scottish Sprinting champion.

The aforementioned events proved to be of great import when Pat Welsh was among the committee that founded Celtic Football Club in late 1887. During a preliminary meeting between the founding fathers, the name of Tom was raised as a possible player that Celtic could attract the signature of. Welsh had vouched for the family and assured the committee that he would be an ideal fit for the club. Therefore, the decision was taken for Welsh to visit the Maley household in Cathcart, where Thomas (senior) had been transferred, with the accompaniment of fellow founders: Brother Walfrid and John Glass.

It is thought that the Celtic delegation only held intention of securing the signature of Tom when they knocked the door. However, Tom was not at home. The Celtic trio then began to speak with Willie and asked that he would ensure that his brother contact them with a response to their proposition of him signing for the club. As the Celtic delegation left the premises, Walfrid turned to Willie and said: "Why don't you come along too?"

Although not of the same ability as his brother, who had featured on occasion for Hibernian, Willie had played for Third Lanark reserves. Once his modesty and doubts over a future in the game were shunned, Willie agreed to put pen to paper for Celtic Football Club immediately. Upon hearing of the visit, his brother contacted the Celtic founders and agreed to join him at Celtic Park. It would prove to be the beginning of an enduring 52-year love affair between the Maley's and the Celts.

Pat Welsh himself went on to become Celtic's first Match Secretary, which ironically was also a position that Willie Maley took up, the latter having been invited to do so due to his qualification as a chartered accountant.

Welsh also made his mark beyond the direct Hoops domain. He was a much-loved parishioner in St Mary's, who was a member of a number of groups that held close ties with the club, including: The League of the Cross, the local conference of the Saint Vincent De Paul Society, the Home Government branch of the Irish National League and he was the leading organiser of the Connaught Reunion in Glasgow.

The following extract is taken from Patrick Welsh's obituary, which appeared in The Glasgow Observer on 12th August 1899:

'The funeral, which was a public one, took place on Sunday to Dalbeth. The cortege was a very large one, all the societies of the parish accompanying the remains to the cemetery.'

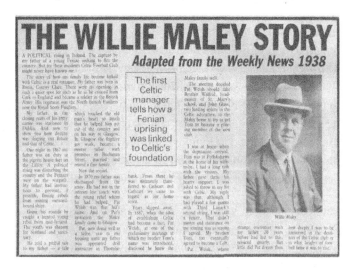

A newspaper article telling the story of Pat Welsh

Willie Maley's grave, a family plot in Cathcart Cemetery

Willie Maley's father (Thomas Maley) and mother (Mary Montgomery) are buried alongside him, as well as his wife (Helen Maley)

FOOTBALL FUNDRAISER

On a balmy mid-May afternoon in 1886, Brother Walfrid held what is believed to be one of his first major footballing initiatives. His hosting of friendly matches at Barrowfield Park, French Street, off Dalmarnock Road, Bridgeton, were the sequel to setting up the 'Penny Dinner Scheme' within the local community.

Brother Walfrid had been the Headmaster of Sacred Heart Catholic School in the Glengarry area of Bridgeton for 12 years. Upon his appointment, he was faced with a trio of issues – the appalling social conditions of Glasgow, a lack of school attendance and Catholic children converting their faith due to proselytism within Protestant ran soup kitchens.

Walfrid identified the school's attendance record as his primary concern, as with greater attendance the government increased the funding that it donated to each educational institution. A rise in government grants would mean that he, as a lead member of the St Vincent De Paul Society, could then seek to tackle wider issues with greater resources.

The 'Penny Dinner Scheme' was one of the projects that Walfrid established in the hope that children would be encouraged to attend school in order to enjoy a substantial meal. The payment of a penny was a suggested token to avoid embarrassment for parents who may feel a loss of pride at being seen to depend on charity, although payment was never compulsory.

To acquire premises for serving these school dinners, Brother Walfrid approached the local St Vincent De Paul

Conference for assistance. The Society obliged, renting a shop property behind Sacred Heart School, in Savoy Street. The shop was turned into a makeshift kitchen and was to be the first location used to provide food for The Poor Children's Dinner and Breakfast Tables.

Brother Walfrid worked closely with his confrere, Brother Dorotheus, who headed St. Mary's Catholic School in the Calton district of the city. Taking over a disused blacksmith in the school yard, Dorotheus also set up the 'Penny Dinner Scheme' for pupils at St. Mary's. As the year progressed, the scheme's success rocketed to such an extent that it became challenging to continue to satisfy the increasing demand, and other initiatives needed to be explored to sustain benefit for the children.

A mark of the problematic overgrowth of the scheme was that Sacred Heart provided 48,500 dinners and 1,150 breakfasts in its debut year. Added to this huge level of service was the fact that the school capacity had quadrupled and was to educate over 1,200 pupils for the school year of 1886. Similarly, St. Mary's started the first six months of 1886 by serving 26,421 meals to students, 17,707 of which were free of charge. Rather than make the suggested donation of a penny compulsory, the decision was made to reach out to other aspects of social assistance.

The Marist Brothers soon branched into football having seen the enjoyment that not only their pupils, but the working-class people of Britain had got from playing the sport. The pair set up youth football leagues for former and current pupils of each school, whilst Walfrid also founded a few teams of his own, which were associated with his other community organisations, including one outfit born from the literary society that he had developed for local Irish linguists.

The rapid growth of football attendances, particularly at Edinburgh Hibernians matches, led Walfrid and Dorotheus to spot a fundraising opportunity. Indeed, Walfrid had already invited Edinburgh Hibernians to travel to the east end of Glasgow on 26th September 1885, where a reserve team fulfilled a charity game against a junior club named Glasgow Hibernian. After that match, the Edinburgh side were fed and entertained by the St Vincent De Paul Society at St. Mary's Church Hall.

The initial match had been disappointing. On the park, Edinburgh Hibernians won 6-0 and off it a small amount of money had been raised. Undeterred, it was on the mid-May afternoon in 1886, mentioned at the top of this piece, that Brother Walfrid managed to get Harp of Dundee, one of approximately 40 Irish teams in Scotland at the time, to accept Clyde's invitation of a charity match at their former home pitch - Barrowfield Park.

Harp of Dundee stole the win with a late goal to make the score line 2-1 in their favour. This time the match's fundraising success was resounding. All proceeds from the event went towards The Poor Children's Dinner and Breakfast Tables, which was the charity within which the 'Penny Dinner Scheme' operated. Therefore, it was fitting that both teams were invited to Sacred Heart School for a post-match meal.

The Marists organised a further match on 18th September 1886, with Walfrid's Eastern Rovers visiting Glengarry Park to face a St Peter's Parish team that he had also become involved with, named Columba. Funds continued to roll in thanks to a crowd of over 1,000 on that occasion.

Interestingly, John Glass (who would later become the founding father who Willie Maley claimed Celtic owe their existence) had formed a club named Eastern Hibernian, who also locked horns with Columba in this period, thus bringing Walfrid, Dorotheus and Glass together within the footballing arena.

Another team of note at this time was Western Hibernians, who played in exhibition matches and were also instituted to The Poor Children's Dinner and Breakfast Tables. The Western Hibernians donned white shirts, black shorts and green and black hooped socks. In an exhibition match in February 1888, they fielded no fewer than seven of the 11 players who would play in Celtic's first match three months later!

Despite the charitable footballing connections between Columba, Eastern Rovers and Western Hibernians, it was Edinburgh Hibernian's defeat to Renton in the 1887 East End Charity Cup replay, that likely culminated in the final realisation that a 'big' Glasgow Irish team could be extremely impactful (see page 23). However, there is a lot of mileage to the theory that the very initial seeds of Celtic were sewn with the success of Walfrid's aforementioned charity match between Harp of Dundee and Clyde, a year earlier.

GRAND CHARITY

FOOTBALL MATCH.

—

CLYDE v. HARP OF DUNDEE

(Holders of the Forfarshire County and the Dundee Burns Club Charity Cups)

IN

BARROWFIELD PARK,

FRENCH STREET, OFF DALMARNOCK ROAD, BRIDGETON,

ON

TO-DAY (SATURDAY), MAY 8th,

KICK-OFF AT 4 P.M.

PROCEEDS FOR THE PURPOSE OF SUPPLYING THE CHILDREN OF THE UNEMPLOYED CATHOLIC HOUSEHOLDERS OF SACRED HEART PARISH WITH

FREE DINNERS & RREAKFASTS.

Poster from Walfrid's charity football match

BRIDGETON.

A meeting was held on Thursday of the young men of the Sacred Heart Parish for the purpose of reorganising the old football club of the parish. There were about 30 present who became members ; besides, several names were handed in of gentlemen wishing to become honorary members. After some discussion it was resolved to adhere to the old name of the Eastern Rovers, which had been raised through the exertions of Brother Walfrid. The office-bearers for the coming season were elected, when Mr. Jas. M'Cann was elected honorary president; Mr. John Gallagher, vice-president; Mr. Wm. Crawley, captain; Mr. John Cavanagh, vice-captain; Mr. James M'Menemy, treasurer; and Robert Stevenson, 30 Howard Street, Bridgeton, secretary. Messrs. John Malloy, James Connor, and Thomas Rooney were elected Managing Committee. On Monday evening they turned out to play a friendly match with the Eastern Hibernians, Parkhead, and after a pleasant game of an hour's duration stood the victors by 4 goals to 1. In the first half, with adverse winds, they succeeded in scoring twice to their opponents one, adding other two in the second half. The secretary would be happy to arrange matches for the coming season.

An article regarding Brother Walfrid's Eastern Rovers, published in The Glasgow Observer newspaper on 11th July 1885. Note the mention of Celtic legend, James McMenemy, as Vice-Captain.

GLORY TO THE HIBEES

When thinking of Celtic landmarks, St. Mary's Catholic Church in the Calton district of Glasgow immediately springs to mind. The club's association with the church building and parish stretches as far back as May 13th, 1870. It was on that date that Brother Walfrid was promoted to an assistant teaching position and was transferred to St. Mary's School, having previously been the protégé of Brother Procope at St. Mungo's.

By mid-1877 another Marist Brother (Dorotheus) joined Walfrid at St. Mary's when he became Headmaster of the school. The working relationship that grew between the pair was to prove pivotal in the development of The Poor Children's Dinner and Breakfast Tables. However, Celtic's more direct connection to the church begins with an event on February 12th, 1887. Edinburgh Hibernians won the Scottish Cup that day by defeating Dumbarton 2-1 at Hampden Park. After the match, a jubilant reception was held in St. Mary's Church Hall.

It may appear surprising that the Leith outfit decided against returning to the capital, but the adulation with which Hibernian were greeted in Glasgow was more than a match for the support that they'd become accustomed to from the Irish communities of Edinburgh. Among the admirers were leading Glasgow Irishmen such as Brother Walfrid and John Glass, who would of course play immense roles in the founding of Celtic Football Club.

Dr John Conway, who would later become the first person to kick a ball for Celtic, led the victory speeches. Conway suggested that "All Irishmen are delighted at Hibernian's victory today," and crucially that he "Strongly urges" his fellow Glasgow Irishmen to "Emulate their example, not only in social but in political matters as well, so that the goal of every Irishman's ambition – legislative independence of his country – will soon be attained."

It is reported in newspapers of the time that Hibernian's Secretary, John McFadden, responded with some final words before raising his hand in valediction. He thanked his Glasgow based compatriots for their "Warming hospitality," and claimed that "Imitation is the sincerest flattery." The reception then concluded with a heartfelt rendition of God Save Ireland, the unofficial anthem for Irish Nationalists at that time.

As the soiree departed, John McFadden is reported to have privately encouraged the Glasgow men to "Go and do likewise" (set up a football team for the Irish community in Glasgow). Dr Conway later said to his parishioners: "As it has become proverbial that imitation is the sincerest flattery, I think we could not please them (Hibernian) better than by following their example." Given that there was a far greater Irish population in Glasgow than in Edinburgh, it made sense to accept the gauntlet that had been thrown down, especially considering that successful football initiatives held within the city for The Poor Children's Dinner and Breakfast Tables were still fresh in the memory.

BROTHER WALFRID'S CONFIRMATION

The organised events in the previous two chapters of this book outline some of the key happenings as a precursor to the founding of Celtic Football Club. One of the final pieces in the jigsaw, serving as confirmation to the idea, happened through a stroke of good fortune.

A charity exhibition match was organised at Glengarry Park on 26th May 1887. This time it was evident that Brother Walfrid and an embryonic committee of men, who would go on to found Celtic, were behind the match. The organisation was much better than previous charity games in Bridgeton. A trophy had been offered up to the winner, which enabled the clash to be labelled 'The East End Catholic Charity Cup'. A major coup was also secured, when the competing teams were announced as Edinburgh Hibernians and Renton. The magnitude of this contest should not be understated, for Hibernian were Scottish Cup holders; whilst Renton held the Glasgow Merchant's Charity Cup (the cup committee invited some teams located on the periphery of Glasgow to compete) and Dunbartonshire Cup trophies.

The improved planning paid off when 12,000 fans paid entry to the fixture, a larger crowd than that which attended the Scottish Cup Final three months earlier. The score finished 1-1, meaning a replay and another pay day beckoned. The replay was pencilled in for the beginning of the new season, on 6th August 1887. A reduced, yet respectable crowd of 4,000 arrived excited at what lay in store. They weren't disappointed as Neil McCallum, who would go on to score Celtic's first ever goal, struck the net five times in a 6-0 win for Renton.

23

Following the match, the Renton and Hibernian parties were cordially invited to the Sacred Heart Boys Club for a post-match reception. There, it was revealed that the combined crowds of 16,000 over the course of the two games, had raised some £120 (equivalent of £15,000 in today's money) which was primarily donated to The Poor Children's Dinner and Breakfast Tables, but was also dispersed among charities in Edinburgh and West Dunbartonshire.

The Sacred Heart parish had witnessed a revolution of football for good. The football became a leather tool introduced to local school playgrounds as a means of encouraging educational attendance, whilst the charitable fundraising power of the sport had confirmed the convictions of those behind the foundation of Celtic. From this point, nothing could stop the founding of Celtic Football Club in November 1887.

(Please see page 352 for additional information in relation to the global achievements of Hibernian & Renton around the time that the East End Catholic Charity Cup took place)

CUP CHAOS

Having defeated Shettleston 5-1, Cowlairs 8-0, Albion Rovers 4-1 and St. Bernard's by the same score; Celtic went into the Scottish Cup Fifth Round tie against Clyde, on 24th November 1888, with a high degree of confidence. Despite such esteem, it was Clyde who started the brighter at Celtic Park, carving out several good chances in the opening 15 minutes. The bulk of the near 8,000 crowd began to relax thereafter as Celtic got a foothold in the game and looked increasingly dangerous. However, the Barrowfield side stunned their hosts when they took the lead just before half time and showed stubborn resistance to keep Neil McCallum and his Celtic colleagues at bay. The match ended: Celtic 0-1 Clyde.

Despite the game being described in The Scotsman newspaper as 'fast and exciting', Celtic lodged an official complaint to the SFA, claiming that the Clyde players had taken too long to change their illegal footwear, which meant that the match commenced late and finished in darkness. The club closed their letter of complaint with a request for the tie to be replayed.

An SFA committee meeting was held at 55 Waterloo Street, Glasgow City Centre, on Wednesday 5th December 1888. The post meeting report was published in The Scotsman newspaper that evening:

Scottish Football Association - Last night the monthly meeting of the committee of the Scottish Football Association was held in the rooms, 55 Waterloo Street, Glasgow—Mr Crerar, the President, in the chair. Attention was called to the circumstance that the Professional

Committee had several matters before it regarding which it had felt it had no power to deal: it was decided by the casting vote of the Chairman that full power should be given to the committee to deal with all professional matters. The Celtic protested against the Clyde being awarded the cup tie played on 24th November, because the ground was unplayable, and that for the last fifteen minutes, the game was played in darkness. Mr Harrison, the referee, explained that the teams started to play a cup tie with the consent of both captains, that for the last eight minutes he could not follow the game, and that the game was late in starting, part of the delay being caused by several Clyde players having to remove bars from their boots. Mr Reid (Airdrieonians) moved that the protest should be sustained, and this was seconded by. Mr J. B. Walker (Renfrewshire Association.) Mr Boag (Partick Thistle) proposed that the protest should be dismissed. Mr Graham (Renton) seconded. On a division, the protest was sustained by 7 votes to 4 and the tie was ordered to be replayed on the ground of the Celtic on Saturday first.

Celtic took full of advantage of being granted a replay and went 2-0 ahead through set piece goals, within ten minutes. Clyde bounced back with tenacity. A deflected shot found its way into the goal, via the post, on the 20-minute mark. By the 21st minute the scores were level! James Kelly of Celtic was in inspired form and regained the Hoops' advantage six minutes later, when he sent a long diagonal ball into the path of Tom Maley, who netted with ease. The score remained that way until the half time interval.

In the second half, Clyde's players showed the reaction expected of a trailing outfit, still teeming with anger at having to re-eliminate the Celts. Indeed, they enjoyed a lot of possession in the early post interval play, but it was in vain as Neil McCallum headed on target to extend Celtic's lead to 4-2.

The match was all but settled when Hart, Clyde's left back, suffered a major shoulder injury, which forced him to leave the field and his team to play with ten men (this was in the days when there were no substitutes). Celtic added another five goals before full time - only Chalmers in the Clyde net prevented double figures and the proverbial cricket score.

The tie's drama did not end there. Celtic had not necessarily prevailed! A meeting was called by the SFA, on Thursday 13th December 1888, to hear an appeal from representatives of Clyde Football Club. The meeting also discussed a similar appeal from Third Lanark, who had lost to Abercorn in a forced replay under identical circumstances. The discussions lasted some two hours before the votes on each case were revealed. Third Lanark's case was dismissed by 8 votes to 2, whilst Clyde's case was also rejected, by 8 votes to 7.

The Bhoys travelled to East Stirlingshire in the Semi-Final two days later, where they again rode their luck. On that occasion, Neil McCallum rescued Celtic with two goals in the final three minutes. The full-time score was East Stirlingshire 1-2 Celtic.

SCOTTISH CUP COMPETITION.
CELTIC v. CLYDE.

This protested tie was played on the former's ground, before 8,000 spectators. Celtic scored twice within ten minutes, and Clyde then twice in less time. Celtic scored a third goal in a scrimmage. The first half ended Celtic three goals, Clyde two. The Celtic had a slight wind in the second half, and scored immediately. Hart, a Clyde back, retired hurt. Celtic scored five additional goals.

Result—CELTIC 9, CLYDE 2.

Snapshot from a report in Lancaster Evening Post - 8th December 1888

FORTUNATE FINALISTS

The drama filled 1888/89 Scottish Cup competition culminated in a Final which was contested between the tournament's luckiest two teams. Celtic and Third Lanark had both won their Fifth-Round ties at the second bite of the cherry, having made successful protests to earn replays against Clyde and Abercorn, respectively. Celtic had also won their Semi-Final clash with two last gasp goals against East Stirlingshire. Therefore, there was forgivable expectation for pandemonium amongst the then Scottish record crowd of 18,000, who had gathered at Hampden Park on 2nd February 1889.

Heavy snowfall from 1pm cast doubt over the final taking place, but a pitch inspection by associate members of the SFA deemed it playable. The snow's persistence and manifestation in the turf delayed the 3pm kick off by 15 minutes. A hurried meeting was held in Queen's Park Pavilion, where the SFA committee discussed the conditions and again ordered play to go ahead. However, both teams had protested that the surface was unplayable in the meantime. A document, rendering the match a friendly, was drafted up, but it was decided to withhold this information from the crowd over fears of a backlash on the terraces.

The confusion was tangible. As far as the players knew, a friendly was being played, yet the authoritative committee had just agreed to consider the match a cup tie. Added to the breakdown of communication was the fact that the fans were cheering with fervour, for undoubtedly this was the cup final as far as they were concerned!

The perplexity of the scene is captured in an article from that day, which reads like a comedy script.

A meeting of the Association was called hurriedly in the Queen's Park pavilion, and it was decided, notwithstanding that the ground was by this time quite unplayable, that the cup tie should be played. Both teams played under protest, and it was understood that a friendly game only should be played.

The Volunteers were the first to appear on the field and received a hearty cheer. They were followed immediately afterwards by the Celts, who came in for even greater cheers. Some amusement was caused by the teams engaging in snowballing each other.

Once the game did get underway it was surprisingly entertaining given the weather conditions. Celtic flew out of the traps and smashed the crossbar courtesy of Neil McCallum's right footed thunderbolt. Third Lanark scored against the run of play though, thanks to a well-aimed cross and instinctive finish from Oswald Jnr inside the box. Oswald Jnr then got his, and Third Lanark's second of the game on the hour mark. An extract from a newspaper match report on the game states:

The Celts replied so feebly to this second reverse that the spectators realised that a cup tie was not being played, and as snow began to fall heavily, hundreds left the field. The play after this calls for little description, the players being barely distinguishable, and, as far as could be seen, play was ruling at midfield.

Just before Mr Campbell blew his whistle, the Third rushed the ball down and put on a third goal.

As shown in the match report, Third Lanark defeated Celtic 3-0. In doing so, it was not made clear as to whether they had won the Scottish Cup until the evening of Tuesday 5th February 1889. That night, the SFA committee assembled to consider the pre-match protests of the teams. An agreement, signed by both clubs before a ball had been kicked, was read out. Its content showed that a friendly had been agreed upon due to the 'unsuitability of the ground.' Despite the document, Mr Reid (Airdrieonians) contended that the SFA does not give legitimacy to agreements between clubs. By contrast, Mr Campbell (Referee) said that the ground was indeed unplayable and not conducive to competitive football. The referee's comments were unanimously corroborated, and the match was ordered to be replayed the following Saturday.

The cynicism of some suggested that rather than altruism and fairness, the real motivation behind ordering a replay was that the seismic crowds from the first encounter had fetched over £920 in gate receipts. Nevertheless, the second attempt to complete the Scottish Cup Final was held on Saturday 9th February 1889. A crowd slightly smaller than that of the previous week turned up, and the cynics were left abashed as a very large share of the combined £1711 gate receipts were donated to local charities.

On the pitch, which was varnished with sunshine, the frantic pace of play was testament to the occasion. The realisation that the destination of the trophy would be decided appeared to motivate Tom Maley, who weaved down the right before being chopped down by a tackle more akin to kickboxing than football. Maley dusted himself down and actually seemed to feel greater pain moments later when he missed from five yards with the goal gaping. Thomson of Third Lanark did likewise with a dreadful miss, before his side took the lead in the 25th minute following a goal mouth scramble.

Celtic had to wait until midway through the second half to draw level, when the ever-reliable Neil McCallum rose highest and headed a looping cross between the posts. Green and white striped joy had been sparked but the tie was very much in the balance. Celtic crafted several opportunities, with which they were wasteful. They'd pay for it, as Oswald Jnr returned to haunt them when he stole victory for the Volunteers with ten minutes to spare.

The cup finally headed home with Third Lanark Rifle Volunteers FC.

Cartoons of the Cup Final - The Scottish Umpire

QUILLANITE QUISLINGS

These days people may have heard the term 'malcontents' being used to describe the rebel shareholders of the 1990s. However, the term was originally used to describe those who would later become 'Quillanites', after the first Celtic AGM a century earlier.

Celtic's first AGM was held in Bridgeton Mechanics Hall on 18th June 1889. The hall was bursting at the seams with most members having much to be pleased about. Celtic had scored 217 goals in the 63 matches that the club had played during its debut season. The Hoops also had a trophy to show for their efforts, alongside the impressive record of reaching the Scottish Cup Final. Impressive though the footballing achievements were, the warmest applause was reserved for Dr John Conway's (Honorary President) announcement that Celtic had raised £421, 16s and 9d for charitable causes. To put that figure into perspective, the sum raised was the equivalent of £25,000 in today's money.

On the copy of the first balance sheet (shown at the end of this piece), you may notice that a man named James Quillan was among the first subscribers with a donation of £10 to help fund the tangible creation of Celtic Football Club. Quillan was the club's first Vice President and in the lead up to the AGM, he had been involved in a public spat with others on the Celtic committee.

News of discontent amongst the custodians of Celtic entered the public domain on 24th May 1889, when The Scottish Sport reported that 'a group of malcontents from the Celtic Club had met in a public house in Bridgeton.'

The newspaper also alleged that this so-called meeting had 'two matters under consideration':

1. *The present committee's mismanagement and the advisability of those present taking charge of the club.*
2. *Should they sever the connection with the Celts and form their own club.*

One of the self-proclaimed 'so called malcontents' wasted no time in responding to the newspaper. In an anonymous letter, he described the claims of this meeting as 'purely fabricated' and 'spiteful'. In contrast to this response, another newspaper by the name of The Scottish Referee, wrote:

While being neither desirous nor able to discuss the affairs of Celtic, we cannot refrain from putting on record our opinion that the scandals which have been too frequently raised about the club and out of which other people have been making capital, tend to show up the management in very bad light.

That dissatisfaction exists and has existed for some time among certain members of the Celtic is proved by the fact that a short time ago arrangements were all but completed for the formation of another Hibernian club in the east end of the city. A ground had been secured and over £500 had been raised in order to give the new organisation a fair start, when it was resolved to abandon the idea temporarily and await certain developments in the Celtic camp. These developments are expected in the next three weeks when we will discover the settlement to the question as to whether we are to have a new club in Glasgow next season.

Should the new club be formed its objects will be the public distribution of aid to charitable institutions, to widen the resources of the working class and to popularise the game generally.

The prime objective of the club – the public distribution of aid to charitable institutions strikes at being a hit at Celtic. That club holds the position it does towards charity and as we have always held, have made known their dealings with various funds to which they contribute. If Celtic showed the distribution in a public rather than private way the present dissatisfaction may never have come.

The annual general meeting of the Celtic will take place in a fortnight, when there will be no doubt some fun over the election of office bearers. Almost all last season's officials will be put up again and there are several prominent outsiders anxious for the posts, the competition is likely to be keen. Some of the players are, we believe, so strongly in favour of re-election of John Glass to the President's chair that they have in private declared that they will leave the club should he be ousted. This says much for Mr Glass' popularity in the playing section. Among the members he has not so many friends and no doubt he will have to fight for the honour.

It soon transpired that the malcontents were led by James Quillan and he outlined his grievances with the Celtic committee in the letters page of The Glasgow Evening News on 28th May 1889.

SIR – As there have been various rumours circulated in regard to the working of this club, will you kindly grant me space for the following remarks; - On the 2nd May, a meeting of the club was held to appoint auditors and adopt rules. I moved that old members should be admitted on payment of 5s, which was seconded by Mr Howie, and carried by 59 against 42 votes. By the rule as read- This majority (including myself) understood that new members were to be admitted on payment of 7s, 6d. On seeing the new rules when published we were surprised to find that instead of 7s, 6d, the sum of 12s, 6d was stipulated.

I protested – and my protest was duly noted – against members who had joined the club previous to 1st September 1888 being excluded from the meeting in direct violation of rules 10 and 24. On the 9th July, 1888 a meeting was alleged to have been held, notice of which was not given to me, although I then held and still hold the office of Vice President, at which another violation of the rules occurred, a resolution being passed making the entry money 10s instead of 5s. Without acting in any way, the part "the captious critic," it seems to me that twelve out of twenty four rules have been disregarded. As a sincere well wisher of the club and in its best interests looking to the good it has accomplished and in the hope that a bright and useful future is still in store for it, I take this opportunity of laying those facts before its many friends.

James Quillan – Vice President, Celtic FC

To produce such a letter regarding internal club matters was a very unorthodox and exceedingly unpopular move. Therefore, it is of little surprise that Chairman of the club, John H McLaughlin, responded in kind to set the record straight:

SIR – I read with great pain, but with no surprise, the extraordinary effusion our Vice President treats your readers to in your issue of last night. As the person directly responsible for drafting and printing the rules perhaps you will allow me space to reply to his misrepresentations. I will refrain from commenting on the indecency of an official in his position, who so loudly proclaims himself "a sincere well-wisher of the club," dragging into print matters which ought never to have been discussed outside of the club but will confine myself to a bare statement of the facts. The rule which Mr Quillan calls in question reads as follows:

"The annual subscription shall be 5s. New members, besides their subscription shall pay an entry money of 7s, 6d."

Now this rule was read over at the meeting on 2nd May no less than five times, and was moreover, discussed clause by clause, and this last clause adopted unanimously. If Mr Quillan didn't understand the rule at the time, it can only be attributed to his inability – which was quite apparent – to grasp the terms "entry money" and "subscription"- a difference he has since seemingly mastered. Through the rest of his rambling letter I do not care to follow him. His alleged grievances have been discussed at many committee meetings, and he has again and again been proved to be totally and hopelessly wrong.

Arguments and facts, however, seem to be thrown away on him, and I shall, therefore not recapitulate what has been explained to him a dozen times over; but for the benefit of those of the Celtic members who do not know Mr Quillan, and might therefore be inclined to attach some weight to

37

his vapourings; allow me to state – firstly that the alleged meeting on 9th July was the usual weekly meeting of the committee, and that if Mr Quillan was absent from it, it was entirely his own fault; and secondly, that that meeting did not pass a resolution to make the entry money 10s, but simply resolved that no new members should be admitted on account of the precarious condition the club then stood in, and this was done on the advice of our late agent, a fact which Mr Quillan is perfectly well aware.

What he means when he says that 12 out of 24 rules have been disregarded, I don't know – probably he does not himself – and until he explains it I shall take the liberty of regarding it as unintelligible nonsense; a fitting ending indeed for a tirade of misstatements, which, in common with the other ebullitions of himself and his friends in print lately, I can only designate as electioneering dodges of the club, or a desire to advertise himself, and to pose as "the poor man's friend," (a role he seems to have a special liking for), that has inspired his precious epistle.

John H McLaughlin

Glasgow, 29th May 1889

McLaughlin's strong rebuttal triggered a lengthy public argument between the pair, which other committee members waded in to. The debate, which revealed much about Quillan's motives at the time, raged in similar vein to the letters shown above, until the eve of the AGM. This despite the fact that McLaughlin had withdrawn from discussing matters in public on 7th June and opted to wait until the AGM to air his thoughts through the appropriate platform.

Throughout the exchanges it became deducible that Quillan's decision to delay the malcontents from setting up Glasgow Hibernian, was a tactical one, allowing himself time to build greater support for the notion ahead of the Celtic AGM. His motive for leading the malcontents away from the club in the first place seemed to be primarily based around management and bureaucracy issues. However, there could also be reason to believe that beyond the matter of rule changes affecting the working class, some of the malcontents may have simply disliked people such as John H McLaughlin being able to shape the ideals of Celtic. This theory stems from 3rd June 1889, when Hugh Murphy partook in the public mudslinging and aimed a few choice remarks at McLaughlin.

Hugh Murphy was heavily involved with the Irish National League and had been a good friend of James Quillan, thanks to their shared enthusiasm for Irish Nationalism. John H McLaughlin however, centred himself around religious groups and tended not to indulge in Irish political matters to quite the same degree.

The following is quoted from a letter that Murphy wrote to McLaughlin via the press:

SIR – although a long-time admirer of the Celtic Club since its inauguration, I may state that the last letter of Mr McLaughlin staggered me. Having copied as much American slang as his fertile brain contains, he makes an attack upon an Irishman who through weal and woe has stuck to "Ireland's a nation." I may tell him that Mr Quillan has had in the past – and, indeed, at the present time – more honourable positions assigned to him than any position the Celtic place him in.

Ironically, Murphy went on to join the Celtic committee in 1890 and the club continued to express an openly political identity. That said, personality clashes and fear of the political aspect of the club not being given continual attention, may have played a part in the desire for some to stray from Celtic.

The final factor to consider is the prominence of the temperance movement at the time. As many as 50,000 people, mostly Irish, were registered members of alcohol temperance societies in the city. In fact, some of the largest public gatherings that Glasgow has witnessed have been those of the Rechabites, abstinence societies and temperance societies demonstrating together at Glasgow Green. The cause of alcohol denial even united the traditionally Republican and Loyalist factions of the immigrant Irish, who marched side by side to deter enthusiastic drinkers during the Glasgow Fair and New Year celebrations!

The malcontents themselves are unlikely to have been concerned with alcohol issues, considering they often met one another in public houses. However, Celtic Football Club was blamed by a minority for facilitating the alcohol problem and Quillan may have outlined this fact as a basis upon which to attract supporters of a new Glasgow Irish club.

A priest from St Mary's of all parishes, actually stated that he "Wished the Celtic club had never come into existence," when commenting on the alcohol problem that was plaguing the east end! Another parishioner, Mr Owen McGerrigan, wrote to The Glasgow Observer and said that football was 'sapping the morality of the youth in St

Mary's, whilst also keeping them from their religious duties.' By contrast, a priest named Fr Carroll lambasted Owen McGerrigan for 'a cowardly attack on Celtic Football Club', in a letter of his own to The Glasgow Observer. Fr Carroll went on to question McGerrigan's authority to dictate his version of morality to the club, its supporters or indeed local Catholics in general. Fr Carroll's comments were further re-enforced by a departing clergyman of St Mary's named Fr Van Der Hyde. In his farewell address, Hyde said: "There has been an increase in membership of The League of the Cross (temperance society) at St Mary's by at least 200 members per half year, and the morality of the parish has improved since the advent of Celtic."

The League of the Cross, to which Celtic fans provided wholesale support, gave birth to the Brake Club phenomenon in 1889 (see page 354). In line with the typically complicated nature of Celtic's history, it was only a matter of months before there were references to Celtic Brake Club carriages being accredited as 'mobile drinking parlours.' The oxymorons that seem to embody Celtic's history were further evidenced by the fact that some Celtic players of the time were given proprietorship of public houses. Although, in the club's defence this was prior to the introduction of professionalism and thus there was little conceivability that Celtic could have attracted the top players (such as James Kelly and Dan Doyle) necessary to draw seismic crowds, without using the assistance of the licensing trade.

The Celtic committee would have to wait until the AGM to discuss these factors that were potentially motivating Quillan and his followers, who were now referred to as

'Quillanites' rather than the malcontents. Was it simply rule changes and management issues? Was it personality clashes? Could it be a battle for the soul of the club and were they planning to use alcohol abstinence as a means to build support for a rival club?

D-day arrived and after the formalities (which are alluded to at the beginning of this chapter) were complete – John H McLaughlin took advantage of the opportunity to resume the debate with James Quillan in person. Sadly, the debate revealed much less than expected but appeared to suggest that Quillan and his band of Quillanites had formed a clique.

The relevant minutes from the AGM read as follows:

...The secretary was then called upon to read the minutes of the last general meeting. On these being read, Mr James Quillan said he would move the adoption of the minutes if a certain rule, (pertaining to entrance fees and subscription money) were omitted, as said rule was not the rule as passed by meeting. (Mr Quillan read his motion). A seconder being found, the chairman received the motion. Mr Joseph Shaughnessy then rose and moved as an amendment that the minutes be held as a correct reflex of general meeting and be passed as such. About a dozen gentlemen sprang to their feet to second Mr Shaughnessy's amendment. A short discussion followed. Few, very few, could understand the position adopted by Mr Quillan, for as fast as one portion of his contention was cleared away, hydra-like another reared its head.

The amendment and motion being placed before the meeting and a vote taken, showed that for Mr

Shaughnessy's amendment 104 votes were given; whilst Mr
Quillan's could only total 17. This early presage of the
feeling of the meeting caused jubilation and dismay to
reign in each of the opposing parties.

The results of the AGM returned that Quillan's position as
Vice President was opposed and he was relieved of his
duties to be replaced by Francis McErlean from Belfast. Of
the 20 Quillanites, none were elected on to the committee.

Six days later, on 24th June 1889, The Scottish Referee
newspaper reported:

At last all is peace and quietness in the camp of Celtic FC.
The Quillanites have been squashed and the original
leaders of the club now go on their way rejoicing. The
doings in the legislative chambers of the Celtic are kept so
quiet that it is hard to say what the row was about. The
objects of the club are praiseworthy, and it is hoped that
the new offices and committee will work towards this end
as one man.

Undeterred, the Quillanites decided to explore the
possibility of relocating Edinburgh Hibernians to Glasgow.
Rumours of a splinter group from Celtic negotiating a
resettlement of their club, boiled the blood of Hibernian
fans. The Edinburgh club had already begun to view the
Glasgow Irish with a degree of contempt, for even though
Celtic donated £45 to Hibernian, it scarcely passed as
compensation for the signature of players, in the eyes of
Hibs fans. This point was demonstrated when the Hibees
support angrily invaded the pitch at Easter Road, whilst 3-0
down against Celtic earlier in the season.

In order to silence the rumoured move of the Edinburgh side, Michael Whelahan, (co-founder of the club) said less than phlegmatically: "Hibernian are the Edinburgh Irishmen and will carry on as the Edinburgh Irishmen. There will be no move to Glasgow or anywhere else." Subsequently, one local newspaper ran the headline - 'The men of the west are unable to come to an agreement with the men of the east.'

The Quillanites persevered, holding a public meeting in Bridgeton to announce their next move. Before a reasonable crowd, James Quillan revealed that he hoped to establish another club of the Glasgow Irishman, with an almost identical raison d'être to that of Celtic.

By the time the curtain was lifted on the 1889/90 season, a new team had successfully applied to become members of the Glasgow and Scottish Football associations. The club, established by James Quillan, had secured a six-acre site near the Oatlands district, south of the River Clyde, with the perk of an entry point from Rutherglen Road. The venue was level, drained and prepared for the erection of an athletic enclosure, complete with a grandstand and cinder athletics track. The arena would be known as Hibernian Park.

The roots and optimisms of James Quillan's club appear very similar to Celtic, yet there was one key difference in ideology. Glasgow Hibernians would have an openly exclusive signing policy, which meant that the club would only adopt the services of players from Irish Catholic backgrounds.

As Celtic represented the Irish Catholic community, whose footballers were generally not given the opportunity to sign for clubs such as Queen's Park or Rangers, the Celts themselves made little attempt to reach outside of the Glasgow Irish domain for players in the first season. However, the door to such possibilities was never closed at Parkhead and despite having an all Catholic team in the club's formative year, the lack of desire to enshrine a sectarian or exclusive policy may have played a role in some of the Quillanites wanting to depart the club. Indeed, Celtic would complete the signing of their first non-Catholic, a goalkeeper named Jamie Bell, in 1890. At that time the goalkeeping position was becoming difficult to fill and it was beneficial to look beyond the Irish community for footballing talent. A year later, Bell was replaced by Orange Order member, Thomas Duff, who was nicknamed 'The Cowlairs Orangeman'! Willie Maley further describes the psyche of the Celtic committee, who stayed beyond the 1889 AGM, in his book, The Celtic Story (published in 1938): *'We have always been a cosmopolitan club since our second year, and we have included in our list of players a Swede, a Jew and a Mohammedan. Much has been made in certain quarters about our religion, but for forty-eight years we have played a mixed team, and some of the greatest Celts we have had did not agree with us in our religious beliefs, although we have never at any time hidden what these are. Men of the type of McNair, Hay, Lyon, Buchan, Cringan, the Thomsons, or Paterson soon found out that broadmindedness which is the real stamp of the good Christian existed to its fullest at Celtic Park, where a man was judged by his football alone.'*

There were predictions from some quarters that the serious ambition of Quillan's Glasgow Hibernian could lead to a decline in gate receipts at Celtic Park. However, any hopes of this feat being achieved by the followers of Glasgow Hibernian, were soon scuppered.

Glasgow Hibernian's audacious launch in opposition to Celtic began with a glimmer of hope when they defeated Shettleston 3-1 in their first game. Interestingly, Shettleston were drafted in as a makeshift opponent, after Edinburgh Hibernians declined the invitation to provide opposition to this latest Glasgow Irish club.

From debut victory, nothing but desperate despair ensued. The club was eliminated from the first round of the Scottish Cup by Thistle, who defeated the Glasgow Irishmen 3-1 at Hibernian Park on 7th September 1889. A solid fan base was not mustered and as few as 500 spectators were among the terraces. Meanwhile, Celtic were prospering with crowds of over 20,000 on a regular basis. The writing was on the wall. Glasgow Hibernian were declared bankrupt quicker than a Buggati Veyron cruising down an open stretch of the Autobahn.

It may have been the end for Glasgow Hibernian, but for James Quillan the story was very much ongoing. In a remarkable twist of events, he was welcomed back to Celtic Football Club a short time later and he stayed committed to the Bhoys throughout the remainder of his involvement in football!

Loans

Mr. J. Brien	....	....	....	....	£30	0	0
Dr. Conway	...	...	...	....	40	0	0
Mr. James Quillan	....	...	...	....	10	0	0
Mr. James Doyle	....	...	...	....	10	0	0
Mr. John Higney	....	...	...	....	20	0	0
Mr. C. McGallagly		...	....	....	50	0	0
Mr. H. Darroch	....	...	...	....	15	0	0
Two Members per Dr. Conway				....	20	0	0

£195 0 0

Interest on Bank Account	...	...	....	....	1	0	0
Sundry Receipts	....	...	...	...	9	4	0

Celtic Football Club.

77 East Rose Street,

Glasgow, 12th June, 1889.

Dear Sir,

The ANNUAL GENERAL MEETING of the Members of the Club will be held in the Mechanics' Hall, Canning Street, Calton, on Tuesday Evening 18th June, at 7.30 prompt, when the Annual Reports will be submitted, Office-Bearers elected, and other competent business transacted. Members are requested to be punctual as the business will be proceeded with at the time stated.

Members will require to produce their Membership Tickets on entering the Meeting.

The Secretary and Treasurer will be in attendance an hour previous to the start of the Meeting to receive Subscriptions.

Yours faithfully,

JOHN O'HARA,

							869	13	1
,, Loans per Contra							195	0	0
,, Donations, Subscriptions, etc.									
Hibernians	45	0	0						
St. Vincent de Paul Society	164	16	0						
Home for Children	50	0	0						
Fr. Dyer, for Vestments for									
PoorHouse	5	0	0						
Poor Children's Dinner Table (St. Mary's)	27	0	0						
Poor Children's Dinner Table									
(Sacred Heart)	15	0	0						
Poor Children's Dinner Table									
(St. Michael's)	9	0	0						
Hand-Loom Weavers of Bridgeton	10	0	0						
Shettleston F.C., Subscription Sale	2	10	0						
Fr. Bird, for Barlinnie Chapel	5	0	0						
Hibernians	18	10	9						
Fr. M'Fadden Defence Fund	10	0	0						
Sisters of Mercy, Lanark	10	0	0						
Little Sisters of the Poor	50	0	0						
							421	16	9
,, Printing							134	12	2
,, Advertising							12	18	2
,, Secretarial Exs., Books, Stationery, Telegrams, etc.							46	7	5
,, Entrance Fees, various Associations							2	11	0
,, Furnishings, Tolls, etc.							23	3	8
,, Trainer's Wages and Expenses							69	18	10
,, Repairs, Washing, etc.							22	16	10
,, Allowances to Players for lost time through injuries							9	7	6
,, Insurance (Stand)	2	12	6						
(1st Team)	7	16	0						
							10	8	6
,, Marriage Present (John Coleman)							10	0	0
,, ,, (M. M'Keown)							10	0	0
,, Mr. James Quillan, Proportion of Expenses London Trip							2	4	4
,, ,, Season Tickets sold							1	5	0
,, Sundries							37	7	7
,, Balance, Cash in Bank	160	15	11						
Balance, Cash in Hand	14	1							
							161	10	0
							£3807	17	8

Hugh Darroch,   *Hon. Joint*
Jno. H. McLaughlin,   *Treas.*

*James Quillan's donation on the first Celtic balance sheet
and a letter to members ahead of the first AGM*

THE FINAL PROTEST

The Scottish Cup campaign had already entailed a multitude of mayhem and the Glasgow Cup Final of 1889 was no different. In the shadow of Hampden, at Cathkin Park, Celtic were up against national, let alone city, giants - Queen's Park, on 14th December.

The game was played at a vigorous pace with Peter Dowds having an early goal disallowed. Many players were warned for 'serious roughness' and both teams scored legitimate goals inside the first half hour. Celtic had certainly been the better side throughout the first half. However, the match exploded into controversy when, after some desultory play, Queen's Park went 2-1 ahead through a header by Sellar. Citing a push on the Hoops goalkeeper, the enraged Celtic players surrounded the referee to plea their case that the goal be chalked off. One Celtic player left the field in disbelief, whilst others threatened to join him. Nevertheless, the referee stood firmly by his decision to award the goal.

Play continued in similarly frantic fashion and Celtic got their just rewards with an equaliser in the 44th minute. Despite dominating the second half, the Hoops conceded again thanks to a 30-yard screamer from Allan Stewart. This time it was a deficit that the Bhoys failed to overcome.

Celtic immediately lodged a protest over the decisive second Queen's Park goal. Therefore, the Glasgow Association decided to present the cup to Queen's Park on a provisional basis, before reviewing the appeal. The cup presentation was made in Royal Restaurant, West Nile Street, during the evening. No Celtic players turned up, blaming their absence upon policy, but a few members of the club's committee appeared throughout the course of the evening. Mr A Kirkwood, President of the Glasgow Association, handed over the cup to the custody of Mr D. C. Brown, President of Queen's Park, and the Queen's Park players were presented with their victory badges.

The much-awaited protest of Celtic was heard on 18th December 1889 in a meeting room on Waterloo Street, Glasgow. Mr A Kirkwood headed the meeting. After listening to what the many truculent Celtic members had to say, the protest was dismissed, and the cup remained in the possession of the Spiders.

The minutes of the meeting close with the following statement: '*As a result of the decision in the protest by the Celtic against the Queen's Park, it is stated that the Celtic will withdraw from the Glasgow Football Association.*'

The remains of Cathkin Park (as of May 2017)

JOHNSTONE VIGILANTE COMMITTEE

At the time of writing, top-flight English clubs often attempt to steal away Celtic's top assets by making lucrative transfer offers, but it hasn't always been that way. In the days before professionalism was introduced to Scottish football, their already professional English counterparts used to send agents up to Glasgow on a kidnapping quest! A player would receive a knock at the door and have a professional contract shown to them by an agent. The player would then either decide to travel down south to the club in question or potentially be jostled into a car and taken to pastures new, in England, ahead of further persuasive talks. Either way, Celtic were never consulted or offered compensation.

The Celtic support in Johnstone, Renfrewshire, decided to act against the theft of top players. In early 1891, they formed 'The Johnstone Vigilante Committee', a unit of passionate fans, who would defend the club from the scourge of English agents.

Johnstone was an area with a strong Celtic connection. Three people associated with the town represented the club in its first year of existence: Willie Dunning, a goalkeeper signed from Johnstone Juniors – Patrick Gallagher, an early Celtic hero who was born in the town and signed from Hibernian – Peter Douds (Peter was born, married and died with this surname but is better known by the surname Dowds, which he acquired through a spelling error when becoming a footballer), a Johnstone born utility man, who was described by Willie Maley at the outbreak of World War II as "The greatest all round player the club has seen."

Shortly after the voided Scottish Cup Final in March 1892 (the game, which Celtic won 1-0, was made void as a result of crowd encroachment among the 40,000 spectators in attendance), Johnstone Celts alerted the local Vigilante Committee to the fact that Peter Douds had been spotted getting in to a car with officials from Everton. The Committee sprang into action and chased the vehicle, before running it off the road and into a hedge. Two men emerged and pretended to have pistols in their possession. They retained Douds and ordered the Evertonians away.

The rescue mission was successful, but a month after Celtic's 5-1 victory over Queen's Park in the Scottish Cup Final replay, Douds had left to sign for Aston Villa. He returned, via Stoke City, in 1894.

SINGING IN THE FACE OF LANDLORDS

The year of 1892 saw some of the earliest controversial events in Celtic Football Club's history. For four years previous, Celtic Park had been situated just 500 metres from its current site - at the north-eastern juncture between Springfield Road and London Road. That initial stadium had been constructed in less than six months by Pat Gaffney and a large volunteer workforce. However, the land on which the impressive original Celtic Park stood was that of private property, owned by Alexander Waddell.

The right to continue utilising the 110 yard x 66 yard pitch, complete with a pavilion, a referee's room, an office, changing facilities and capacity for 1,000 spectators, was costing Celtic Football Club £50 per annum. Despite the club's charitable endeavour, Alexander Waddell began to take note of the rising Celtic fortune and, rather iniquitously, raised his rental demands by some 800% from £50 to £450 per annum. Such demands were not feasible for a growing club like Celtic and thus the club explored alternative options.

The Celtic committee viewed sites in Springburn and Possilpark before taking advantage of a disused brickyard, adjacent to Janefield Street Cemetery. Productive talks were held with the brickyard landowner, an unlikely saviour, named James Hozier or Lord Newlands as he later became titled. Hozier had been an active Unionist politician, who had worked as Foreign Secretary and Private Secretary for the Prime Minister. He was an enthusiastic establishment figure, who was President of the Lanarkshire Territorial Forces Association and even went on to become the Grand Master Mason of Scotland in 1899 until 1903.

A deal for a ten-year lease had initially been struck, but James Hozier was later persuaded to sell the land to Celtic permanently. A lasting reminder of Hozier's involvement in the transaction can be found in the shadow of Celtic Park, off London Road, where Mauldslie Street (named after his former home, Mauldslie Castle) exists.

Once the club confirmed their decision to relocate, a large band of volunteers were once more required to construct the new stadium. 100,000 cartloads of earth were used to plug a 40-foot quarry half filled with water. Two tracks were installed, the outer to be used for cycling events and the inner to be used for running. Both were among the best of their kind in the world. A 15-tiered stand spanned the touchline, and a two-storey pavilion was added.

The new Celtic Park was officially opened on Saturday 13th August 1892 with the club's third, of what would prove to be annual, sports days. Newspaper reports of the time describe the weather that day to be of 'the most disagreeable kind.' Indeed, a thunderstorm hovered above the new ground at 3pm. However, the wet conditions were not enough to stop star attraction, Bradley (of Huddersfield), winning the 150 and 100 metre sprint races. Edinburgh distance runners, Hume and Hunter, claimed the top two spots in the mile race; whilst the day saw further distance runs and cycling jousts won by Englishmen.

A quote from the 1932/33 Celtic handbook reflected on the day: '*The old trouble landlord brought about a change of field, and it was in keeping with it, too, that a seeming impossible site was converted into a splendid enclosure. A case of leaving the graveyard to enter the paradise. A happy title did that pressman strike. The lessons learnt and the experience gained on the old monument to the loyalty and fidelity of the pioneers of the club – did they not give their labour to construct it- were not lost. The splendid pedestrian and cycling tracks, which surround the playing area on which champions the world over showed their paces, added another title: 'The home of sport.' It was an auspicious occasion and great day when the late Fenian, Michael Davitt, laid a fresh centre sod of turf from Donegal with a handsome silver spade presented to him by the club.'*

As seen in the extract from the handbook, Celtic invited Michael Davitt to perform the penultimate action of the day, when he laid the first sod of shamrock smothered turf, imported from the town of Mullachdubh in Donegal. Michael Davitt was the founder of the Irish National Land League and had served 15 years in a Dartmoor prison for 'Fenian agitation'. He was appointed Celtic Patron at the club's AGM in 1889 and was a natural choice to perform such a symbolic act in terms of extenuating the Irish identity of the club.

Davitt was accompanied at the new Celtic Park by MP Timothy Daniel Sullivan, who concluded the occasion when he turned to the crowd and sang the unofficial Irish national anthem of the time: God Save Ireland. MP Sullivan had penned the song himself, in tribute to the three Manchester Martyrs, who were executed after a sham trial on November 23rd, 1867.

The grand opening was epitomised by a poetic east end headmaster in the following way:

On alien soil like yourself I am here;
I'll take root and flourish, of that never fear;
And though I'll be crossed sore and oft by the foes,
You'll find me as hardy as Thistle or Rose.
If metal is needed on your own pitch you'll have it
Let your play honour me and my friend Michael Davitt.

Sadly, the turf was stolen hours after it was ceremoniously laid and the culprit was never found.

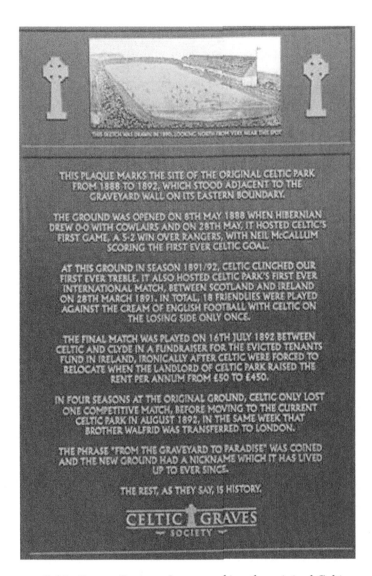

Celtic Graves Society plaque marking the original Celtic Park site.

FLOODLIGHT FAILURE

A myth has circulated the Celtic support recently regarding the club being British football's pioneers of floodlighting. In actual fact, Celtic were relatively late to have floodlights installed at Parkhead and experiments with the system had taken place in England as early as 1888. The myth likely grew from the story of Celtic's first attempt to host an illuminated match, during a friendly against Clyde on Christmas day, 1893.

The Christmas clash drew a crowd of 5,000 spectators due to the novelty of a football match taking place under the aid of electric light. Football had been played under artificial lights in Scotland before, particularly at the Edinburgh Exhibitions, but this was the first match of the kind in a club owned stadium such as Celtic Park. Some 16 arch lights were suspended above the pitch on wires, which were fixed to a dozen, 50 feet high, wooden posts. Meanwhile, almost 100 gas-jets provided additional illumination along the covered enclosure.

Apart from the obvious eyesore of multiple wires hanging across the pitch, the cables also tended to sag too low and interfere with lofted passes. Eventually, in January 1894, the issue came to a head when St Bernard's FC were beaten 8-1 by Celtic in the Quarter-Finals of the Scottish Cup. After the match, St Bernard's lodged a protest with the SFA, regarding the ball striking the electric lighting wires. By virtue of the fact that the ball had only struck the wires twice during the game, St Bernard's withdrew their protest, but maintained that their initial objection had been based on principle. Taking note of the clear failure of night time football at Celtic Park, the club swiftly abandoned the notion.

The next time that the Bhoys played a match under floodlit conditions was against Michigan All Stars, during a tour of the USA, on 25th June 1931. However, Celtic would have to wait until October 1959 to switch on their own floodlighting system again. The system was installed at a cost of £40,000 by Edinburgh firm Miller and Stables Ltd. Despite many UK grounds already having floodlighting in place, the Celtic board boasted that the Parkhead lights were the best in football and that the four pylons, towering at 208 feet high, were the tallest such structures in the world.

To mark the timely upgrade, the Hoops organised a glamour friendly with Wolverhampton Wanderers on October 12th, 1959. The club had preferred to bring Real Madrid to Celtic Park for the game, but the Spaniards wanted double the £5000 guarantee, which Celtic had offered them. Wolverhampton Wanderers were a welcome replacement, considering that the black country outfit were champions of England. 45,000 Celtic fans braved the rain to enjoy the new facilities, but witnessed their team receive a footballing lesson. The Englishmen triumphed 2-0, which subdued the Celtic support, who were already feeling frustrated by the rumour that Bobby Collins and Willie Fernie were only sold to Everton and Middlesbrough in order to pay for the new lights, during the previous season.

IRISH RACE CONVENTION

One of the greatest Scots-Irish men, James Connolly, once said: "The cause of labour is the cause of Ireland and the cause of Ireland is the cause of labour." He could easily have replaced the word labour with Celtic during the embryonic years of the club and nobody in Glasgow would have batted an eye lid.

Ireland and her contemporary cause of the 19th century was proudly fastened to Celtic Football Club from the outset. Before Celtic had been endowed to the diaspora in Glasgow, Dr John Conway stated that: "All Irishmen are delighted at Hibernian's victory," and crucially that he strongly urges his fellow Glasgow Irishmen to "Emulate their example, not only in social but in political matters as well, so that the goal of every Irishman's ambition – legislative independence of his country – will soon be attained." Dr Conway, who would later become the first person to kick a ball for Celtic, articulated that phrase as he led the victory speeches during a jubilant reception at St. Mary's Church Hall on February 12th, 1887. The soiree had taken place after Hibernian's success over Dumbarton in the Final of the Scottish Cup at Hampden Park that day. (See page 21)

Whilst most nations value full independence, Home Rule is undoubtedly the next best thing. In 1896, Ireland had not been afforded either privilege by the British establishment. However, the famous emancipator, Daniel O'Connell, had some success in his tireless campaign to improve the civil rights of his fellow Irish people. Most on the island had begun to receive slightly fairer treatment at that period in history, though the wounds of repressive penal laws, plantations and slaughter were not yet healed.

The liberal British Prime Minister, William Gladstone, attempted to pass Irish Home Rule Acts in 1886 and 1893, to no avail. His failure to grant Irish self-determination, thanks to Unionist resistance in the House of Lords, effectively stalled the struggle for Irish autonomy until 1896. It was then that the campaign was rekindled by the Archbishop of Toronto. The Archbishop, a Kilkenny man in exile, had sent a letter to Edward Blake. Edward was the son of the great Irish jurist and politician, William Hume Blake, who had swapped life in Wicklow for Ontario and became a leader in the Liberal Party of Canada.

Following in his father's footsteps, Edward Blake grew to become a QC and lead the Liberal Party. After a long political career within that domain, he became a chancellor of Toronto University before emigrating to restore his political work ahead of the 1892 election, as an Irish Nationalist MP for the constituency of South Longford.

By the time Blake received contact from the Archbishop of Toronto, he had been appointed to the Royal Commission on the Financial Relations between Great Britain and Ireland. The letter he received read as follows:

St. Michael's Palace, Toronto, 8th October 1895.
To Hon. EDWARD BLAKE, Q.C., M.P. Humewood, Toronto

My Dear Mr. Blake,

I regret exceedingly to learn that you are very much run down in health and challenged by some in my old land. I assure you that the leading citizens of Toronto wish to give public endorsement to the course you have pursued in advocating the cause of Home Rule for Ireland. The sacrifices you have made in the cause of Home Rule ought to have been more than sufficient to shield you from mean insinuations and vindictive calumnies and should also have proved to the most suspicious and incredulous your absolute devotion to the Irish cause.

Will Irishmen never give heed to the warning of our national poet, which is also the teaching of our sad history?

Erin, thy silent tear never shall cease,
Erin, thy languid smile ne'er shall increase,
Till like the rainbow's light
Thy various tints unite
And form in Heaven's sight
One arch of peace.

How is this necessary union to be affected? How are the Irish National forces to be focussed into a great centre of strength and power? It seems to me that to the solution of this problem, Irish patriotism and Irish statesmanship should now devote themselves. The Home Rule cause has cost the Irish race too many sacrifices, it has been pushed too far towards realisation to be now abandoned because of the difficulties that beset it. These difficulties are for the most part the direct result of personal jealousies, animosities and ambitions indulged in by certain of the Irish representatives, and doubtless they can be pushed out of the way by the united and determined action of the Irish people.

As an Irishman interested in the destinies of my native land, I trust I may, without presumption, venture to make a suggestion, which if acted on, would, in my opinion, be instrumental in securing that unity of counsel and of action

63

amongst the Nationalists of Ireland so necessary for the success of the cause they have at heart. My suggestion is this: Let a great National Convention be held in Dublin, composed of chosen representatives of the clergy and people of Ireland and of an advisory representation of the Irish race abroad. In that Convention let Ireland speak out her mind, let not her voice be like a broken musical instrument emitting discordant notes and jarring sounds, but let it on the contrary be clear, loud, and emphatic, insisting on unity and condemning faction. Let her point out and uphold the Parliamentary representatives whose methods and conduct she approves, and let her mark out and condemn those whose intolerance of control, personal jealousies and animosities have done so much to break the unity and waste the strength of the National Party. In that Convention let the voice of Ireland's sons abroad be heard and advice considered. They live under free institutions and are accustomed to the workings of deliberative assemblies and representative governments, and hence the advice and experience of their chosen delegates in the present condition of Irish affairs would be of the utmost value and importance.

A great National Convention, such as I venture to suggest, speaking with the authority of the nation, and voicing its fixed and unalterable purpose to labour for and to win the right of self-government, would give new hope and heart and energy to Irishmen at home and abroad, and it would be able to restore unity amongst the ranks of the Irish Nationalist representatives, to make of them once more a compact body and an irresistible power in the Imperial Parliament. When Ireland speaks to Englishmen through such a body her just demands cannot be long refused her.

Wishing you a safe and prosperous voyage to the sunny lands of the Southern Cross, and with sentiments of sincere esteem, believe me to be, my dear Mr. Blake.

Yours very faithfully,

fc JOHN WALSH,
Archbishop of Toronto.

The Archbishop's suggestion of a national convention was enthusiastically received, serving as the birth of a new movement, which vowed not to relent in its quest to realise the aspiration of the Irish around the world. An event aptly named the Irish Race Convention was arranged in September 1896 – held in Leinster Hall on Hawkins Street, Dublin. Thousands of delegates from Europe, Canada, USA and Australia attended the Convention, each asserting that the right to sovereignty be restored in Ireland. Renowned Celtic man and Fenian, Michael Davitt, chaired the meeting. Irish freedom's man of the moment read telegrams of support from Quebec and the National League of Great Britain, before he inspired the huge crowd in attendance with a rallying cry: "I have undergone over ten years imprisonment because I have been a rebel against misgovernment from the moment I was first taught that, next to my duty to God was my duty to Irish liberty, and I say here today that during seven long years of that imprisonment, under England's system of punishment, I never for one hour ceased to feel the pangs of hunger."

Davitt need not look far around the room to find familiar faces from his trips to Scotland. One such face was that of John Ferguson, an Ulster Protestant, who had moved to Glasgow and founded the Home Government Branch of the Irish National League. One of Celtic's most important founding fathers, John Glass, served as Treasurer to Ferguson's Home Government Branch. This is none too surprising, for James Quillan (see page 33), Tom White,

Hugh and Arthur Murphy, and John and William McKillop all held pivotal roles on the club's early committees, whilst simultaneously undertaking political positions within the realm of Irish Nationalism. Like John Glass and co., William McKillop had been a founding member of Celtic Football Club. However, his political work surpassed that of his confreres, evidenced when he ultimately became MP for North Sligo in 1903, despite living in Glasgow.

John Ferguson was called to the stage to have the penultimate word before Davitt would adjourn the Irish Race Convention himself at 4pm. Ferguson used the platform to explain that in spite of the initial problems posed by anti-Irish racism, his work in Glasgow had "Roused the spirit of Celtic kinship amongst the Scottish people, and today Scotland stands solid for Home Rule."

Ferguson continued with a lengthy oration, in which re-affirmed the task at hand before concluding in typical Irish fashion: "England in these days cannot afford to rule Ireland with the sword; England must appreciate Ireland, and here we offer her the hand of friendship, but we must have national self-government.

Oh brothers, gather close to keep
The land we'll win once more;
Division were the direst curse
That darkens now our door.
The God of Nations musters us,
And leads us forth once more;
Now who can break what he has bound,
While each to each is true?
And when the nations onward march
In better days to be,
Our Irish flag shall float
Amongst the banners of the free

Its colour then will speak of hope
Like sunshine's glistening sheen,
And all the world be better for our wearing of the green."

The heartening comments of this passionate patriot were met with warm applause from his fellow Scottish based representatives. Incredibly, ten separate branches of the Irish National League had travelled from Scotland. They found themselves joined by a delegation representing the only sporting consortium of the Irish diaspora at the event – Celtic Football Club. Celtic's deputation included John Glass, who was then acting as President of the club, as well as Treasurer, James McKay, and Secretary, Willie Maley. To send such an esteemed contingent to a convention of that nature was a strong statement that the club's early identity would reflect the community from which it emanated.

That the official representation of Celtic at the Convention had full support of other club members is deduced by noting their attendance under varying guises. Indeed, other Celts at the event included: Club Captain - James Kelly, Club Lawyer - Joseph Shaughnessy, former player - Mick Dunbar and committee men - Dr Joseph Scanlon, Thomas Colgan, MP William McKillop, Joseph McGroary and John McGuire.

Of course, much has changed in the boardroom since 1896 and the club no longer expresses these types of unassuming political views. Nevertheless, this particular event should be remembered by Celtic supporters when trying to understand the psyche of the men who steered the early Celtic ship.

A picture of the McKillop brothers' grave in Dalbeth Cemetery

WORLD CYCLING CHAMPIONSHIPS

The Sir Chris Hoy Velodrome sits in the shadow of the colossal Celtic Park stadium, but remarkably little is known of the connection between track cycling and Celtic Football Club.

Celtic Park's association with cycling dates to the early years of the club and its quest for survival. The club had spent its earliest years raising funds for charities such as The Poor Children's Dinner and Breakfast Tables, to which it had been instituted. To fund such ambitions, the Hoops needed to find additional sources of revenue to finance stadium maintenance and to pay functional staff. Cycling events were one of a few ideas that the club trialled in 1891, and they provided a vital lifeline.

A year later, in 1892, after ground rent rose by 800% from £50 to £450 per annum, Celtic relocated 500 metres from their original home to a disused brickyard - the current Celtic Park site. The move was a huge operation, which required the assistance of a large volunteer workforce.

The club's committee held a meeting to look at ways of increasing revenue in their new home, to fund floodlighting experiments and install a press box. The popularity of cycling was discussed and given its previous success with the club, the sport was looked upon as a positive revenue stream. With that in mind, a cement track, as opposed cinder (a feature of many football grounds of the time) was constructed. The track circulated the field and measured at three and a half laps to the mile.

Cycling events took place at the new Celtic Park from 1893, throughout the decade. Headline contests included

Scottish/Irish meetings. Scottish Championship winning riders such as R A Vogt even used to practise at the stadium. The decision to build the track proved a success and the vision to act on cycling's popularity was rewarded, with race attendances regularly surpassing 10,000 people. However, the pinnacle of Celtic Park's cycling history was still to be reached.

The Track World Championships had been held since 1893 but had yet to take place in the UK. All that, however, was about to change. The cement track, along with the facilities to accommodate enormous crowds, made Celtic Park an excellent choice to host the competition. The Scottish Cyclists' Union approached the club in 1895, offering £500 to hire the stadium for the World Championships two years later. Significant expenditure would be needed to upgrade the track to championship standard, but the club ultimately agreed once limited company status was secured in March 1897.

According to contemporary reports from The New York Post, Celtic spent the equivalent of £900 to build banks nine feet high, specifically for the competition. It was a bold decision by the committee to risk so much money, but their confidence again paid off when a crowd of over 8,000 spectators paid entry to the championships. The risk of spending almost double the earnings received from leasing renumerations played a key role in determining the constitutional status of the club.

The debate over professionalism and the soul of the club had been rumbling on at Celtic Park for some time. Yet it is a little-known fact that the prospect of holding major cycling events was also a topic that was used to push for change, by the more business minded committee men such as Joseph Shaughnessy. In particular, at a half yearly meeting in December 1895, Tom Maley attempted to mute discussion on the limited company issue, calling for a separate meeting to discuss such a serious matter, much to the chagrin of those in the room with greater financial foresight. Maley's obstruction was overruled and Shaughnessy said that limited liability must be investigated given the club's financial necessities. At this point, John H McLaughlin stepped into the discourse, remarking that £500 from the Scottish Cyclist Union hinged on the outcome of the question, for it would not be plausible to carry out alterations to the cycling facilities without the safety net of having limited liability. Nevertheless, the majority of members were sceptical of such a move, despite being in favour of hosting the World Cycling Championships.

There would be much discussion on the pros and cons of limited companies and the potential impact of such status for Celtic Football Club. The battle turned fierce with those wanting to keep charity as the priority being referred to in such terms as 'soup kitchen cranks' and 'dinner table soreheads'. As the Championships drew closer, cycling was the talking point at the top of the agenda again. On 25th February 1897, the committee told approximately 100 members that they were no longer willing to be subject to personal liability when it came to balancing the books of the club. The outcome of the meeting, chaired by John Glass at St. Mary's League of the Cross Hall, meant that there was a final choice to be made: either track improvements would not go ahead with Celtic in its current form, or the club would need to become a limited company to facilitate and finance the alterations. As previously alluded, the club was given approval to become a limited company following a meeting back at St. Mary's on 4th March 1897. This enabled the World Championships and future prestigious cycling events to take place.

As the years went by and Celtic Park underwent various renovations, not least after two fires, the look of the stadium changed drastically. Despite this, a flattened track could still be seen surrounding the perimeter of the pitch up until the 1990s, when Celtic Park was dramatically upgraded to an all-seated stadium with capacity for 60,000 supporters.

A cycling event taking place at Celtic Park in the early 1890s

WON BY RANGERS FC

In 1901, 8 Scottish clubs were invited to compete in the Glasgow Exhibition Cup as part of the cities' International Trade Fair. Celtic reached the Final at Ibrox Park, drawing 2-2 with Rangers in a match that attracted a crowd of 40,000 and fetched £1067 10s 9d in gate receipts. The Ibrox meeting room was the scene of a bitter argument in the aftermath of the game as officials from the Govan club demanded that the replay be staged at Ibrox once more. In contrast, Celtic's representatives insisted on the game taking place at Parkhead. A settlement could not be reached so the matter required the interjection of the Glasgow Association, who deemed Celtic's refusal to return to Ibrox as a forfeiture of the competition. Crucially, the tournament was won by Rangers FC.

Following the first Ibrox disaster in 1902, in which 26 people died and 547 people were injured during an England v Scotland international; (Rangers had been able to host the match by virtue of a single vote favouring Ibrox to Celtic Park) Rangers put on a competition with the trophy from the Glasgow Exhibition Cup offered as the prize. As English champions, Sunderland were invited to participate and were joined by Everton, who finished the season three points behind the Black Cats, in second spot. Scottish runners up, Celtic, were invited; whilst the champions, Rangers, partook themselves.

The competition, aptly named 'The British League Cup', was altruistically designed to raise funds for the families of the Ibrox disaster victims. In the opening game, a Celtic side spearheaded by Johnny Campbell, thrashed a Sunderland team consisting of nine Scotsmen (5-1 at

Ibrox). Meanwhile, Rangers scored two goals in the last ten minutes to see off Everton by three goals to two, in a replay at Celtic Park. The pair had drawn the first game 1-1 at Ibrox.

The stage was set for a Glasgow derby finale, though the match was delayed by a month until 17th June 1902, to coincide with the coronation of Edward VII. Cathkin Park was the venue for the Final, where 12,000 people were treated to a tense tussle between the Scottish giants. Jimmy Quinn netted a quick double for the Hoops, but Rangers were level pegging before the interval. This was how the score line stayed until the end of normal time. Interestingly, multiple newspaper reports across England and Scotland reported upon the game as a draw. However, Celtic did go on to win the match 3-2 in the final minute extra time, courtesy of the lethal finishing of hat-trick hero, Jimmy Quinn.

The Bhoys celebrated becoming the champions of Britain by parading the very same trophy that Rangers had held aloft a year earlier when they triumphed in the Glasgow Exhibition Cup. Celtic felt they had suitably earned the prize on offer by beating the champions of both England and Scotland. Thus, the club deemed the trophy theirs to keep. On the other hand, Rangers contested that they had offered the silverware as a mere showpiece item to display to the crowd. The matter came to a head when directors from Rangers Football Club visited Celtic Park to collect the trophy but were sent away in a less than phlegmatic manner. After legal exchanges, which are rumoured to have continued into this decade, the trophy remains in Paradise. It is still engraved with the words 'Won by Rangers FC'.

GLASGOW EXHIBITION CHARITY CUP.

FINAL.

GLASGOW RANGERS v. CELTIC.

At Cathkin Park, Glasgow, last night, before 10,000 spectators, Celtic started, and, after some even play, opened the scoring through Quinn. The Rangers pressed for some time, but could make no impression on the defence of Celtic, who added a second point, Quinn again being responsible. The Rangers retaliated vigorously, Smith scoring their first goal, and he equalised before the interval. The second half was devoid of scoring. Result : — Glasgow Rangers, 2; Celtic, 2. The receipts for the match were £314, making a total from the competition of £900, which goes towards the Ibrox Fund.

Newspaper report in Sunderland Daily Echo 18th June 1902

The Glasgow Exhibition Cup in the trophy cabinet at Celtic Park

CORONATION CUP TIE FINAL.

CELTIC V. RANGERS.

These teams met last night at Cathkin Park, Glasgow, to decide which Club will become owner of the Coronation Cup, which was won by Rangers during the tenure of the Glasgow Exhibition, and presented by that Club for competition with a view to the money drawn being handed to the Ibrox Disaster Fund. Both teams scored twice in the first half. No scoring took place in the second portion, and the match ended in a tie, two goals each.

Extra time was played — ten minutes each way. The Rangers had the pull in the opening period, but they could not score. In the closing minute Lonie essayed a great run on the right, securing a corner, which culminated in Quin scoring the winning goal 30 seconds from time amidst a scene of the wildest excitement.

The gate realised £265, while £49 was taken at the stands. This, with the sum previously drawn, makes a total of about £900 as the result of the competition, the proceeds of which go to the Disaster Fund.

Newspaper report in Dundee Evening Telegraph 18th June 1902

Dalbeth Cemetery - Grave of Johnny Campbell, who scored two goals for Celtic in The British League Cup Semi Final

PARKHEAD FIRE

The new Celtic Park was troublesome at times in Celtic's early years. Problems first arose with the stadium when the disastrous Grant Stand was opened ahead of a 5-0 league win over St Bernard's FC, on 28th October 1899. The stand required the road we now know as Kerrydale Street to be constructed, so that the huge gallery could link to London Road. It had a number of modifications made to it to try and overcome the issue of condensation. The fitted windows may have been a retardant against weather blemishes but when the stand was full, they had an unfortunate tendency to steam up and prevent occupants from being able to see the match.

Worse was to come on May 9th, 1904, when a separate yet similarly named structure, the Grand Stand, and Pavilion caught fire. The Grand Stand was on the north side of the field and ran the length of the pitch, as opposed to the Grant Stand which stood at the opposite side of the stadium.

The Evening Telegraph provided the following information in a report on 10th May 1904: *The Grand Stand was constructed with terraced seats rising backwards from the cycling track up to the height of 50 feet. It provided seated accommodation for 3,500 spectators, and had a corrugated iron roof, supported on steel struts and girders. The pavilion, which stood a little to the north-west of the stand, was a comparatively small building, being only about 40 feet by 30 feet and two storeys in height. It included the rooms of the club, a billiard room, in which was a table which cost £75; retiring rooms for the players, bathrooms, and other apartments. In the pavilion was a large quantity*

of what in football parlance is described as "stock,"
consisting of players' clothing, hurdles and other athletic
apparatus, and seats for the track, to the value of about
£500. When erected about ten years ago the stand and
pavilion cost about £6,000. The erections, however, have
from time to time been strengthened and improved to meet
the requirements of the Dean of Guild Court. So recently as
the International football match, which was played on 9th
of last month, the stand was completely renovated, and
having been officially inspected by the Master of Works, the
liners of the Court declared it to be safe and sound in every
respect.

The fire originated near the east of the stand and, fanned by
a slight westerly wind, the flames were blown across the
stadium with terrible rapidity. The wind carried sparks in
the direction of the Grant Stand and there was serious
danger of that structure also becoming ignited. Fortunately,
the breeze was not of sufficient strength to carry the embers
such a distance, but the scorched and blackened grass bore
testimony to the danger in which the erection was placed.

A local man, named James MacDonald, quickly raised the
alarm on London Road before the fire brigade were again
informed of the emergency by a man named Mr. Anderson
in Great Eastern Avenue. However, when the firemen
arrived via the small road between Janefield Street
Cemetery and the back of the stand, they were met with a
sight not too dissimilar to Blackpool illuminations. There
was no chance of saving the Grand Stand or the Pavilion.

The Grand Stand was insured to the extent of
approximately £2,000 but there was no insurance on the

contents of the pavilion. The loss to the club, therefore, amounted to £4,000.

The Pavilion next to the Grand Stand prior to its destruction by fire on 9th May - 1904

MALEY'S DANISH PUNISHMENT

Celtic were undeniably international from an early age. The club had already enjoyed two successful tours encompassing Austria, Czechoslovakia and Germany, by the time that the decision was made to embark on another continental expedition at the end of the 1906/1907 season. This time the Hoops would swap central Europe for Denmark - a new region with a fresh opportunity to exhibit the 'Celtic way' to football fans abroad.

First on the Danish menu was Boldklubben 1893, who Celtic disposed of by five goals to two. The crowd-pleasing outside left, Bobby Templeton, ran the show that day and stole all the local newspaper inches. Templeton had joined Celtic from Woolwich Arsenal for £250, just over a year previously. His wizardry on the wing justified such a price tag and made him a firm favourite with the faithful.

Next for the Hoops was a København Select side, who defied the odds and defeated Celtic 2-1. Although their team overachieved with their performance, the Danish supporters screamed for Bobby Templeton to continue his dribbling exploits throughout the match, such was the show that the Scottish international was putting on. Bobby's compliance with the crowd infuriated Willie Maley, for if such genius artistry did not result in goals then it was futile as far as the Celtic boss was concerned. Nevertheless, Templeton continued showboating. Dribble after dribble. Dummy after stepover. This defiant behaviour comes as no surprise when one explores the character of the man. Afterall, he was the footballer who once famously took a bet at Bopstock & Wombwell menagerie in New City Road, to step into a lion's cage and twist its tail!

An incensed Maley, whose Celtic team had travelled to Denmark without a recognised goalkeeper, punished Templeton by placing him between the sticks for the remaining two matches of the tour. Celtic oversaw the same København Select side 5-1 and 4-2 respectively in those closing games, yet by the time the squad had returned to Glasgow, Willie Maley had announced that Bobby Templeton would be transfer listed. Despite being surplus to requirements, he did play a handful of matches at the beginning of the new season. Although, he was finally sold when an offer from Kilmarnock was accepted on 18th October 1907.

THE ORIGINAL HAMPDEN RIOT

When thinking of the rivalry between Celtic and Rangers, 'the Hampden riot' of 1980 is rarely far from one's thoughts. However, this fixture has a history of mayhem at the national stadium, which stretches back much further. Many historians deem the original Hampden riot, on 17th April 1909, to be a major development in the rivalry. On this occasion, the Glasgow clubs were playing out a Scottish Cup Final replay. The match finished 1-1 and everybody had assumed that there would be extra time, including the players, who stayed on the pitch. However, this assumption did not take in to account the fact that SFA rules did not permit extra time until a second replay had been played.

Rumours of conspiracy quickly spread around the stadium, sending fans on both sides into splenetic rage with the conviction that the game had been deliberately drawn to ensure a third pay day. Many supporters spilled onto the pitch to remonstrate, charging in the direction of the changing rooms, where the players had sharply headed. So palpable was the anger among the pitch invaders that dozens of police officers had to use truncheons to stop them from advancing beyond the field.

Suddenly, bedlam erupted! Wooden terracing was set alight, goal posts were hauled down and punches flew at intervening police officers. The rioters set pay boxes ablaze and slashed the fire brigade's hoses when they arrived at the ground. Turf was also uprooted, and ambulance staff were even assaulted when trying to treat injured police officers.

Reinforcements had to be called from the local constabulary, yet the relief they brought in managing to move the mobs away from the stadium was only temporary, as rioting continued for a further two hours on the streets of Glasgow's south side.

Disorder on such a large scale was never going to avoid punishment. Indeed, the SFA called an urgent meeting on the Monday morning to decide upon appropriate action. The meeting revealed that the rioters had used knives and bottles as their weapons of choice, which had injured no fewer than 54 police officers. The committee also calculated total damage costs at £800. The SFA decided to donate £500 to Queen's Park FC to repair their Hampden Park Stadium, whilst Celtic and Rangers were both fined £150 each to split the remaining cost of repairs. Considering that the match tickets raised £4000, this was a pittance for each club to pay. Following payment of the fines, representatives from both clubs made it clear to the SFA that they were against holding another replay. Therefore, the 1909 Scottish Cup was made void.

A REMORSEFUL VASE

'Good things come to those who wait' is a phrase extolling the virtue of patience. Celtic certainly exemplified this proverb during The Budapest Cup shenanigans of 1914. It was during that year that Celtic had sealed a league and cup double, whilst Burnley had won the FA Cup in England. Both clubs happened to be touring Hungary prior to the beginning of the 1914/1915 season and as British teams were regarded the finest in the world at the time, Ferencvaros Football Club took advantage of these top side's visiting their home city.

Ferencvaros decided to hold a charitable match between Celtic and Burnley at their FTC Stadion for the benefit of Balkan War refugees. A silver trophy in the shape of a lighthouse was donated by Hungary News newspaper, to be awarded to the winner of the clash, which had been alluringly named 'The Budapest Cup'. Astonishingly, the hosts didn't notify Celtic of the match in advance, but fortunately the club were able to shuffle their plans to fulfil the fixture when the late news came through.

The game took place amid scorching conditions. The pitch was dry and the crowd of close to 10,000 saw an aggressive encounter. Jimmy 'Napoleon' McMenemy put Celtic in front through a 20th minute penalty. Burnley then equalised with a penalty of their own in the second half, after 'Sunny' Jim Young handled in the box. The match finished that way, with the game tied at 1-1.

Reports in the press allude to the fact that Celtic refused to play extra time. The Hoops, weary in the mid-May sun, instead opted to travel to Burnley at a later date, where a replay could be held, and the Hungarians agreed to forward the trophy to the eventual victors.

On September 14th (1914), four months after the original game and almost seven weeks after the outbreak of World War I, Celtic finally travelled to Turf Moor. The Bhoys took the game to Burnley and dominated the first half without tangible reward. At the break, Peter Johnstone had to be withdrawn from the Celtic team with a foot injury and due to there being no substitutes in those days, the Hoops played on with ten men. Nevertheless, Jimmy McColl netted a blinder just shy of the hour mark and the ever-reliable Patsy Gallacher doubled Celtic's lead ten minutes later. As the game drew to its close, Burnley livened things up when they pegged a goal back from the penalty spot. It wasn't enough for the Clarets though, as Celtic held out for a 2-1 win and the unofficial title of 'World Club Champions.'

Speculation ranges in regard to the aftermath of Celtic's victory. It is clear that a share of the gate receipts were sent from Turf Moor to Hungarian charities and it is also unquestionable that the trophy was not sent over from Hungary as promised. However, there is ambiguity as to the reason why that silver lighthouse did not find its way to Burnley. Some say it was raffled off to raise funds for the Red Cross, whereas others claim that the trophy was lost after the outbreak of the war. Regardless of the reasons, all would be atoned for, in May 1988, almost exactly 74 years after the original Budapest Cup clash took place in Hungary. It was then that the Chairman of Ferencvaros, Zoltan Magyar, marked Celtic's centenary celebrations by presenting his Parkhead counterpart (Jack McGinn) with a large majestic vase in recognition of their triumph. It may not have been a silver lighthouse trophy, but it certainly made amends for the unanswered issue in 1914.

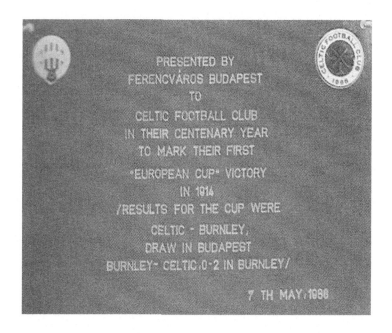

An engraved gift, along with the vase, presented to Celtic 74 years after winning The Budapest Cup. The result incorrectly shows a 2-0 win, as opposed 2-1.

BRITAIN'S BRAVEST

On 12th June 1915, near Givenchy-lès-la-Bassée (northern France), William Angus and the men of D Company were ordered to attack. Led by Lieutenant James Martin, the troops launched a night time offensive designed to capture the enemy trench in the early hours of the morning. As the bombing party approached enemy lines, they horrifyingly found the earth littered with landmines. An explosion quickly followed, causing a 4.5 metre hole to form across the slope in front of the German position. Lieutenant James Martin was missing. As the smoke cleared and the sun rose, Martin could be seen lying yards from the German trench. It is said that the Germans aimed a periscope at him, stalking him as if he were carrion being watched by a ravenous vulture. Only the Lieutenant's position being too close to the parapet to be shot, meant that British troops, by now retreated to their own trench, were spared the sight of his execution.

A rescue plan was denied on the basis that crossing the 64-metre stretch, sandwiched between the opposing trenches, in the daylight, was analogous to a suicide mission. There was no hope... until Martin made an astonishing attempt to crawl back to his trench. The Germans opened fire and a response was instantly issued in kind.

Owing to the bullet scattered sky, William Angus insisted that he utilise the opportunity to go and retrieve Lieutenant James Martin. His stand-in officer initially refused the notion, but bravery and stubbornness were concomitant with Angus' character. Angus forced senior leaders to rethink the order, stealthily leapt the parapet and crawled along the chilling bog referred to as 'no man's land'. The

Royal Scots' commanding officer wrote about the scene in a letter to the soldier's father: *It seemed so hopeless. With a rope 50 yards long, your son crept out. Owing to the clever way he crept, he got to Martin without being seen. Martin staggered to his feet and, directed by Angus, made a dash for our line.*

The pair were eventually spotted by enemy forces. Angus shielded Martin and paid the price by having multiple grenades thrown at him. Against a backdrop of smoke, bombs and bullets, the men ran for their lives. When they finally reached safety, Angus lowered his colleague and sprinted to another point of the trench so as to divert enemy fire. Lieutenant Martin was in remarkably good shape for a man who had been thrown across the soil by an explosive device. William Angus was less fortunate. He had 40 gunshot wounds, shrapnel injuries to his legs, arms, head and shoulders, whilst he had also lost his sight in one eye thanks to a grenade blast. His wounds were patched up in a military hospital in Boulogne-sur-Mer and he extraordinarily survived. It was from that hospital bed that Angus wrote a short letter to his sister:

I am still in France and they might keep me here for some time yet. They are doing their best to save the sight in my left eye. The best eye specialists in the world are in this hospital. They have given me great hopes of getting my sight all right, so I will just have to hope for the best. My other wounds are getting on all right, but it will be a long time before I am able to get up and walk about. However, I will get on all right, never fear, and some day your battered old brother will come back to Carluke as cheery as ever.

William Angus was born in Carluke, three months before Celtic played their first ever match. After leaving school he found work as a miner but was soon able to ply his trade on a part time basis at Carluke Football Club. He moved on to Celtic in 1911 but failed to break in to the first team. He was released by the Hoops in 1914 and joined Wishaw Thistle, where he was made club captain until war was declared in July. As a member of the local Territorial Battalion of the Highland Light Infantry, he was sent to Dunoon to undergo training. Upon hearing of the loss of many men in France, Angus volunteered to transfer to the 8th Battalion Royal Scots and was mobilised immediately.

Two months after his heroic deed in France, Carluke's streets were packed at Angus' homecoming ceremony. Flanked by Lieutenant James Martin and the Lord Newlands, he received a hero's welcome. His colleague, Lieutenant Colonel Gemmill, described his act as "The bravest in the history of the British Army." Willie Maley, who was then Secretary of Celtic, also remarked: "No club ever had a more willing or conscientious player, and one who always showed that fine spirit." Yet perhaps it is most telling to quote William Angus himself, when asked why he risked his life to save Lieutenant Martin: "I had to go back to Carluke. I could not return if I left someone from Carluke to die there."

The ceremony, noted above, came weeks after Angus had been presented with the Victoria Cross award by King George V at Buckingham Palace, on 30th August 1915. When the King commented on his 40 injuries, Angus was said to have answered "Aye sir, but only 13 were serious." At that same ceremony, Lieutenant Martin also spoke a few words in front of the King: "I know you will bear with me if I do not make a long speech. My heart is too full for words. When I lay on the German parapet that Saturday in June my plight seemed hopeless, but Angus at the risk of his life came out and saved me. Carluke may well be proud of her hero. For it was an act of bravery second to none in the annals of the British Army. Corporal Angus, I thank you from the bottom of my heart. I hope you will soon be restored to your wanted health and strength and that you may be long spared to wear this watch and chain which I ask you to please accept as a small memento of that day."

Once settled back into normal life, William Angus was invited to Celtic Park and Ibrox, where he received standing ovations. Following the war, he began a new career as a goods carrier and became President of Carluke Rovers FC, a position he held until his death in 1959. Throughout each year of his life, from 1916 onwards, he received a telegram of thanks from Lieutenant Martin's family, which often opened with an unfamiliar line in Celtic circles: 'Congratulations on the 12th'. Meanwhile, Angus was also bought an annual gift on the anniversary of the incident, by those within the Racecourse Betting Control Board, on which he served as a Master of Works.

A commemorative stone for William Angus in Carluke

William Angus at hospital in France

LADIES BATTLE WITHIN THE WAR

Celtic Park was a focal point in Scottish society when it came to the war effort. The club played their part by holding recruitment rallies at the stadium and even putting on an exhibition of trench warfare ahead of one match. Football was encouraged to go ahead whenever possible to boost morale during this turbulent period, and the pressure to fulfil fixtures was so intense that Celtic had to play two games in a day on 15th April 1916. The Hoops defeated Raith Rovers 6-0 at Celtic Park in the morning (reaching a domestic record 104 goals in 34 games, which eclipsed Falkirk's 103 goal tally amassed in the 1907/08 season), before beating Motherwell 3-1 at Fir Park in the afternoon.

Some solely attribute the club's public support for the war effort to the global struggle against tyranny. Whilst this was true for many Celtic fans and players enlisting with the forces, the politics surrounding Irish Nationalism at the time should not be overlooked either. Celtic had numerous key people at the club who were prominent members of Irish Nationalist organisations in Glasgow. These organisations had strong links with figures such as Joseph Devlin of the Irish Parliamentary Party (IPP), who were encouraging people in Belfast and across the island of Ireland, to fight for Britain due to the promise of Home Rule being granted in return. Indeed, during Celtic's visits to Antrim in the late 1920s to play against Belfast Celtic, there are reports of Devlin thanking the club for all their support during the Home Rule crisis when he was second in command of the IPP behind John Redmond. There was certainly not the same type of recruitment drive at Celtic Park when it came to the second world war; whilst 22 members of staff did still serve or enlist with the forces.

Celtic Park held an unusual social role in World War I when the stadium played host to an England versus Scotland football match on 2nd March 1918. The match was unusual at the time as it was played between women. Players were drawn from local munition factories, which were dominated by women, as many male workers had been conscripted to fight in WWI.

The Scottish women were all selected from William Beardmore's iron and steel works in Glasgow (Cardonald, Mosspark and Parkhead). Within Beardmore's factories there was a strong welfare focus, which sought to make the most of many newfound opportunities for women. One aspect of his welfare scheme led to the formation of ladies' football teams in 1917. Celtic were very supportive of the revolutionary concept of women's football, largely helped by the fact that Beardmore's Parkhead factory was based next to the stadium, at the Forge. In lending their support, Celtic made a huge contribution to the rise of the female game. There was little respect or public interest in allowing women to play football back then, but by permitting the local ladies' team to use the changing rooms, communal baths and pitch for training, the club did much to change that attitude.

The English team came solely from the Vickers-Maxim factory in Barrow-in-Furness, which operated a similar project when it came to providing sporting opportunities for women.

The match was played in order to raise funds for the war effort, which was essential because resources were depleting by this late stage of the conflict. Fans were enticed to Celtic Park by being offered additional entertainment in the form of artillery displays, donkeys and an aerial fly-past. Over 15,000 people turned up, a quite remarkable feat, especially when one considers that Celtic travelled to Clydebank and Rangers hosted Kilmarnock at Ibrox that same day. The bulk of the supporters appear to have enjoyed themselves as local reports talked of 'an explosive atmosphere' throughout the game. That said, England took the lead through an own goal, before compounding their advantage as they thrashed Scotland 4-0. The sides met a further two times in England that month, drawing the second game 2-2 before England won 3-2 in the final contest.

An image of the poster advertising the match – taken at Hampden Park Museum

THE HEART'S BATTALION

The 1914 Heart of Midlothian team is widely recognised as the finest in their club's history. The Jambos were sitting pretty at the top of the Scottish League when the Great War broke out, putting football clubs under intense pressure. Nobody felt that pressure more than Hearts, when a letter implying that their players were cowards surfaced in the press in November of that year. The article was headlined: 'The White Feathers of Midlothian' and its content had been sent in by 'A soldier's daughter'.

Might I suggest that while the Heart of Midlothian continue to play football, enabled to pursue their peaceful play by the sacrifices of the lives of thousands of their countrymen, they might adopt, temporarily, a name of fame, 'the white feathers of Midlothian'...

The words of 'A soldier's daughter' echoed the discontent felt by Airdrie Chairman, Thomas Forsyth, who called on the SFA to cancel the season when he stated that "Playing football while our men are fighting is repugnant."

As the Hearts players were subject to severe scrutiny in the wake of the article, they convened a meeting among themselves to address the matter. They wanted to show that they were as tough and patriotic as any other working-class member of society. Therefore, 16 members of the squad signed up to the 16th Royal Scots Battalion (also known as McCrae's Battalion). The decision to jeopardise their pursuit of the Scottish League title, in answer to the call of duty, proved an inspirational one. Indeed, many supporters of the club signed up to accompany their heroes on the battle ground: 500 of the 1,350 who bolstered the ranks of the battalion that week to be exact. This was made possible by the unit being the first of 'the Pals' battalions in World War I, which were specially constituted battalions of the British Army comprising of men who enlisted on the promise that they would be able to serve alongside their friends, colleagues and local heroes, rather than being outposted at random.

Though Hearts led the way, it should also be noted that 150 fans (and some players) of Hibernian, seven Raith Rovers players and footballers from Falkirk, Dunfermline Athletic, East Fife and St Bernard's also enlisted with the 16th Royal Scots. Fans from each of those clubs were encouraged to follow in their heroes' footsteps and fight alongside them, which they did, albeit in fewer numbers than the Hearts support.

The war-bound Hearts players trained in the Pentland hills, performing night manoeuvres, sometimes before playing Scottish football fixtures the next day. The tough workload caused blisters and other injuries, which affected performances on the pitch and caused unavailability. As a result, the club's trainer, Jamie Duckworth, started attending the night manoeuvres with the team to nurse any ailments. The stress took a toll on Duckworth's mental health and it was no surprise that the intense pressures manifest themselves in a dip in form for the Edinburgh club.

News from the battlefield often filtered back to Edinburgh via the postman. Certainly, if the opening words of a letter were: 'I regret to inform you', it was a horrifying sight. Over 1,000 families from the 16th Royal Scots, including those of seven Hearts players, received such letters throughout the conflict.

The names of James Speedie and James Boyd, aged 21, Henry Wattie and Duncan Currie, 23, Tom Gracie, 26, Edgar Ellis and John Allan, just 30 years old – make up the tragic roll of honour for Hearts in this period. James Speedie was killed at Loos in September 1915 and Currie, Ellis and Wattie all fell at the Somme. Tom Gracie had managed to play through the season, finishing up as the league's top goal scorer with 29 goals, but he played the closing weeks of the campaign with leukaemia before he died in a military hospital. The careers of Paddy Crossan, gassed and wounded twice at the Somme, and Alfie Briggs, who returned from war with two machine gun bullets lodged in his back, were also compromised at this time. Yet amidst the devastation, the Jambos held on to their lead at the top of the table for 36 matches! A remarkable title was then painfully snatched from their clasp on the final week of the season when defeat against St Mirren and Morton saw Celtic win the league by four points.

It was fitting that a charity match, to raise money for the War Memorial Fund, was arranged at Tynecastle on 22nd May 1920. On account of Celtic's charitable proclivity, the Bhoys were invited to provide the opposition. Celtic were more than glad to oblige, having had seven players of their own lose their lives in WWI. The Hoops were also the holders of the Navy and Army War Fund Shield (1918), played to raise money for the families of those who had fought in the war. (However, Celtic weren't presented with the shield as it was not ready on the day of the final. The competition was originally planned as an annual event but with the war finishing just months later it was never staged again and Celtic were never presented with the silverware.) The Bhoys named a strong starting 11 to add numbers to the gate. 14,000 spectators arrived, contributing £760 (approx. £33,000 in today's money) towards the funding of a Scottish National War Memorial at Edinburgh Castle.

In terms of the footballing facet of proceedings, the crowd was not bequeathed with sterling stuff in the first half. The second half was brighter, with McLean giving Celtic the lead through a tidy right footed finish from the corner of the penalty box. Hearts went close to an equaliser, but their hopes were dashed when McInally doubled Celtic's advantage with a header from close range.

After the match, which Celtic won 2-0, the Lord High Commissioner showed his appreciation for the two teams. A report in The Scotsman newspaper on 24th May 1920, summarises the scene:

On arrival at the ground, His Grace (Lord High Commissioner) *was received by Mr Furst, the chairman of the Club, and the club directors and the manager, Mr W. McCartney. At the close of the play, in the Tynecastle Board-room, which was tastefully furnished and decorated for the occasion, the players of both sides were introduced to the Duke, who shook hands with each of them, and thanked them for taking part in the game in aid of memorial funds. As soldiers, he thought it was their duty to put up a memorial to the Scotsmen who had fallen in the war. When he was out in the East, football always came next in importance to duty, and he could say that the best men he had had were the football players. They were always an example to the others. When soldiers got into the dumps, as they sometimes did, a game at football set them all right again.*

They had a splendid "gate" and he liked the spirit of the giving on such an occasion. If he could get 10d. from each man in the country they would have all the money they would require for their purpose. He would greatly prefer 10d. from every man than a thousand from a comparative few. It was very gratifying to have the assistance in this memorial scheme of the people who had fought for the country. Medals were presented to both teams, the gift of Sir J. T. Cargill.

What those young Heart's players sacrificed was remarkable. Their memory was suitably honoured during this exhibition event and their story lives on in Edinburgh circles to this day.

SHIPYARD SATURDAY

It was the final day of the 1921/22 season, Celtic and Rangers were separated by a single point and both teams were playing away from home. Scottish football held its collective breath and pondered on where the title may be heading.

A last day title decider is something that many Celtic fans will remember well. Those memories will be fond when recalling our clinching of the league at Tannadice in 2008, as Rangers capitulated at Pittodrie. Fans a little older will have less happy memories of Celtic losing the title on 'Black Sunday' in 2005 and doing likewise, on goal difference, in 2003. Those older still, will also recall the sheer jubilation at Love Street in 1986 as the Bhoys snatched the title from Hearts, who squandered control of the championship at Dens Park. However, in 1922, last day title deciders were a somewhat exotic phenomenon.

Willie Maley's team had to make the short journey through Port Glasgow and along the coast to Greenock, where a less than hospitable welcome greeted them and the travelling support. Rangers, meanwhile, travelled to Shawfield to take on Clyde. Celtic were favourites for the league as a victory would seal glory, whilst a draw would ensure a play-off, regardless of how Rangers fared.

The Celtic support turned out en masse. The club organised two trains to run from Glasgow at discounted prices and the bumper support was well required as this would be a record attendance for a Morton home game. Morton's crowd had been boosted, along with the team's confidence, due to their first and only Scottish Cup success, against Rangers at Hampden Park, two weeks prior.

Morton historians record that '*by kick-off time, Cappielow was a seething, solid, noisy mass. The official attendance was 23,500 but it was suspected that many more had gained admission by more devious routes than the turnstiles. Hundreds of youngsters had been spilled out and were crouched around the track.*' Loose security provisions had been made to prevent confrontation within the unsegregated crowd, which was typical of the time. By prohibiting banners and flags, Morton felt there would be reduced problems. Celtic fans didn't concur with the provisions nor comply with them, thus their congregated masses in three quarters of the stadium were easily identifiable.

The Celtic support had long travelled in large numbers to away fixtures, where they carried the flag of Ireland and sang Irish rebel songs. Their unwavering beliefs were almost always met with open hostility and the people of Greenock reacted in much the same way. The recent partition of Ireland and the ongoing civil rights abuses in the six counties caused significant tension in Western Scotland. Placing a largely Irish Republican support amongst a hostile and resolute host club, on a day to determine the destination of the title, provided the perfect recipe for animosity to ensue. Given the non-stringent measures that were in place for the fixture, it comes as little surprise that the match became noteworthy for battles off the park.

Fighting broke out among rival fans in the west terrace before kick-off. As the match got underway, the tension momentarily eased. Celtic got off to a stuttering start and metaphorically speaking, the tension had been transferred to the players in hooped jerseys. Indeed, the Celtic players visibly felt the pressure of the occasion. The Greenock Telegraph reported that *'For once the Celts were outdone in nippy forwards. McKay and Brown were full of it. They manoeuvred about, dodged, swerved, and did all the other things that are generally credited to the inimitable Patsy Gallacher.'* The buoyant Morton team were enjoying their post cup final celebrations and relaxing into the game nicely. Celtic had been restricted to a single attempt on goal and, on the 35-minute mark, a powerful strike from Morton's striker, Brown, near burst the Celtic net. Half time: Morton 1-0 Celtic. Meanwhile, at Shawfield: Clyde 0-0 Rangers.

The Celtic support had no time to dwell on the bleakness of their team's situation, for trouble flared again on the west terracing. This time it was severe. The younger fans, traditionally stood at the front of the terracing, had to leap the barriers at pitch side to avoid the fighting. A small group of Celtic fans were being assaulted but gave as good as they got. Stones filled the air and each set of supporters tried to wrestle the others' flags. A vast group of Celtic fans ran across the pitch from the opposite terrace, but the Morton support met them on the Cappielow turf to engage in battle.

The Greenock Telegraph reported of the scene: *'Hundreds ran onto the field and a number of boys who had been seated on the track fled as if for their very lives. At one stage men with flags could be seen lining up and then charging. Confusion followed. Stones and other missiles were thrown, and groups could be seen struggling and fighting.'*

Many casualties required hospital treatment for serious head and facial injuries. Police intervened and were assisted by the players in terms of clearing the pitch and helping injured supporters to reach the pavilion, where they could be given medical assistance.

Chaos aside, the game re-started but Celtic continued in similar fashion. The Hoops pressed for an equaliser, but they were having little success and struggling to contain multiple Morton counter-attacks. Finally, Celtic managed to get hold of the ball and the noise from the stands grew. The clock struck 4.35pm - luckily for Celtic, the score at Shawfield had remained deadlocked at 0-0 - not that anyone was aware (this being a time before the Walkman radio was commonplace).

Celtic forced the Morton defence to retreat. The noise followed with a raucous cacophony of The Dear Little Shamrock. In the 82nd minute, a hopeless looking cross was booted into the Morton box. The keeper, Edwards, who had little to do all afternoon, lost his focus and fumbled. Celtic's right-winger, Andy McAtee, was on hand to head the ball into the empty net. Cappielow erupted to the discord of thousands of delighted Glaswegians.

Celtic had one hand on the title but, symptomatic of the club's philosophy, they relentlessly chased a winner. Moments later, at Shawfield, Rangers were presented with a golden opportunity. Meiklejohn, of the Govan outfit, struck a powerful shot, only to see it deflected over the crossbar by his own team-mate. Rangers' chance of winning their game had evaporated, whilst Celtic assuredly achieved their draw. Both teams had tied their matches, meaning Andy McAtee's late header was enough to clinch the championship for Celtic.

The Celtic support had little chance to celebrate before they again had to be warier of alternative matters than the success of their team. The departing Celtic brake clubs were attacked on Port Glasgow Road. One Celtic brake club banner was seized and burnt close to the stadium. Those who retained their material emblems were bricked and had to dodge the steel rivets that were being flung in their direction from the neighbouring shipyard. It became apparent that this level of organised attack had been pre-meditated. It was a vicious, structured assault, motivated by the contempt in which Morton fans held those of Irish Catholic stock. The attackers may have done their homework, for rivets had been the weapon of choice when groups of Catholic workers were forcibly expelled from shipyards in the North of Ireland a decade earlier. Thus, rivets were nicknamed 'Belfast confetti'.

A light breeze and hand to hand combat was the order of the short walk to Cartsdyke Station for those Celtic fans returning by train. There was further trouble on the train itself and one man was arrested in Central Station for a slashing attack with an open razor.

When the trouble finally subsided, The Glasgow Observer made it clear where the blame lay: '*Those who know Greenock and have had experience of the local crowd were not surprised to hear that the Celtic brake-clubmen, being a comparative minority, were attacked by the big battalions of Orange hooligans.*' The Shamrock fanzine touched on this aspect in a recent edition of their popular Celtic history magazine. Within their phenomenal article, they stated: '*A letter to the Observer some weeks later from an 'Irish Greenockian' pointed out that the year previous, Rangers fans had thrown stones and bottles at Morton players and the referee in an encounter at Capplielow (even bursting the match ball at one point!) without being confronted by locals during or after the match. Interestingly, this Greenock correspondent also pointed out that the Rangers fans were more tactically aware than their Celtic counterparts when it came to terrace warfare: "Let it be a warning to Celtic brake-clubs in future visits to Greenock that the Rangers' brake-clubs, on the occasion referred to, were all together in one compact body, well up the slopes, and presenting to the Cappielow heroes a position too formidable to attack. On the Celts' visit recently, the brake-clubs were divided into three separate bodies, the party attacked being the smallest of the three, and so low down the terracing as to be an easy victim for the kind of Morton supporters who come from Port Glasgow."*'

Perhaps the most alarming issue of the 'Cappielow Riot' was that Morton fans had a history of using military tactics, learned during the first world war, to orchestrate trouble. The security, therefore, was incredibly lax at the time. Nevertheless, the Celtic faithful, battered and bruised though they were, could eventually enjoy the status of their team being champions of Scotland.

HALF TIME SPEEDWAY

Most speedway historians contend that the second official speedway meeting in Britain was held at Celtic Park on 28th April 1928. Many of the sport's enthusiasts believe that the sport began in proper stadia, on cinder tracks. Therefore, with this in place, coupled with the stadium's classic oval shape, Celtic Park would have been an ideal venue. The new motorsport was almost a month old in Britain when, in March 1928, it was announced that Celtic Park would indeed be used for speedway, the announcement coming from no less a Celtic legend than Manager, Willie Maley.

The motorcycling correspondent for The Glasgow Herald wrote: *'So the Australian dirt-track specialists are to come north after all and show us the real thing which attracts thousands to the trackside in the Antipodes. McKay and Galloway, who also are to promote meetings twice a week at the famous Celtic Park Grounds at Parkhead. These meetings will be open and the prize money to the amount of £200 per meeting will be forthcoming they say.*

The racing will be conducted according to the regulations approved by the ACU which prohibit betting and it will be interesting to see if the excitement and interest of the sport itself will prove sufficient to attract the Glasgow public although the promoters have no doubt on the matter. The track is to be loosened so as to allow 'broadsiding', a protective fence will be erected, and electric lighting will be installed if necessary.'

The arising motorsport was booming throughout the UK. New tracks firstly opened in England, then in Scotland and Wales. A meeting, widely regarded as the very first in

Britain, was held at High Beech in February 1928. There were other speedway events held in Manchester and Surrey a year earlier, but those races were conducted in a clockwise direction and thus are not considered as being 'true speedway' occasions, in retrospect.

The first speedway event at Celtic Park was organised by Dirt Track Speedways as they sought to promote the sport further in Scotland. A crowd of 5,000 turned up for the meeting, a small number compared to the 30,000 spectators who attended High Beech in England, two months earlier. The disappointment went against the script and efforts had to be redoubled north of the border.

An excellent promotional opportunity presented itself when Celtic hosted Rangers in a Glasgow Charity Cup tie on May 5th, 1928. Knowing a seismic crowd was in store, Dirt Track Speedways put on a brief exhibition of speedway during the half time interval. The promoters then staged the first charity speedway meeting in the UK, at Celtic Park, in aid of St Andrews Ambulance service, who required funds for a new headquarters. Despite such efforts, it was soon clear that the Parkhead track was not rivalling the drawing powers of similar ventures down south, and the twice weekly events in Glasgow were reduced to once. Even this was too frequent and, given an excuse, like the Prince of Wales' visit to the city, meetings were cancelled.

In total, 11 meetings took place at Celtic Park and when riders complained about the quality of the surface, in addition to the lack of pulling power at Parkhead, racing was halted at the stadium. The doors on Celtic Park speedway were officially closed as of 21st July 1928.

A report in a 1929 newspaper article suggested that stadium alterations at Celtic Park encroached on the track, rendering it unsuitable for speedway again. Scottish speedway moved to a track on Janefield Street, just yards from the home of Celtic Football Club. The new venue initially fared better, as local teams such as Glasgow Tigers and Coatbridge Monarchs began to establish themselves. However, it was a false dawn and the sport seemed to be in decline again, soon attracting little more than a cult following in Scotland (which has remained the case until recently). The final meeting at the alternative Glasgow track was held in May 1932.

A bid to bring speedway back to the home of the Hoops was made by Trevor Redmond in 1963. Trevor was a former Scottish Open champion and successful rider, who was about to finish his career at Glasgow Tigers. He sought to secure the rights to use the stadium, but his attempt proved fruitless. However, the connection between Celtic and Scottish speedway was momentarily rekindled in 2008, when Glasgow Tigers were invited to Paradise to pose for a photograph to mark the speedway club's 80th anniversary.

The speedway programme from the first ever meeting held in Scotland.

PARADISE IN FLAMES AGAIN

There are countless books about the history of Celtic Football Club, each taking a unique angle. A lot of this history would not be able to be retold, at least authentically, had a pavilion fire in 1929 been slightly more extensive. After the 1904 fire (see page 78), damage to the pavilion side of the stadium had been repaired. However, in May 1929, the job was finished when Celtic Park befell further bad luck and caught ablaze.

Construction workers, architecting a new South Stand, spotted flames bursting through the pavilion windows. They quickly raised the alarm but the ruthlessness of the fire, combined with the wooden composition of the structure, meant that the pavilion was condemned before so much as a fire serviceman could arrive. Stowed in the building were the early photographs and documentation from the first 40 years of the club. Valuable photographs including the original Celtic team, the first Celtic players to win the Scottish Cup and league title, and single photographs of Micky Dunbar, John H McLaughlin, John Glass, and other prominent Celtic men, were irretrievable.

The fire destroyed everything but a safe. The safe, of which all hopes hinged on the contents of, had been damaged having struck a radiator as it fell from the above floor. Thankfully, the club's early records of charitable contributions, committee members and plans to find land for a stadium etc. were found inside it in good condition. Their survival allows us to tell the Celtic story.

PRINCE OF GOALKEEPERS

Throughout all the incidents and events in this book, little if any will be as entwined with tragedy as this infamous story. Indeed, where there is sunshine, there must be shadow. That shadow fell on 5th September 1931, when Johnny Thomson, 'The Prince of Goalkeepers', received a serious head injury while playing against Rangers at Ibrox. He died later in hospital, having never regained consciousness.

Thomson was a formidable young goalkeeper who earned his 'prince' nickname even before he lost his life. He was spotted playing local football for Wellesley Juniors by Celtic's chief scout, Steve Callaghan. Such was his belief in Thomson, Callaghan persuaded Willie Maley to sign the goalkeeper that same evening. Maley obliged and Thomson rose to prominence for Celtic in 1927. However, his debut as an 18-year-old did not go according the script. He made a howler, but told his teammates: "Don't worry, I have been taught not to make the same mistake twice, I'll be fine for next week." How right he was, as Thomson would go on to represent Celtic on a further 187 occasions, earning a shutout rate of 34% and collecting five honours, which is somewhat impressive when one considers that Celtic were a team in transition during that era.

Renowned for his bravery and unfaltering fearlessness, Thomson's dive at the feet of the Rangers forward, Sam English, was his devastating downfall. As English shot, John Thomson's head took the full impact of the Rangers player's knee, leaving the goalkeeper unconscious with his skull bleeding.

113

As the youngster was being stretchered off, a section of the home support was unaware of the seriousness of the injury and cheered until they were silenced by one of the Rangers players. Owing to the severity of the injury, the match petered out to a 0-0 draw amid a rare eerie silence, not often associated with a Glasgow derby.

Thomson was taken to the Victoria Infirmary in Glasgow. He had a lacerated wound over the right parietal bones of the skull, which meant that there was a depression in his head of two inches in diameter. At 5pm he suffered a major convulsion. Dr Norman Davidson carried out an emergency operation to try and lower the amount of pressure caused by the swelling to the brain, but the surgery was unsuccessful, and the 22-year-old was pronounced dead by 9.25pm.

Johnny was laid to rest on 9th September 1931. Roughly 40,000 people attended his funeral in Cardenden, a considerable number of which had walked some 55 miles from Glasgow. A further crowd about half the size turned out at Glasgow Queen Street Station to watch two trains set off, carrying 2,000 mourners. When you consider that the club's average attendance never rose above 18,000 from 1930 until the suspension of football in 1938, the turnout to remember one of its most loved sons was nothing short of remarkable.

A week after Johnny's death, a poignant tribute was held before the match at Celtic Park. Though there had been huge press coverage of John's tragic accident, The Glasgow Herald only gave a very brief synopsis of the pre-match tribute at Parkhead the following week. The report was as follows:

'An impressive tribute was paid to John Thomson at Celtic Park on Saturday. The flags were at half mast and all round the ground there was a subdued air. Celtic came out first, filing slowly from the pavilion, followed by Queen's Park. The twenty-two players formed an unbroken line as they took to the field in their positions. All wore black armlets. The crowd did not know how to welcome the players, there was a moment's hesitation and then a half-hearted cheer rippled round the field. Players and spectators stood while a lament, 'The Last Post' and 'Lead Kindly Light' was played. There was silence for a moment, then a cheer for the teams and another for Falconer as he ran towards the west goal. Then play began…'

As much as Johnny had earned his status with fantastic performances for club and country, he was an incredible character too. One such exemplification of this was when Celtic hosted Queen's Park in the late 1920s. A fierce shot was struck by the Spiders' forward, prompting Thomson to dive to his right. The ball deflected and Thomson twisted his body in mid-air to change direction and pull off an extraordinary save. As the front man moved to congratulate Thomson from the resulting corner, he let out a scream of pain as the goalkeeper stood on his toe!

Another well-known tale, which is testament to Johnny's sense of humour, comes from a time when he was called a Fenian b*****d by an opposing player. Johnny reported the matter to James McGrory. McGrory replied: "Don't worry, I get called that all the time." Thomson's retort: "Yes but that's ok for you, you are one!" The joke being that Johnny was of course a church going Protestant.

John Thomson's legacy both as a player and a man, lives on through the John Thomson Memorial Committee. The Committee was established by Alec Burns in 1983, to promote the memory of John Thomson in his hometown of Cardenden. The organisation was instrumental in having Johnny recognised by being inducted into the Scottish Football Hall of Fame in September 2008. They also run an annual tournament in John's memory, which has courted the participation of close to 6,000 local children since its inception.

Countless plays, books and quotes have been written to chart the life of The Prince of Goalkeepers. Most famously, The John Thomson Song was penned many years ago and was covered on a record disc by Glen Daly. However, most Celtic fans don't realise that another song tribute, titled The Laddie Frae Cardenden, was written by Alexander McGregor and recorded by Douglas Robb - at 62 Glengall Road, Peckham, London, in September 1931. The record disc can be found on display at the Scottish Football Museum.

It is safe to say that John Thomson will never be forgotten. His epitaph is fitting of the legend that remains: 'They never die who live in the hearts they leave behind.'

A rare photo of Johnny Thomson in action, taken from my first book – Our Stories & Our Songs: The Celtic Support

BRIDGETON BILLY BOYS

During the 1930s there was a significant move by the government, in conjunction with the Church of Scotland, to send Irish born immigrants back across the sea. There was also an epidemic of razor gangs fighting in working class districts of Glasgow, often for sectarian reasons. The prominent Protestant gang, The Bridgeton Billy Boys, were founded and led by Billy Fullerton, a former member of The British Fascists. The Billy Boys adopted a militaristic style of behaviour, marching on parades, forming their own bands and singing their own songs. The gang also formed a youth wing, whose members were termed The Derry Boys. Hence the infamous song heard on the terraces at Ibrox:

Hello Hello we are the Billy Boys,
Hello Hello you'll know us by our noise
We're up to our knees in Fenian blood
Surrender or you'll die
For we are the Brigton Derry Boys

Against such a backdrop there was always going to be trouble at football matches and Celtic's Scottish Cup clash with St Mirren, on 3rd March 1934, was no different. A huge travelling support was heading to Love Street, hoping to see the Bhoys advance to the Semi-Finals and salvage the campaign, considering that the Hoops were floundering in 10th position in the league. A special train service had been put on for supporters in Glasgow and the surrounding areas, to take them to Paisley. With each passing stop the carriages became more and more filled, each with a fine atmosphere… that was until the train pulled into Bridgeton Cross Station.

Suddenly, five doors were thrust open by a mob of 200 men. The gang produced bayonets, razors, knives and axes – attacking all, as suspected Celtic fans, indiscriminately. It soon became apparent that the attack had been the work of The Billy Boys, who conducted their latest act of sectarian fuelled violence prior to attending Rangers' cup match at Ibrox against Aberdeen that day.

With the Celtic support terrorised, they continued their journey on to Love Street, seeking respite in the form of victory. 33,434 people clicked through the turnstyles, earning St Mirren £1273 in much needed gate receipts. The bumper crowd weren't disappointed. Celtic began the match poorly, McStay and McGonagle in particular, had dreadful matches in defence. This allowed 16th placed St Mirren to capitalise and earn themselves a 1-0 lead through Jimmy McGregor. The match was a very exciting affair thereafter with a multitude of missed opportunities for both sides. Celtic missed two penalties, the first taken by Peter McGonagle and the second by Peter Wilson. In response, St Mirren missed a penalty of their own when Jimmy Knox blazed wide, but his blushes were spared by John Latimer, who made sure of St Mirren's victory with a fine goal to put the Paisley club two ahead.

Two days had passed to allow the dust to settle before the Glasgow based media picked up on the story of the pre-match train station debacle. Perhaps a sign of the times, the story didn't make the front or back pages. Rather, it was treated as a customary incident. Nevertheless, a detailed report did appear in The Scotsman newspaper on 1st May 1934, which read as follows:

GANG TERRORISM IN GLASGOW

119

*Revelations regarding terrorism by gangs in the Bridgeton
district of Glasgow were made by Detective-Lieutenant
William Dudgeon Paterson, of the City Police, during a
trail in the High Court of Justiciary in Glasgow yesterday.*

*The trial was a sequel to an attack made by a mob, in
Bridgeton Cross Station on March 3, on a train which was
conveying passengers from Maryhill and Possil to Paisley,
where the Celtic Football Club were playing St Mirren FC.
The accused, John Traquair, was charged with mobbing,
rioting, and assault. It was alleged that being a member of
a gang known as the 'Billy Boys' or by some other name or
names, he did, on March 3, at Bridgeton Cross Station,
form part of a riotous mob and invade a compartment of a
railway carriage with intent to assault passengers therein.
The charge also alleged that he assaulted John McVey, 277
Saracen Street, by striking him on the arm with a razor or
other sharp instrument to the effusion of blood and that he
also assaulted Ranzo Buonaccorsi, 136 Barloch Street,
Possilpark. He was found guilty of all the charges and
sentenced to four years' penal servitude.*

*Detective Paterson, in evidence, said it was practically
impossible to get witnesses in the Bridgeton district. The
reason was "Pure terror. There is a general campaign of
regular terrorism to prevent the giving of evidence. The
shopkeepers and residents are concerned."*

The piece continued with details of the formalities of the
court proceedings before showing further testimonies:

SCENES IN THE TRAIN

*John McVey aged 21, 277 Saracen Street, stated that he
and Ranzo Buonaccorsi caught the 1.30pm train on the day*

in question for Paisley. When the train reached Bridgeton Cross two men and two women came into the compartment. A number of passengers were wearing Celtic colours, such as green rosettes, and in the front part of the train some of them had green scarves as well. Witness wore no colours of any kind. There was a crowd at Bridgeton Cross Station and some of them wore blue rosettes and badges. Some of the crowd carried sticks and missiles. As the two women came forward to enter the compartment, the witness got up to open the carriage door. As he was doing so he got a blow on the left forearm. He did not see who struck him. A man jumped into the compartment and hit witness on identical spot where he had been struck before, it was a heavy blow. At the police station on March 5 he identified Traquair as the man who struck him, and he also struck Buonaccorsi in the face.

At the time the assault was committed the Rangers' supporters were forcing their way in behind Traquair. He did not think they wanted in for any peaceful purpose. There was panic in the station and witness heard shouting "Papist ----." There was a mixture of Roman Catholics and Protestants in the Celtic FC but the majority were Roman Catholic.

SHELTERING UNDER SEATS

The guard came along and pulled Traquair out. Afraid of being struck by stones, the people in the compartment got under the seats. When the train began to move again a passenger drew attention to his sleeve and then he saw he was bleeding from his left forearm. By the time train got to Dalmarnock he had lost a considerable quantity of blood. He was taken to the Royal Infirmary, where stitches were

121

put to his wound. The cut went right through his jacket, shirt and semmit. Cross examined by Mr Campbell, witness admitted that a good number of the Celtic supporters in Glasgow were Irish. He denied that a good deal of bad language was used by the Celtic supporters that day. He did not hear anyone shout an abusive remark about Traquair's face, nor did he hear a man named Campbell shout out that the Rangers were a dirty lot.

MAN WITH A BAYONET

Ranzo Buonaccorsi, 136 Banlock Street, Possilpark, also gave evidence regarding what occurred in the railway compartment. When the train came to Bridgeton Cross Station there was a big crowd on the platform showing blue scarves and blue handkerchiefs, shouting filthy expressions such as "Dirty Papist -." Witness saw stones in their hands. One man had a bayonet and another a hammer. He formed the impression that the filthy language was directed towards the people in the train and that it was an organised affair. A man entered the compartment and struck McVey, it was not a punch, but more of a stab. Then the assailant struck at the witness and the first blow landed on his face. He put his arm out to defend himself. He was afraid to retaliate, owing to the attitude of the crowd.

STRUCK WITH BATON

Thomas Campbell, 23 Glamis Road, Newbank, said that as the train was slowing down he saw a passenger who was leaning out the window being struck by what appeared to be a wooden baton. Later he saw accused strike a blow at McVey, but he did not know if the man had anything in his hand. Robert Keir, 13 Willock Street, the guard said that there was a commotion in the second carriage of the train. When he went along he saw a man with his right arm raised and trying to strike another. He was afraid there would be trouble at the station and he signalled to the driver to start the train. The train left a minute before it was due to start.

EVIDENCE FOR DEFENCE

The first witness for the defence, Thomas Duncan, 50 Charlotte Street, said he had known the accused for over thirty years. Witness was Vice-President of a junior football team called Barrowfield Thistle, of which accused was Treasurer. He could say positively that accused was not a member the 'Billy Boys'. James Simmons, 9 Binnie Place, also stated that the reference to gangs had tended to create a certain atmosphere of suspicion in the case. He regretted to have seen articles in the Glasgow newspapers on the scandalous conduct of those alleged gangs. He contented that association with a gang was completely disproved in the case of the accused.

THE INDIAN JUGGLER

In the empire days of old when the British were claiming superiority over India's population, some Indian Nationalists responded to the colonial jibes that they were not man enough to rule themselves, by proving a point on the football field. Mohammed Salim was one such Indian. He was born in Calcutta in 1904 and began kicking a ball with his peers in an impoverished local village as a teenager. Like many of his countrymen, Salim became part of a football team, who played matches, in bare feet, against locally stationed British forces. Such matches were a safe and symbolic method of subduing the sense of pre-eminence that Britain had attempted to enforce over the Indian people.

By the mid-1930s, Salim was an integral part of a 5-time Calcutta title winning team, which earned him a spot in the national squad for two friendlies against the Chinese Olympic side. Salim starred in the first match, earning himself many new admirers. Among them, his own cousin, who had travelled from England to witness him play for the first time. Such was the indelible impression that he had made, Salim was persuaded by his cousin to try his hand in Europe, rather than play for India in the second friendly.

Salim and his cousin landed in England, having sailed from Cairo. No Indian had ever played football in Europe before, let alone Britain. Therefore, the enormity of the challenge to overcome contemporary racist and imperial attitudes should not be understated. Salim's cousin knew of Celtic's uniquely inclusive credentials and took Mohammed to Parkhead to meet the club's Manager, Willie Maley. It is thought that he pleaded with the Celtic boss: "A great player from India has come by ship. Will you please take a trial of his? But there is a slight problem. Salim plays in bare feet." The Celtic Manager appeared momentarily discombobulated. It was certainly unorthodox for an amateur player to travel from Calcutta with hope of staking a claim in the Scottish professional game, especially whilst professing to play without boots! Nevertheless, after some awkward laughter, Maley granted Salim a trial, in which he would have the opportunity to showcase his talent for the reserve team.

The Daily Record epitomised the ignorance of the era when they broke the story of the trial. Bizarrely headlined, 'Can he swallow a sword?', the piece shows the type of mentality that Mohammed Salim was up against:

'On Friday evening Celtic play Galston in an Alliance game at Parkhead. There is nothing startling about that, but the game is going to draw a bigger crowd, much bigger, because Celtic will play at outside right a dark-skinned young man, Bachchi Khan of the Mohammedan Sporting Club, Calcutta. Mr. Khan has been playing football since he was 14 years of age. He is now 23. Nothing startling about that. He has played for his club against British Army teams. Nothing startling about that. But, luvaduck, the man plays in his bare feet – AND THERE'S SOMETHING STARTLING ABOUT THAT. His cousin is a storekeeper at Elderslie docks and this week he made contact with Willie Maley asking that Bachchi, who is here on holiday be given a run out with Celts. The Celtic manager agreed to give our coloured visitor a place in a trial game, and he took the field sans boots, sans shinguards. And played a delightful game. His crosses to the goalmouth were pictures. The only "protection" he has

are elastic bandages – two-and-a-half inches deep – round his ankles, a fact that should make our bandaged toed, heavily booted shin-guarded players think. And if my information is correct Mr. Khan doesn't give a rap if the pitch is covered with broken glass!' (Note the reference to Mohammed Salim as 'Bachchi Khan'. His real full name was Mohammed Abdul Salim Bachi Khan.)

Salim's first appearance came against Galston on 28th August 1936. He dazzled on the wing and made a trio of assists as Celtic triumphed 7-1 in front of a bumper 7,000 crowd. The Glasgow Observer waxed lyrical of him the next day, with the following report:

Ten twinkling toes of Salim, Celtic FC's player from India, hypnotised the crowd at Parkhead last night in an alliance game with Galston. He balances the ball on his big toe, lets it run down the scale to his little toe, twirls it, hops on one foot around the defender, then flicks the ball to the centre who has only to send it into goal. Three of Celtic's seven goals last night came from his moves. Was asked to take a penalty he refused. Said he was shy. Salim does not speak English, his brother translates for him. Brother Hasheem thinks Salim is wonderful – so did the crowd last night.

By the time the West Bengal winger had shirked his shyness and scored a penalty to help ease Celtic to a 5-1 victory in his second game against Hamilton Academicals 'A', The Scottish Daily Express had him dubbed: 'The Indian Juggler'.

Salim soon signed for the club, another display of how Celtic broke social barriers in the days of the Empire. Yet, a week after his successful trial period, he became very unsettled. The Calcutta man had been impressive, making early strides towards the first team with his fine crossing, but the media attention he received had been hyperbolic because of his unique story. The Indian was struggling with the public attention and adaption to the cultural changes of Glasgow life.

The club did their best to keep hold of the South Asian starlet, even moving to put on a charity match for the winger with an offer of 5% of the proceeds going his way. However, Salim was desperate to return home and not knowing the significance of the 5%, he suggested that the club donate the money to local orphans, who were to be special guests for the match. The 5% of gate receipts amounted to £1,800 in today's money, which staggered Mohammed, but true to his word, he donated every penny to the orphaned children.

Mohammed duly departed the club having played just two reserve games, yet his tale resonated with Celtic supporters for years to come. As much as the Celtic support cherished Salim, his feelings were reciprocal, as evidenced by edition number 58 of The Celt fanzine, in which it was referenced that Salim had written to The Evening Times in 1949 to request a copy of Willie Maley's book: The Story of Celtic.

In 2002, Mohammed Salim's son, Rashid, revealed that he wrote to Celtic Football Club back in the 1980s to request financial assistance for his father's medical treatment. In an interview with The Telegraph, Rashid said: "I had no intention of asking for money. It was just a ploy to find out if Mohammed Salim was still alive in their memory. To my amazement, I received a letter from the club. Inside was a bank draft for £100. I was delighted, not because I received the money but because my father still holds a pride of place in Celtic. I have not even cashed the draft and will preserve it till I die."

This tale began on the dusty crack ridden fields of Calcutta, where football matches were staged against British Army regiments stationed in the city. Salim and his team-mates demonstrated then that regardless of footwear, they were not just equal, but could also better their imperial masters. His move to Celtic was the embodiment of the club's ethos and a poignant illustration of triumph over tyranny. As the September sun set on his short Celtic career, it is beautifully symmetric that we began to advance towards post-colonial times with the sun also setting on the British empire around the globe. We may be left wondering just what might have been if those brilliant bandaged feet had stayed in Glasgow and forced their way into the Celtic first team. However, the event of his signing for the club is one of the most symbolic reported in this book and is the epitome of that famous Willie Maley quote: "It is not his creed nor his nationality which counts – it's the man himself."

Salim getting his feet bandaged by Celtic legend, Jimmy 'Napoleon' McMenemy

CELTIC PARK CLOSED

1939 saw the world at war for a second time, resulting in the suspension of the Scottish Football League. Wartime football then took the form of regional leagues and Celtic had not fared too well in the first season of the Southern League format. Indeed, the Bhoys finished in 5th place in 1940/41, whilst Rangers took the trophy.

Unfortunately, the 1941/42 season didn't start off much better for Celtic and trouble flared at the first derby match of the campaign. Rangers had dominated proceedings at Ibrox on 6th September 1941. The Govan side led 2-0 towards the end of the first half, but Celtic began to fight back as the interval neared. The Bhoys sought to get the ball wide, where they had so often found success through the mesmerising skill of Jimmy Delaney. The world class outside right, who later played for Manchester United, weaved his way through the Rangers defence and peppered the full back with tantalising trickery. He found himself inside the penalty area with a chance to strike at goal, only to receive a violent push in the spine. The referee had little choice but to point for the spot. Despite the clear foul, the match official was immediately surrounded by a host of Rangers players protesting against his decision. When order was restored after considerable delay, Frank Murphy missed the penalty.

The Celtic support was apoplectic at the antics of the Rangers team, which had hampered the penalty kick from being taken for so long. The fans' collective fuse detonated as disorder erupted in the Celtic end throughout the interval and continued into the second half. Bottles flew at the pitch and rival supporters, amid disturbing scenes.

The behaviour of the Celtic support led the SFA, on 17th September, to close Celtic Park for one month. Given that the offending match was held at Ibrox, some viewed the punishment as unjust. However, as newspapers pointed out, the idea of clubs being responsible for the conduct of their fans had been noted and agreed at a meeting between the SFA President (Tom White, Celtic) and the Scottish League President (Willie Maley, Celtic) back in 1922. The incident had occurred on the West Terracing at Ibrox, where the Celtic supporters had been housed. Thus, by the mandate of the 1922 meeting, the imposition of a stadium ban at Parkhead was not unreasonable. Bob Kelly, then Director of Celtic, initially concurred with the SFA's verdict and stated that the governing body had "Acted according to the rules," and were "Within their rights."

In contrast to the above, Glasgow's Lord Provost (Sir Patrick Dollan) told The Glasgow Herald: "I hope the government and police, who will have the final say on this matter, will correct the judgement which is more like Nazi philosophy than British fair play." The Lord Provost went on to say that the closing of Celtic Park should not be acceptable to the public authorities in this circumstance. Instead, he felt that fair minded citizens would take the view that both clubs should be punished because both clubs were responsible. This view taken because the provocation of the Celtic faithful came from Rangers players "Contravening the laws."

The Lord Provost's position on the issue was clear, but there was more to his comments than meets the eye. The true nature of this establishment figure's remarks become clear when one listens to the end of his statement: "My sympathies go out to Rangers and their followers. The

131

Celtic have been made martyrs. The sporting world may think that Rangers have been treated with favouritism, but, knowing them, I believe this would have been the last thing that they would desire."

Ultimately, Bob Kelly and Celtic did challenge the SFA. Board member, Colonel John Shaughnessy, said: "It is because of what the opposition did that we are hung up. That seems to be a very material factor. Nothing was done by our team to give any excuse to our fans to start bottle-throwing." Regardless of Celtic's prevailing sense of injustice, the SFA issued the club with a notice for the foreclosure of Celtic Park. The conditions outlined in the notice were as follows:

(I) Celtic FC ground to be closed for all football from this date until October 17th, 1941, during which period Celtic will not be permitted to play on an opponent's ground in Glasgow.

(II) Celtic to post bills on all parts of their stadium intimating to the supporters on re-opening (a) that the ground was closed by this association because of serious misbehaviour of supporters at Ibrox stadium on September 6 and (b) warning their supporters that more serious punishment must fall on the club in the event of reoccurrence on any ground.

In light of the decision to close Celtic Park, the SFA warned all clubs over their player's conduct due to 'increased prevalence of showing dissent towards referee's decisions'. The organisation also liaised with the Chief Constable of Glasgow to ensure that necessary steps were taken to avoid a 're-occurrence of misconduct' in future matches between Celtic and Rangers.

Celtic's next scheduled home game, v Morton on 27th September 1941, was reversed to be held at Cappielow. Celtic won by three goals to two on that occasion. The Bhoys then played a Glasgow Cup Semi-Final against Rangers, which the SFA ordered to be played at Hampden, in line with the terms of the stadium closure that forbade Celtic to play at an opponent's home ground if the opponent was located within Glasgow. Although Hampden Park was a neutral ground, the fact that it is also in Glasgow made a mockery of the scenario. Nevertheless, the game went ahead and Celtic lost 3-2 to their bitter rivals.

The last home match to be reversed before the Paradise ban was lifted came on 4th October 1941. Celtic faced Motherwell and had to travel to Fir Park, where they were beaten 2-1. The Celts finally returned home to entertain Partick Thistle on 25th October, with the Glasgow sides playing out a 1-1 draw.

GUT WRENCHING BOYCOTT

The 1949/50 season got off to a great start for Celtic. Bobby Collins' impressive debut in the curtain raiser against Rangers saw the Hoops unexpectedly triumph in the Scottish League Cup. The Bhoys had received high praise for their entertaining style of play as they attacked their way to a 3-2 win against the age-old foe. Praise was again heaped on the Celts after the next League Cup clash at Pittodrie, when the team epitomised 'the Celtic way', with a 5-4 win against Aberdeen. Some fans even began to wonder if a trophy-less decade and the near relegation in 1948 could be replaced with a return to the silverware laden successes of the early 1900s. However, initial optimism was soon eroded when the Hoops failed to score against St Mirren a week later. Only the woodwork and a great penalty save by Willie Miller denied the Buddies a larger victory than the 1-0 win they achieved on that occasion.

Next up was a continuation of the League Cup group stages with a short trip to Ibrox on 27th August 1949. In front of 95,000 hostile fans, Celtic were holding their own. The scores were locked at a stalemate on the half hour mark, when suddenly the match acquired a negative tone. A Celtic attack was fizzling out as an overhit through ball was rolling towards Brown in the Rangers goal. Charlie Tully gave pursuit, whilst Sammy Cox of Rangers, shielded the ball back to the safe clasp of his goalkeeper. Cox then turned and booted Tully in the stomach. Football boots weren't of the modern-day design and were more akin to leather daggers back then. Unsurprisingly, Tully went down in agony as a result.

With as little patience as one might expect, the Celtic support waited for the penalty and a red card to ensue. Neither was forthcoming and just as earlier in the decade, anarchy arose at the Celtic end of Ibrox stadium. Bottles flew and fighting followed. In response, the referee stopped the game and allowed the trainer to attend Tully.

Play continued when the police restored order. Rangers then took the lead ten minutes later. Shortly after half time, the Govan outfit were awarded a penalty after Waddell had been tackled by Alec Boden. Rangers' Young hit the crossbar from the spot kick, but the blues went on to get a decisive second goal late in the match. Play didn't finish without Cox and Tully finding time to continue their spat, and both were cautioned for 'handbags' before time was up.

Celtic appealed to the SFA for an investigation into the events which caused the chaos. The inquiry's findings were announced on the 7th September 1949. Astonishingly, both Cox and Tully were formally reprimanded for 'provoking violent disorder'. Celtic Chairman, Bob Kelly, was seething. He demanded an explanation as to how Tully could possibly be responsible for an incident in which he was the victim of assault. The SFA claimed that the Ulsterman had 'exaggerated any slight injury he may have received.' The hilarity of this outlook from the governing body became all the more laughable when the referee's match report was released. The report showed that the official had not seen the incident. On this basis, one wonders how Tully could be punished for exasperating his injury.

To add fuel to the fire, Rangers were to visit Celtic Park a week after the SFA's disgraceful verdict, on 13th September. This time the match was a Semi-Final in the Glasgow Cup, which was a keenly contested tournament back then. In contrast to the concerns of the police, the match had passed in relative peace. However, all was about to change with 87 minutes on the clock. Celtic were on the attack, a late tackle came in and as the cries for a free kick went up, the referee waved play on. The ball found its way to the feet of a Rangers player, whilst Celtic's squad crowded around the referee. Anger turned to disbelief as the 'Gers striker ran towards the net, without challenge, and slotted home.

Charlie Tully was absolutely sickened and tried to lead the Celtic players off the field. The team discussed the issue but decided not to follow. Instead, they furiously played out the final minutes of the game, which resulted in a 2-1 defeat and the end of Celtic's Glasgow Cup campaign. Despite the hollow nature of Rangers' victory, the authorities decided to act against nobody – apart from Charlie Tully again. This time he was persecuted for 'incitement'.

Celtic tried, to no avail, to get the match replayed. Bob Kelly then made a final speculative plea to the SFA, to postpone another upcoming game between Celtic and Rangers, which was scheduled for 24th September. Given the poisonous anger and injustice felt by Celtic supporters at the treatment of their club, Kelly feared for public safety. Nobody was shocked to see the request denied and the game was obtusely set to go ahead amid a malevolent atmosphere.

As far as the Celtic Supporters Association (CSA), which had only been formed five years earlier, was concerned - this was the final straw. The fledgling organisation arranged urgent meetings to decide upon immediate action. The club had exhausted official channels, without the hostility towards Celtic or the bias against the club becoming any less apparent. The Celtic support had to make some form of protest and the CSA drew inspiration from the club's first patron, who gave rise to the concept of a boycott, a century earlier.

Michael Davitt was not only Celtic's first Patron, but he was also a political associate of the club's founding fathers. It was Davitt's Land League organisation who, in their campaign for fair rent and treatment for Irish tenants, sought to isolate the Earl of Erne and his agent (a former British Army Captain called Charles Boycott) after the pair had started serving notices of eviction on the local population. The campaign to isolate them included labourers withdrawing from the estate and local shops refusing to open. This gave rise to the political protest termed: 'boycott'.

The notion of asking Celtic supporters to withhold support for the team during the next Glasgow derby would be a massive gamble. If a boycott was met with a poor response, then the CSA would effectively be finished. Undeterred, the CSA showed their bravery and announced that its member clubs would not attend the Rangers game. They urged all Celtic supporters to do the same.

35,000 fewer fans turned up at Ibrox than on the previous occasion between the teams. The successful boycott had reduced the Ibrox crowd from 95,000 to 60,000 and cost

Rangers £2,000 in lost gate receipts. Charlie Tully also boycotted the match himself, whilst the team were apparently instructed by Bob Kelly to avoid physical contact with the opposition. It is therefore, none too surprising that Celtic lost the shambolic game 4-0. However, this first example of large scale boycotting in football, was the real measure of Celtic's success that day, even if it did little to change the decades of questionable officiating that followed.

The Belfast Celtic Society remember Charlie Tully

Charlie Tully at rest in Milltown Cemetery, Belfast

OPEN AIR MASS

Catholicism is an undeniable aspect of Celtic's origins. Such a reality was something that Celtic Football Club never denied and whilst promoting inclusivity, members of the clergy were granted free entry to matches in the early years of the club. By extension of the esteem in which leaders of the persecuted Glasgow Catholic people were held, Celtic supported many Catholic charities and organisations too. One such organisation was The Catholic Young Men's Society, which was founded by Father Richard O'Brien in Limerick. The Society's history explains that Father O'Brien established the social and spiritual movement when he met 24 labouring men in the upper room of a small two-storey cottage on May 19th, 1849. His motivation was simple - The Young Men's Society of the Immaculate Heart of Mary was set afloat with the following raison d'être: *To foster by mutual union and co-operation, and by priestly guidance, the spiritual, intellectual, social and physical welfare of its members.*

The organisation captured the interest of the youth in Ireland with a penchant for snooker, darts and trips to Knock. Volunteers of the Society also instilled valuable morals and ethical guidance into its membership base. On account of these merits, it came as no surprise when branches began opening across the Irish sea, the first of which in Sheffield in 1854, before the organisation eventually encompassed vast parts of the world, not least South Africa and Australia.

The Catholic Young Men's Society expanded into Scotland through Irish immigration. During the second decade of this migrating wave across the sea, Cannon Edward Joseph

Hannan (nephew of Father Richard O'Brien), visited Edinburgh on holiday, in 1861. He was persuaded to stay in Scotland by the Bishop, who had pleaded with him to run the recently re-inaugurated St. Patrick's Church in the Cowgate area of Edinburgh. Hannan had already displayed the necessary qualities to undertake this role, having devoted large periods of his time in the capital to addressing the social problems that poorer Catholics faced in the city. Pivotally, one such measure that Hannan took to improve the lives of young parishioners was to found a local branch of The Catholic Young Men's Society in 1865. Hannan then went on to become a priest in St. Patrick's Church six years later.

Like many key facets of Scots-Irish life, it wasn't long before the Cowgate branch of Hannan's established Catholic organisation immersed itself in the sporting hub of the community. Father Hannan had centred most of his work within priesthood around the inhabitants of his parish, which were ultimately the Irish community of Edinburgh. In 1875, with the assistance of 21-year-old Michael Whelahan, (whom he had met through The Catholic Young Men's Society); he founded Hibernian Football Club. Hannan himself served as the club's first Manager and latterly as President, until his death in June 1891. Despite only starting as a small church team, Hibs were refused entry to Scottish football competitions due to being an 'Irish club'. However, Cannon Hannan had done much lobbying to the governing body, which resulted in acceptance of the team participating in the 1877 Scottish Cup, just two years after the club's foundation.

The Catholic Young Men's Society played a strong role in the early history of Hibernian. It was a disciplined organisation, whose Edinburgh branch insisted that Hibernian players were practising Catholics. This policy led to the club being referenced by some as Scotland's first sectarian club. To balance this negative view, it could also be argued that the insistence on Catholic faith brought a sense of philosophy, spirituality and education to the early life of Hibernian and those who supported the club.

At Celtic Park, there has always been fierce opposition to a sectarian policy and Celtic remains a club open to all people regardless of their faith. Nevertheless, it goes without saying that the majority of supporters had/have an Irish and therefore naturally, Catholic, background. It was with this in mind that the club allowed The Catholic Young Men's Society to use Celtic Park as a venue for open air masses on numerous occasions. Paradise was used on a particularly frequent basis between the world wars and was the arena chosen to hold a large event to celebrate the centenary of the organisation in 1949. The event took the form of another open-air mass and attracted no fewer than 27,000 worshippers.

The western world is becoming increasingly secular today, as reflected by the decrease in membership numbers for The Catholic Young Men's Society. At its height, in the 1950s, the movement boasted more than 100 branches throughout Ireland. Today, its spiritual home has as few as 17. Incidentally, the period of those peak membership figures coincides with one of the last and largest open-air masses held at Celtic Park. Indeed, the club hosted the Marian Day celebrations of 1954 at Paradise, with the Archbishop of Glasgow - the Most Reverend Donald Campbell, leading the ceremony on that occasion.

Open air mass at Celtic Park - 1954

THE FLAG THAT FLIES ON HIGH

It may have been the post-war years, but Celtic were locked into a battle of their own. Season 1951/1952 had seen the club loitering four points above the relegation zone by the time that Rangers came to Parkhead for the traditional New Year's Day derby. Despite the Hogmanay festivities, many in Glasgow had little cause for celebration, at least until the match had passed and the city could breathe a sigh of relief. This unease stemmed from a decade of high profile incidents whenever Scotland's two biggest clubs had met. In a bid to minimise violence, the match was made an all ticket affair and newspapers across the city urged Celtic fans to avoid bringing bottles, banners or ill-mannered tongues with them.

The match proceeded like many Glasgow derbies of the time – frantic, frenetic and with Rangers controlling the game. Aside from the customary vehement atmosphere in those days, the game had passed with little trouble until the 70th minute, when fighting broke out in the North enclosure. Bottles were thrown, a sight that had become such a common backdrop in these games that the objects were like derby day confetti. 11 spectators were arrested, two of which were sent to prison, whilst others were fined for their part in a number of incidents that took place outside of Celtic Park at full time.

Enough was enough and the Glasgow Magistrates invited representatives of the Scottish Football Association and the Scottish League to consider the following proposals:

1: The Rangers and Celtic clubs should not again be paired on New Year's Day, when passions are likely to be inflamed by drink and more bottles are likely to be carried than on any other day.

2: On every occasion when the clubs meet admission should be by ticket only and the attendance limited to a number consistent with public safety, the number to be decided by the chief constable.

3: In the interests of safety of the public Celtic F.C. should be asked to construct numbered passage-ways in the terracing at each end of Celtic Park.

4: The two clubs should avoid displaying flags which might incite feeling among the spectators.

The final point was the one that was taken forth by the SFA, courting immeasurable controversy with its vague wording and likely reference to the tricolour. The old Irish flag with a golden harp on a green background had flown at Celtic Park from the opening of the stadium until Ireland became a Free State in 1922. The new emblem of Eire was then flown on the roof of the Jungle thereafter.

The national flag of Ireland was, and still is, an essential symbol of the club's Irish heritage. The particular flag flown at the stadium at the time had been handed to Celtic Football Club by the first Taoiseach of Ireland, Eamon De Valera. It was not a gift that would be readily removed.

Knowing the value of Irish identity to Celtic Football Club, many fans were concerned that some within the SFA would seize the opportunity to use the recommendations against the club. Those fears were realised when, after consideration, the Referee Committee of the SFA ruled that 'Celtic be asked to refrain from displaying in its park any

145

flag or emblem that had no association with the country or the sport on match days.' While expressing dissatisfaction that other recommendations had not been adopted, the Glasgow Magistrates endorsed the decision of the Referee Committee, as did the SFA council, by 26 votes to 7. However, Mr. John F Wilson, Chairman of Rangers, told the council: "The emblem has never been of any annoyance to Rangers. Don't delude yourselves." Wilson's stern contention that the flag of Ireland should be permitted to ripple in the wind above Celtic Park should not come as any surprise. Indeed, for Rangers to prosper they needed that badge of Irishness across the city: a representation of the very thing that their club had become the antithesis of in order to manufacture an identity and attract support.

Bob Kelly defended Celtic's traditions in less than phlegmatic fashion. He claimed that he would rather remove Celtic from Scottish football and start playing Gaelic games at Celtic Park than comply with the order. Kelly felt that to ignore the historical significance of the club would render its existence meaningless. This was not a mere matter of a flag. It was the surface of a wider battle against anti-Irish racism and institutionalised bigotry. Kelly's abrasive resistance ultimately led to the flag issue being voted on by all teams in the league.

Hibernian voted in support of the SFA, a disappointing move from a so called 'fellow Irish club'. Amid incredible irony, the deciding vote lay in the hands of Rangers. As previously alluded, Rangers had the foresight to consider the financial implications of the situation and determined that they wished for the tricolour to stay at Paradise.

The SFA Council convened a meeting to discuss the outcome of the vote, which had favoured Celtic's stance. Despite, the Hoops having a mandate from the rest of Scottish football, the council decided to hold a vote of their own, as to whether they should reverse their ruling on the flag issue. It was a disgraceful mark of the organisation's bigotry that their internal vote rejected the democratic voice of Scottish football.

The battle lines were well and truly drawn. If Celtic continued to fly the Irish flag in defiance of the SFA ruling, and any misconduct by their supporters took place, then the club would face a fine, closure of the ground, or suspension from the league. As ever, the Celtic board would not give in. Desmond White (Celtic Chairman in the late 70s) commented to The Evening Times: "It is indeed a sad commentary on the bigotry which still exists in the West of Scotland that this flag should be looked upon as an act of provocation. Eire is after all, a friendly country. Many of our supporters are wholly or part of Irish origin and naturally are proud of their Irish ancestry and would have every right to feel slighted if the tricolour was singled out for removal."

The genuine threat of expulsion hung over the club for the remainder of the 1951/1952 season. George Graham (SFA Secretary and Grandmason) led attempts to punish Celtic further, a move which Desmond White later said: "Will see him roast in hell." The bitter clique led by Graham continued to press for Celtic to take down the flag and submit to the SFA's demands. Celtic had taken legal advice on the matter and were confident about the outcome. However, Graham was not an easy man to tackle with his masonic connections. Surprisingly, Hibernian were the club that publicly backed the SFA Secretary at this time. The Hibees' position was largely held because their Chairman, Harry Swan, was an acting SFA President at a meeting on the issue. Swan was also rumoured to be a Freemason, which may have provided additional motivation for the direction of his vote. Either way, it appears that he was acting to further his personal ambitions and strengthen his relationship with the top brass of the game's governing body in Scotland.

No matter what was thrown at the club, Bob Kelly stood up to pressure from his colleagues on the SFA council and remained staunch in his quest to uphold the roots of Celtic Football Club. His persistence finally paid off when clubs and authorities alike, realised that Celtic were not going to budge, and their expulsion would have huge financial repercussions for Scottish football. Speaking to a lay Catholic organisation years later, Bob Kelly stated: "We had no need to be ashamed of our fathers, nor had we any cause to be ashamed that those founders (of Celtic) came from that country that has provided protagonists for liberty wherever they have settled."

Bob Kelly's defence of the flag is immortalised in a fantastic song named The Flag That Flies on High. The song was performed by Derek Warfield in 2005 for his Songs for the Bhoys collection. It documents the flag controversy and celebrates the fact that Celtic 'overcame all obstacles and kept their flag on high'.

THE FLAG THAT FLIES ON HIGH – DEREK WARFIELD

In Glasgow, back in '88
poor children needed fed
and some big-hearted Irish men
who lived around Parkhead
decided in their charity to silence
hunger's cry, so they started
Celtic Football Club and raised
the flag on high

and they raised the flag on high x2
(they started Celtic football club)
and raised the flag on high

Then bigots who did hate their race
and most of all their creed
used their power to hinder them
in spite of children's need
but Celtic's spirit - then as now
despite each pressman's lie
they rose above all obstacles
and kept their flag on high

They kept their flag on high
and they kept their flag on high
they rose above all obstacles
and kept their flag on high

They carried on from strength to strength
from fame to greater fame
now all who've heard of football
know the Glasgow Celtic name
But still the same old bigotry will let
no chance go by to blacken this great football
name and the flag that flies on high

When in 1953 the ruling SFA
they said that Celtic football club
must take their flag away
But Kelly and his Celtic men said
they would rather die
than to disgrace their forefathers
and the flag that flies on high

and the flag that flies on high x2
than to disgrace their forefathers
and the flag that flies on high

And still the Irish tricolour
it waves o'er Paradise
where proudly it's admired and loved
by Irish exile's eyes
God grant men like Bob Kelly
all attacks we will defy
from the enemies of Celtic
and the flag that flies on high

and the flag that flies on high x2
from the enemies of Celtic
and the flag that flies on high

The Irish tricolour proudly waving above the Jungle

JOHN 'JACKIE' MILLSOPP

When it comes to fallen Celts, the names of John Thomson and Phil O'Donnell are rightly remembered by the Celtic support. However, the loss of another young player in similarly tragic circumstances, is often overlooked. John Millsopp, or 'Jackie' as he was better known, was cut down in his prime at the tender age of 22. He signed full forms with Celtic in 1948 and was a versatile talent, able to deputise for wingers, defenders and central midfielders.

Millsopp cemented a permanent role in the side after four years of waiting, albeit he still operated under the tag of a utility man. Nonetheless, the fledgling prospect had learnt from the likes of Bobby Evans and Charlie Tully, developing into an all-round talent. Having got a solid run of consecutive starts, Millsopp took to the field against Falkirk at Celtic Park on 6th September 1952. The flags were at half-mast that day and the Celtic players wore black armbands, a tribute to the magnificent Frank O'Donnell, who had passed away earlier in the week. The former forward, who scored 58 goals in 83 games for the club, was just 41 years of age when his life was prematurely taken. Little did anyone associated with Celtic know that the scene would sinisterly repeat itself a fortnight later.

A match report from The Glasgow Herald on 8th September 1952 encapsulates the excitement once play got underway: *A Baillie-Millsopp-Tully movement put Scott's charge in danger and the keeper was fortunate to see Tully's attempt go narrowly passed. Delaney then took Falkirk in to engage Bonnar, who had little trouble dealing with a Plumb shot.*

The reference to (Jimmy) Delaney leading the Falkirk attack was a sight that invoked nostalgic memories amongst the 20,000 Celtic fans in attendance. It had not been too long since many of them had seen the outstanding outside right burst down the wing in green and white hoops before his move to Manchester United. Nevertheless, Delaney was powerless to stop his former side taking the lead in the 9th minute, after stupendous play from Tully led to McPhail driving home from just inside the box. Celtic doubled their lead moments later. This time Fernie dispatched another Tully delivery. The Bhoys further turned on the style when McPhail bagged his second of the game to send Celtic into the break with a 3-0 lead.

The Glasgow Herald report, referenced above, described the second half in the following manner:

In the first minute Scott was in trouble again from a Tully cross but managed to clear at the second attempt. Falkirk then made track for Bonnar and 90 seconds after the restart they had reduced the lead. Although Plumb was the scorer, Delaney takes most the credit for a beautiful back heeler, which enabled the centre to drive past Bonnar.

Eight minutes later Falkirk again struck with success. A neat slip from Plumb to Morrison opened the Parkhead defence and Bonnar had little chance with Morrison's drive.

Celtic became a bit rattled and the defence uncertain and it was no great surprise when in the sixteenth minute Plumb accepted from McCabe and prodded a smart equalising goal for Falkrik.

*Now came the fight for the leading goal and after McPhail
had shot over, a Brown cross brought the Celtic rear into
action. With a roving commission Delaney was giving
concern and the old Celt was disgusted when a McCabe
score was ruled out for offside.*

*Nine minutes from time Tully pounced on a Baillie free kick
and flashed a hard effort past Scott for Celtic's fourth goal.
One minute from time McPhail headed a fifth goal for
Celtic.*

What the match report failed to mention about the eight-
goal thriller, was that John Millsopp had complained of
chronic stomach pains during the game. The omission of
this detail is understandable, as many assumed it to be a
minor issue considering that the youngster completed the
match. It soon transpired that Millsopp had a problem with
his appendix and, following training on 9th September, he
reported to Glasgow's Royal Infirmary where he underwent
an operation for appendicitis. Anticipating a routine
procedure, it was an absolute shock to everybody
connected with the club when the news surfaced that there
were fatal complications with Millsopp's surgery and that
he had passed away due to a burst appendix.

Multiple newspapers broke the sad news to the wider
football world the next day. Yet The Evening Times did so
in their 18th September edition, with a footnote entitled
'Jackie Millsopp's death':

*Glasgow's football supporters, players and officials have
been shocked by the death of young Jackie Millsopp of
Celtic in a Glasgow Infirmary last night. He was only 21*
(should have read 22). *He had made his way in to the first*

team and only 10 days ago (should have read 12 days ago) *played against Falkirk.*

The sympathy of everyone goes to the boy's relatives and to his club. Jackie's death will cast a gloom over the Celtic and Rangers match on Saturday, when the players of both sides will pay their tributes before the game starts.

Mourning had scarcely begun when Celtic played host to Rangers, two days later. It would be unthinkable for the game to go ahead in today's world, given that the funeral took place in Cambuslang that morning. Yet that is exactly what happened.

A delegation from Rangers (Geroge Young, Sammy Cox, Ian McColl and Jock Shaw) along with the entire Celtic team, excepting John McPhail and Bobby Collins, attended the funeral service at St. Bride's Roman Catholic Church. Hundreds of mourners looked on as Weir, Tully, Evans, Fallon, Stein and McGrory bore the coffin after requiem mass. The 200 strong cortege then followed the hearse, led by James McGrory, to Westburn Cemetery, where John 'Jackie' Millsopp was laid to rest.

The Celtic players and their Rangers counterparts had no time for sorrow, as they made the short trip to Parkhead for the match that afternoon. There, the flags were again at half mast, hooped jerseys were once more haunted by the presence of a black armband and a minute of silence was held before kick-off. The mood amongst the Celtic team was one of determination and disconsolation in equal measure. This oxymoron illustrated itself through the ability of Celtic to earn a 2-1 win, whilst Alex Rollo and James Walsh refused to celebrate their decisive goals.

Off the field, there was a subdued atmosphere in terms of vocal support from the 48,000 people in attendance. Although, even a backdrop of heartache failed to totally punctuate the violence that coincided with this fixture. The Glasgow Herald ran a headline 'Hooligan Element At Parkhead', whilst The Evening Times focused on 'Why Are The Old Firm Crowds Falling Off So Much?' Each newspaper had a small subsection to pay tribute to John Millsopp, whilst The Glasgow Herald piece covered his passing within the context of crowd issues.

The Glasgow Herald article, published on 22nd September 1952, first praised Celtic fans for their behaviour since being permitted to fly the Eire flag, before laying the blame at the door of a pocket of Rangers supporters. Below is the relevant section of said article:

...The vast majority of Rangers fans were as shocked as anyone when during a most impressive minute of silence in tribute to the late John Millsopp, the Celtic player who died in midweek, a profane exhortation thundered over the ground. The rumble of disapproval that followed indicated how easily that spark could have started a conflagration.

At half time the disturbers of the peace continued their provocative behaviour but to the great credit of the opposite camp the only retaliation was a round of slow handclapping. An attempt was made to hoist a miniature flag of Eire but those nearby obviously put an end to it. Rangers Football Club have no desire that the hooligan type of follower should be linked with them...

In spite of the behaviour of some at the derby match, most people were moved by such a tragedy. None more so than

Sean Fallon, who speaks of his despair at the death, in his biography by Steven Sullivan. Fallon said: "I'm not ashamed to say that I shed a few tears around that time. I had got to know him well because we'd shared a cabin on the boat over to America the summer before, when the club took us over for a tour after we had won the Scottish Cup. We became good friends and Jackie was a lovely lad. Everyone at Celtic liked him, and it affected us all for a long, long time."

The scenes of anguish around the club correspond with Fallon's recollections, reportedly being reminiscent of the desolation experienced at the 1930s funerals for young Celts: John Thomson and Peter Scarff. (Peter Scarff was a great inside-left for Celtic, who contracted TB disease around the time that Thomson passed away. He died two years later.)

SHAWFIELD DISASTER

Beyond the incredible 7-1 League Cup Final, little is known about Celtic in the close of 1957. The triumph of that never forgotten October afternoon was soon contrasted by tragedy when the Celts played against Clyde two months later.

A large and buoyant Celtic support made the shortest trip of the season to Shawfield stadium. The ground is said to have been overflowing, with children needing to sit on top of the boundary wall at pitch side to avoid being crushed. The match got underway with the referee's whistle momentarily punctuating the Celtic support's fine rendition of Kevin Barry.

In the third minute, Neil Mochan, who scored a brace in the famous 7-1 demolition of Rangers, combined with the hat-trick hero from that famous day - Billy McPhail. McPhail found himself unmarked on the left-hand side of the area and took a touch inside on his right foot, before rifling into the roof of the net. Pandemonium ensued, in a momentarily joyous manner.

Suddenly, things turned sinister.

The crowd had surged with catastrophic effect. The weight of the huge Celtic support falling forward caused a mass pile up on the pitch side wall, which toppled the brick work and crushed the children, who had been sat on top of it. Screams of panic pierced the air as all available ambulance units were dispatched to the scene.

The game was halted immediately, but due to the fog being so severe, those on the side of the ground furthest from the collapse had no idea what was going on. It was only when police pleaded for help from spectators that people began to realise that something serious had happened.

Men from both supports urgently tried to lift sections of the wall to allow the buried children to escape. Try as they might, the sound of helpless tears caused horrifically distressing emotions and so the police intervened, utilising their training to show calm leadership. The fire brigade joined the effort, desperately doing all in their power to help.

One father was seen, head in hands, weeping as the horror unfolded before his eyes. His son was among the 12 children who had to be taken to hospital for treatment. Their ages were all between nine and 15. A 54-year-old man was also hospitalised, whilst a further 24 boys and 14 adults were treated for minor injuries.

Despite the macabre scene, play was resumed half an hour after the last ambulance left Shawfield. The players coped well in the circumstances, and Billy McPhail soon scored his second of the afternoon with an outrageous right footed strike into the top corner from an acute angle. The match looked to be all over in the 23rd minute, when Neil 'Smiler' Mochan belted a shot against the crossbar, which cannoned off a defender into the net. However, Clyde weren't willing to give up yet. They responded with two quick fire goals to go into the break trailing 3-2.

Clyde started the second half on the attack but a fluent move on the counter saw McPhail round the keeper… only for the centre forward to miss an open goal. John Smith redressed matters for the Hoops when he extended Celtic's advantage in the 57th minute, but plucky Clyde responded again, making the score 4-3 just after the hour mark. It took a beautiful volley by Sammy Wilson and a late second for Smith to confirm victory for Celtic. Those in hooped jerseys had certainly been made to fight for their 6-3 win, though the result had been secondary in the circumstances.

The day after the match, on Sunday 15th December, a test was carried out on a part of the wall that was still standing. 18 policemen stood on a ten-yard stretch of the wall without issue, but when they closed in to two yards, the wall shook and parts of it trembled. Clearly it was not fit for purpose, especially as there had been a 26,500-strong crowd bearing down upon it.

Unbearable anxiety hung over the city throughout the weekend, before there was a clamour to obtain a copy of the Monday newspapers. Devastatingly, the red tops told of a 12-year-old named James Ryan, who had not been as lucky as others at Shawfield. The child from Bridgeton had lost his life just minutes after seeing his hero score for the club he loved. The hospitalised fans were being visited by players of both teams when the sombre news was confirmed to the clubs, who immediately decided that they would send officials to the funeral.

A Fatal Accident Inquiry went ahead on 27th February 1958 and statements were taken in open court. Bizarrely, statements came from both the Rutherglen and Lanarkshire Police forces as 95% of Shawfield stadium was located in Lanarkshire, whilst the turnstyles fell within Glasgow. As such, the main man power was supplied by Lanarkshire Police but both forces had been involved. Eventually, the jury returned a formal verdict that the accident had occurred 'through the actions of an unruly element in the crowd'. The verdict failed to give closure on one of the saddest days in the history of Celtic Football Club.

THE RIGHT TO REPLY

Throughout the annals of Celtic history there are countless legendary figures. Bobby Evans was one such player. A skilful inside right, Evans was reluctantly converted into a no-nonsense centre back due to his aggression, tough tackling and aerial prowess. These traits made him a fine Celtic captain, yet his real forte was turning defence in to attack with an excellent range of passing.

As great as Bobby Evans was for the club, he let himself down during a 1960 Scottish Cup tie in Paisley, at a time when his career was coming to an end. Bobby was getting dominated by the St Mirren striker, Gerry Baker, who peeled off Evans in the box, just as a well-placed cross was making its way to the far post. Evans was caught under the ball and opted to catch it with both hands. This led one incensed Celtic fan, Mr. Mackenzie from Gallowhill (Paisley), to write a letter to The Evening Citizen newspaper expressing his dismay at the Celtic stalwart's actions. The letter, which was published on 16th February 1960, read:

I left the St. Mirren-Celtic cup-tie at Love Street with a firm opinion on one aspect of our future international sides – Bobby Evans is no longer the man to fill Scotland's centre-half jersey. I have long been an admirer of Bobby Evans, both as a footballer who never gave up trying and as a sportsman. It may have been a good tactic to jump into the air and catch the ball like a goalkeeper (as he did on Saturday) but it was a surprisingly graceless act from a no.1 player. Bobby, slow on the turn these days, has been relying on his positional sense. Now it seems, even that is suspect.

As a leader and figurehead for many years, Evans was never one to shy away from his critics. Owing to the fact that the newspaper offered a 'right to reply' opportunity for any player that was singled out and reproved, the editor no doubt felt he would be in for a treat with the story that would emanate from the Celtic man's response. However, Bobby Evans had more class than to react in such a public way.

A day after the letter was published, Mr. Mackenzie heard a knock at his door. He promptly strolled along the hallway and twisted the handle. A look of disbelief and discomfiture was immediately etched across his face as standing in front of him was a displeased man looking to set the record straight. Celtic and Scotland's centre half had gone to Paisley to reproach Mr. Mackenzie about one area of his letter. There was no shouting or raised voices, but after Evans introduced himself, he supposedly stood before Mr. Mackenzie and authoritatively said: "I don't mind you saying I am past it, but don't ever question my sportsmanship." A mark of the man's character is that once Evans had said his piece, he stayed for a drink and the pair parted on good terms!

POLICE CONDEMN THE CELTIC SONG

Picture the scene: Celtic on the cusp of glory. By hook, crook, bus, plane, train and automobile, thousands of supporters had made it to Lisbon for the final of the 1967 European Cup. The faithful had won the hearts of the Portuguese people with their exemplary conduct and incredible atmosphere before the match. As the Celtic players lined up alongside their Italian opponents in the tunnel, Bertie Auld cleared his throat and began to sing: "Sure it's a grand old team to play for…" Each of the Lisbon Lions joined in and Glen Daly's immortal anthem was soon heard by the supporters. The support sang with the players as the team came into view: "Sure it's a grand old team to see and if you know the history…" The enjoyment of the occasion by players and fans, in unison, appeared to mesmerise the Inter Milan outfit and gave Celtic the upper hand. That moment is regaled as one of the most iconic in the history of Celtic Football Club.

Throughout the years, supporters have enjoyed singing The Celtic Song at many other great times. It is synonymous with the club. A vocal monument to Celtic. However, it is an often-overlooked fact that fans are actually singing a combination of two different songs on the terraces – Hail Hail The Celts Are Here and The Celtic Song. The latter is played on its own over the tannoy at Celtic Park before every home match, as the teams emerge from the tunnel.

The lyrics to The Celtic Song are said to have been written by Liam Mallory, though nobody has been able to identify the man, and there are two popular theories as to his true identity. It is thought that Liam Mallory is either a pseudonym for Glen Daly himself, or for Mick McLaughlin

– better known as 'Garngad Mick'. McLaughlin is also alleged to have written Hampden In The Sun. The latter theory extends that the rights to the song were sold to Glen Daly for a fiver!

Glen Daly eventually produced the iconic Celtic Song at Pye Record's Marble Arch Studios in London, in August 1961. On his visit to record the immutable track, he had an hour to kill and reportedly went for a roast dinner in The Strand restaurant, which was among the most reputable in the city and boasted a guest list that was littered with celebrity names. Upon devouring the meal, the Calton born artist is said to have pondered over the second verse of The Celtic Song, which he felt was inadequate. It was at the restaurant table that a desperate Daly became inspired, when he recalled the voice of Belfast Celtic fanatic, Charlie Tully, who had sung the Antrim club's classic song at a party in Kenilworth one evening. The lyrics that Glen Daly remembered hearing Tully slur were part of a short ditty that had been a favourite of Belfast Celtic's support for years: 'We don't care if we win lose or draw. Darn the hare we care because we only know that there's going to be a show and the Belfast Celtic will be there.' The words were a perfect fit. Glen Daly's anthem was complete, and the song was released on a 45rpm single record in October 1961.

Much like the attachment of This Land Is Your Land to Let The People Sing, Hail Hail The Celts Are Here was connected to The Celtic Song by Hoops supporters in the early 1960s.

Hail Hail The Celts Are Here can be traced back to a 1917 military marching song by D.A. Estron and Theodore

Morse, called Hail Hail The Gangs Are Here. It was set to the tune of With Cat-like Tread, Upon Our Prey We Steal, which was a song featured in an 1879 Gilbert & Sullivan opera, named The Pirates of Penzance. The song had been largely plagiarised by Gilbert and Sullivan, who stole the original version, entitled The Anvil Chorus, from Italian opera composer - Giuseppe Verdi. Verdi had written The Anvil Chorus for an 1853 opera: Il Trovatore (The Troubadour), which in turn was based on the play, El Trovador, written by Antonio García Gutiérrez in 1836!

The lyrics to the 1917 adaption, from which the Celtic chant arose, were:

Hail! Hail! the gang's all here,
What the deuce do we care,
What the deuce do we care,
Hail! Hail! We're full of cheer,
What the deuce do we care Bill!

A swift modification to make the version appropriate for Celtic Football Club was made and the song was then used on the terraces as a preamble to The Celtic Song.

As is aforementioned, The Celtic Song, as a standalone match day anthem, holds a historic and enduring place in Celtic folklore. It was first played over the tannoy at Celtic Park on 14th October 1961, prior to a league match against Stirling Albion. However, following its release, it was immediately under threat from the establishment. The media reported on the song in a very peculiar manner, instantly describing it as 'inflammatory', 'potentially offensive' and 'a possible catalyst for old firm trouble'. The Daily Mail even ran a story in October 1961 with the

headline: 'Police Condemn New Celtic Rallying Song'.
The piece went on to say:

*Glasgow police attacked yesterday, an Englishman's plan
to give Celtic supporters two rallying songs. One of the
songs – both have already been recorded – tells of the
death of Celtic and Scotland goalkeeper John Thomson,
who died 30 years ago. The recording company and who
organised the recording session is C.P Stanton who runs
Glasgow Jazz Club Promotions Ltd.*

*"It is ridiculous to suggest these records could cause more
trouble," he said last night.*

Common sense eventually prevailed, and The Celtic Song
lived on as the soundtrack to the Bhoys becoming
champions of Europe six years later. It continues to have an
impact, and for that Celtic fans owe a debt of gratitude to
the elusive Liam Mallory, and Glen Daly, unless of course
they are indeed the same person.

HIDDEN AGENDA

The idea of players using fake names and disguising themselves with false beards sounds like a crazy tale harking back to the Victorian era. However, it was the reality during Donegal's Kennedy Cup competition of 1964.

The links between the Glasgow Irish and Donegal are well renowned. For decades there has been a daily bus service that runs both ways between Donegal and the Gorbals, whilst many of the Irish community in Scotland can trace their ancestral roots to Ulster and the county specifically. Despite the region being associated with keen support for Gaelic games and Irish language speaking, there had always been considerable interest reserved for the non-native code of football. Therefore, many towns in Donegal hosted summer time football tournaments to boost tourism from Scotland. Moville was one such town.

The Kennedy Cup, held in Moville, was notorious for local and touring teams paying to attract ringers because the tournament drew large crowds (up to 5,000 for finals) and paid huge prize money. In the summer of 1964, the competition hit the headlines thanks to one team making a wild attempt to cheat their way to glory, by adopting the services of Scottish professional footballers. Carfin Emeralds were the side in question. The small Scottish club had been founded by a monsignor named John Gillen, who was born in Donegal but moved to Motherwell to conduct church duties as a Parish Priest. Gillen's brother lived in Moville and was responsible for organising the annual Kennedy Cup competition.

John Gillen was desperate for his team to lift his brother's trophy as the £2,000 prize (approximately £36,000 in today's money) would go a long way towards funding his parochial projects in Motherwell. Gillen set about the task, confident that he could use his contacts to enlist the services of multiple Celtic players. However, a major stumbling block would be overcoming the contractual conditions, which prohibited professional footballers from playing for any other club.

Quite comically, a plan was hatched for any willing Hoops stars to avoid detection by wearing make-up, boot polish and false beards. Perhaps because of the altruistic reasons behind Carfin Emerald's pursuit of victory, many contracted Celtic players agreed to participate. Even a certain Jimmy Johnstone, who was a regular churchgoer in Viewpark, agreed to join the Carfin club for a game on their venture after the local priest had requested his assistance on Gillen's behalf.

Remarkably, the Bhoys and a few amateur players, boarded a boat bound for the Emerald Isle in July 1964. They took to the pitch at Bay Field in ambitious disguise such as false goatees and facial scars. The 1-1 draw against Tonnage Dockers from Derry may have helped preserve anonymity, but there was certainly curiosity about the strange looking faces among the Carfin squad. The majority Celtic XI, ironically donning the green and white hoops of Carfin Emeralds, rectified matters in the replay by racing into an unassailable lead within half an hour. The incognito Celts would go on to win 7-3 on that occasion.

Carfin Emeralds and their covert Celts were as good as caught when the local media reported the full names of the

Derry team's players but didn't mention the name of a single player for the Scottish club. The Derry Journal then compounded the difficulty for the Celtic players to conceal their identity, when they explicitly namedropped Neil Mochan and Frank Haffey from the Carfin team that defeated Rosemount 3-2 in the Quarter Final in September.

Unbelievably, John Gillen remained undeterred and ordered the team to play on, regardless of being uncovered by the media. His last-ditch attempt to see the plan through meant that Carfin Emeralds didn't submit a team sheet for the Semi-Final against Foyle Rovers. The match was very tight, with Neil Mochan scoring a superb solo goal to take the game by virtue of a 1-0 victory. The team had played at 50% to try and keep the disguise alive but there could be no risks in the Final now that one hand was on the £2,000 prize money.

The Final, held on 11th October 1964, would be played against Manchester Athletic. It was billed 'A Scottish v English, cross-channel affair.' Celtic had beaten Aberdeen at Pittodrie a day earlier so no first teamers could travel or risk playing, although some Hoops reserves had an instrumental role in the Carfin club triumphing 7-0 against their English counterparts.

The Derry Journal's coverage of the Final included several photographs, one of which was captioned 'Members of the Carfin Emeralds team, most of whom wore false beards side-whiskers and make-up are introduced to Rev. H Gallagher C.C. Moville before the kick-off.' The article also outlined Rainey, Mitchell, Ward, Howley and Coyle as Carfin Emeralds team members.

The Kennedy Cup headed to Motherwell, bringing the cash with it. Despite all Celts being caught out in North Western Irish circles, it seems that each guilty party avoided retribution from the Parkhead hierarchy.

The secret Celts pictured prior to a match for Carfin Emeralds in the Kennedy Cup, 1964. Note the dodgy disguises and a clearly familiar face in Billy McNeill.

GEORGE CONNELLY DAZZLES THE CROWD

The story of George Connelly is one of the saddest in British football. A flawed genius, he signed provisional forms for Celtic, joining from Tulliallan Juniors, in July 1964. It would not be long before he'd dazzle the Parkhead crowd.

Jock Stein had been impressed with the young holding midfielder and sent him onto the pitch at Celtic Park just before the start of a European Cup Winners' Cup Quarter-Final match against Dynamo Kiev on 12th January 1966. The 16-year-old was tasked with thrilling the crowd in return for a fiver and he obliged the Manager with a delightful display of 'keepy-ups'. Connelly had the fans looking on in awe as he danced around the full perimeter of the pitch, keeping the ball aloft without fail. Stein had been confident that Connelly would excite the faithful, given that his average at juggling with the ball was said to be 2,000 consecutive 'keepy-ups'.

Connelly was one of a number of exciting prospects at the club in this era. Indeed, there were high hopes for the next generation coming through on the conveyor belt, though the challenge of filling the huge shoes of the Lisbon Lions was always going to be immeasurable. Barely two years had elapsed before Connelly emerged as an ever-present in the Celtic side and perhaps the most important player of the Quality Street Gang- no mean feat when you consider that other breakthrough talents included Kenny Dalglish, Danny McGrain and Lou Macari.

So high was the esteem in which he was held, Connelly was touted as the successor to Billy McNeill thanks to his defensive abilities, which meant he was utilised at the back as well as in midfield. This belief was reaffirmed in the 1969 Scottish Cup Final against Rangers, when Connelly played a lead role, walked the ball into the net for his goal and again performed an exhibition of 'keepy-ups'... this time inside his own penalty box! Rangers supporters were furious at his showboating antics, as the Ibrox side were trailing 4-0. However, Jock Stein claimed that Connelly's performance had shown that he was on a par with Franz Beckenbauer.

Despite his domestic prowess, the pinnacle for Connelly was to come in the European Cup Semi-Final of 1970 against Leeds United. It was then that the Hoops legend really made the world stand up and take note of his incredible ability. Leeds were dubbed 'the greatest English team of all time' and the press south of the border had Celtic marked as underdogs. With the help of a sublime team, and the immortal Jimmy Johnstone, Connelly put Leeds to the sword by netting the winning goal at Elland Road in the first leg. Celtic went on to defeat Leeds in front of a European record 136,505 crowd at Hampden Park in the second leg, two weeks later. The Bhoys had won 'the battle of Britain' by three goals to one on aggregate. It saw Celtic reach their second European Cup Final in three years. Astonishingly, Connelly was left out of the Final, which Celtic lost in extra time against Feyenoord.

Tragically, George Connelly was soon seeking solace from a range of mental health issues, through the consumption of alcohol. By 1973, the shy star was finding it very tough to live in the limelight, this despite his earning of the player of the year award.

The troubled star reported injured ahead of the Scottish League match against Partick Thistle on 17th November 1973, yet in reality he had not turned up for training the day before and had remained missing for the game. Connelly soon returned but walked out on Celtic again ahead of a Glasgow derby on 14th September 1974. On this occasion he stayed away from football for two months until he returned to training on 9th November.

Connelly's eventual return to first team action was short lived. He walked out on the club a further three times and also performed one of his disappearing acts before what should have been his Scotland debut, exiting the airport just as Willie Ormond's squad were boarding a flight to Switzerland in May 1973. After experiencing issues with his marriage, everything became too much for George. He played his last game of football for Celtic on 13th September 1975 at Fir Park, and after failing to turn up at Celtic Park for the clash with Stenhousemuir on 24th of that month, he announced his retirement.

George Connelly's unique talents continue to be revered, cementing his place in Celtic folklore. However, we all wonder what could have been if his mind was in a positive place. The Celtic support finally got to pay tribute to him when he returned to Paradise for the first time, to perform the half time draw, during a Celtic v AC Milan Champions League Group Stage match in October 2007.

FIGHT LIKE LIONS

After steering the club to its first league title in 12 years, Jock Stein took his Celtic team on a tour of North America. Just five days had elapsed since the close of the 1965/66 season when the Bhoys embarked on their transatlantic journey to round off the campaign. The Manager wanted to allow the team to bond properly away from the scrutiny of the media, which had intensified during the title run in. He saw the forging of an unbreakable team spirit as the next step towards building on the newfound success that he had brought to the club during his first two seasons at the helm.

The soon to be Lisbon Lions began their tour by flying from Glasgow to Bermuda, via London, on 11th May 1966. The squad, minus Jim Craig who was unable to travel due to his dental studies at the University of Glasgow, stayed overnight in the British overseas territory and played a match against Bermuda the next day. Tommy Gemmell found himself in an experimental centre forward role on that occasion, where he bagged a brace as the Hoops won 10-1. The footballing aspect of the stay on the island was then rounded off with a 7-0 win against Bermuda YMCA a few days later, on the 15th May.

Having spent six days tanning themselves and enjoying the blend of British-American culture, the Celtic contingent left Bermuda and flew to New York. Upon landing in the Big Apple, the team boarded a bus bound for New Jersey. Indeed, it was during the bus journey that Jock Stein learned of the news that he was about to become several hundred pounds richer, thanks to a panel of football writers in London, who had voted him British football's manager of the year. Stein had received the award for combining

175

domestic success, securing the league championship and League Cup double, with an excellent European campaign, only halted by an incorrect decision to disallow a Bobby Lennox strike for offside. That decision to rule out the goal against Liverpool at Anfield, ultimately denied Celtic a place in the European Cup Winners' Cup Final against Borussia Dortmund at Hampden. However, the Hoops' exploits abroad that season had shown Stein that he could achieve greatness.

Once the squad arrived in New Jersey, Stein made it clear that whilst there would be laughter, swimming pools and relaxation, his players needed to get down to business on the field. His instructions were promptly carried out in the form of New Jersey All Stars being smashed 6-0 by the Celts in their opening match on US soil. The Bhoys then moved on to Toronto, where they defeated Tottenham Hotspur 1-0 in front of a 26,000 crowd. The Spurs side, which included Terry Venables, were reportedly enraged that Celtic had broken a promise not to bring Jimmy Johnstone on. Although, 'Jinky' only played the last 20 minutes of the match due to an injury to John Hughes.

Days later, Stein's blossoming team travelled to Ontario, where they destroyed a Hamilton Primo XI, by 11 goals to nil. In keeping with the pace of the tour, Celtic arrived back in New Jersey on 27th May to face Bologna at the famous Roosevelt (baseball) Stadium. The sight that greeted the teams before the match left them flabbergasted. According to Ronnie Simpson, who wrote the match reports on behalf of the media throughout the tour, a corner flag lay rested against a concrete boundary wall, the grass was bare, and the touchlines were not within the regulatory dimensions. Despite the disappointment felt by the Celtic team and

Bologna's branding of the pitch "An insult," both clubs agreed to fulfil the fixture due to the large crowd that had turned up.

The game itself was a very tempestuous affair. Celtic showed the attacking initiative and Bologna defended with aggression. The mark was overstepped 20 minutes from time when the Italian's outside right, Giancarie Morrone, was ordered off for persistent fouling. Bertie Auld and Bobby Murdoch had been his particular targets. When both midfield enforcers sought retribution, they received the full wrath of a largely Italian immigrant crowd. Bottles were thrown at the Celtic players and Billy McNeill bore the brunt of the onslaught. The captain required a couple of stitches above the eye after he was struck by a glass object, which effectively ended the game as a footballing contest. Like most 0-0 draws, the football was forgettable, but the day will be remembered for the shocking scenes at full time when mounted police were forced to protect Jock Stein. The commanding Celtic boss was jostled and shoved by Bologna supporters as he tried to escape towards the tunnel to carry out his post-match debrief.

Big Jock was keen to move on from the Bologna controversy and refocus his attention on getting his team back to playing attractive football. He was given that opportunity two days later and due to the horrendous condition of the pitch at the Roosevelt Stadium, Celtic's match against St Louis CYM All-Stars was moved to Roosevelt High School. There, it was playground football as the Bhoys cruised their way to a 6-1 win and swiftly headed on to San Francisco ahead of another clash with Tottenham Hotspur.

The second match against Spurs had been feared to court more controversy after the issue over the Jimmy Johnstone substitution in the previous encounter between the sides. The basis of the complaint from Spurs, it had been clarified, was that it had been agreed that substitutions were only to be made in the event of injury. Stein insisted that John Hughes had picked up an ankle knock, but the North London club clearly felt otherwise. Despite the nervous anticipation, this game was free of animosity and amounted to nothing more than two good teams playing a competitive match in front of 12,000 locals at the Kezar Stadium.

Bertie Auld gave Celtic the lead after 25 minutes, when he intercepted a stray pass and unleashed a rocket into the roof of the net from the edge of the area. Just a minute later, Mackay equalised by tapping home the rebound from his penalty, which was saved by Ronnie Simpson. The first half talking points were rounded off with an injury to Bertie Auld, who was ironically carried off with an ankle knock, just prior to the interval.

Celtic sought to restore their advantage after the break and did so within 14 minutes. Bobby Lennox crashed the ball low into the net after receiving a square pass from Stevie Chalmers on that occasion. Spurs battled back and dominated the late stages, however, attack after attack was thwarted by a resolute Celtic defence, which was buoyed by the return of their skipper, Billy McNeill. In the dying moments, Terry Venables breached the wall of green and white before him and hit a piledriver from 26 yards, which beat Ronnie Simpson, only to strike the post. By hook, crook and goalpost – the Hoops managed to hold out for a 2-1 win.

Celtic completed a trilogy of games against Spurs at the Empire Stadium in Vancouver, on 4th June 1966. This third match against the English club was due to be the last game of the tour for Jimmy Johnstone and Ian Young as they needed to head home for their weddings on 6th June. However, by the time kick off came around the pair had been persuaded to stay until the penultimate match of the tour due to injuries within the squad. The game got underway and was typically hard fought. Bobby Lennox gave Celtic an early lead and the match remained very cagey thereafter. However, the game was to spring into life in the final five minutes as a Terry Venables equaliser served as a spark to light the proverbial fuse. The referee's choosing to ignore a push by Venables on Bobby Murdoch in the lead up to the goal left the Celtic players incensed. Jimmy Johnstone was the most vocal of those disputing the decision, so much so that the referee sent him off for dissent. The tricky winger was seething. He refused to leave the field and after both managers intervened, it was agreed he should stay on the park. The contentious equaliser was enough to earn Spurs a draw and ensure that Celtic failed to win for only the second time on tour. There was to be no simmering of the fire after the game, for Jimmy Johnstone was so enraged at his treatment that he insisted to return home as soon as possible to prepare for his wedding. His wish was granted, which meant Ian Young was also allowed to join him on the flight home.

12 players remained in America, two of which were goalkeepers. Undeterred, the threadbare Celtic squad returned to the Kezar Stadium in San Francisco for the penultimate and arguably biggest game of the expedition. This time the opponents were footballing giants, Bayern Munich, who had selected a young prospect named Gerd

Muller to play at right back! The reported (approximate) 12,000 spectators in attendance got their $3.75 entrance fee's worth with the most ferocious match of the tour yet.

Celtic dominated the first half but found themselves a goal down at the break. The second half is summarised by Joe McBride, who recalled the game years later: "We (McBride and Gerd Muller) spoke about the game Celtic played against Bayern in San Francisco in 1966. It was a pre-season friendly, but it was not especially friendly. Gerd was just a kid starting out and it still is amazing to recall at that time one of the world's greatest goal scorers was playing at right back. He got himself into an argument with Steve Chalmers and hooked Stevie, who chased him round the pitch. But before Stevie could get to him, a big guy wearing a kilt had jumped the barriers and stuck one on Gerd - he was flat out on the track. When we spoke about the incident, he recalled every detail - apart from the time he was unconscious."

In contrast to Joe McBride's account of the events that day, Ronnie Simpson's report claimed that it was in fact Bayern's full back, Adolf Kunstwadl, who struck Chalmers, before being chased behind the goal and knocked out by the Celtic striker himself, rather than any pitch invading fan. Notwithstanding this confusion, one thing that is certain is that approximately 100 fans did invade the pitch during the commotion and play was consequently halted for seven minutes. The running battles and free for all was frankly emblematic of the trouble that had marred the Bhoys' time in North America, yet there was still room for action on the pitch to steal the headlines.

At the time of the incident, Celtic had pulled a goal back through Lennox but were trailing 2-1. The Hoops faced an incredibly tough task in breaking down a nine-man Bayern defence, within the ten minutes that remained. Yet it took just 89 seconds for Joe McBride to steal the march on the army of German defenders and finish superbly from an acute angle. American stadia had never seen anything like it and the crowd erupted in ecstasy. Despite the trouble that had occurred, American journalists centred on what they viewed as 'the most exciting match ever played in San Francisco', against a backdrop of 'an atmosphere of tremendous excitement'.

The tour closed with a rare amicable game in Los Angeles against Atlas FC. The fatigued players had just one last game to survive in order to maintain Celtic's unbeaten run. Willie O'Neill played with a hefty knock from the Bayern game and Joe McBride had his thigh strapped in plaster. The blazing sun also showed little consideration for Celtic's plight and it is, therefore, unsurprising that the team played poorly. Nevertheless, the Glasgow outfit battled bravely. Their incredible fighting spirit was encapsulated when the Glasgow Irishman, Charlie Gallacher, scored in the 88th minute to hand Celtic a 1-0 victory. The result marked the end of an astonishing tour ahead of what was to be an astonishing season.

The Celtic party headed to New York on the night after the game, where they were permitted a day of shopping, before flying home to Glasgow on 15th June 1966.

The stats from that trip are quite incredible: Played 11, won 8, drew 3, lost 0, scored 47, conceded 6.

THE BATTLE OF MONTEVIDEO

It goes without saying that May 1967 saw the east end of Glasgow revel in the international spotlight as Celtic became the first non-Latin team to win the European Cup. A mixture of pretty football and Glasgow gallusness had ensured that the Lisbon Lions conquered the continent in a way that had never been seen before. The squad then went on to prove themselves as the unquestionable kings of Europe in the Bernabeu, by beating Real Madrid 1-0 during Alfredo Di Stefano's testimonial.

The new season brought new challenges in terms of securing the club's legacy. Indeed, a mouth-watering tie against the cream of South America awaited Celtic in October, for the chance to be crowned undisputed world champions. Yet before the Bhoys could think about global stardom, they were given a rude awakening by Dynamo Kiev, who ended their status as European champions at the first hurdle. The Russians advanced to the second round of the European Cup by virtue of a 3-2 aggregate win.

The early exit from Europe placed even greater importance on the World Club Championship and Jock Stein immediately took on the thankless task of preparing his team to face Racing Club. The board had obtained minimal video footage of their opponents and without the television coverage that we take for granted today, Celtic had little chance of knowing what lay in store for them. Jim Craig reflected this fact years later when he spoke to Celtic TV about the build-up to the match: "We knew that as an Argentinian team they were probably going to be animals because Alf Ramsey had said that of the Argentina national team after his England side beat them in the World Cup

Quarter-Final the year before. Other than that, we knew very little about Racing Club."

Nevertheless, Stein endeavoured to prepare his team in the best possible manner. He had already organised a friendly against South American opposition in the form of Uruguayan outfit, FC Penarol. Celtic won the friendly 2-1 and the gaffer was confident of achieving victory through his man management skills thereon. His excellent Celtic side had already responded to being eliminated from Europe by thrashing Hibernian 4-0, Morton 7-1 and Partick Thistle 5-1, in the three consecutive games that followed. Make no mistake, this was a very confident squad that was preparing to host the Argentinians.

Over 100,000 people crammed into Hampden Park for the first leg on 17th October 1967, where the game had been moved to accommodate the crowds. Emboldened by the support, Celtic attacked a rugged, animalistic defence, throughout. Racing punched, kicked and spat on the Celtic players, so much so that when Jimmy Johnstone returned to the dressing room at half time his hair was matted with mucous. No man in a green and white jersey was safe from a beating, as the first recipient of a headbutt on the night, Bertie Auld, will testify.

Celtic managed to keep their composure, and Billy McNeill headed the only goal of the game from a John Hughes corner in the second half. McNeill took the opportunity to let the Racing defender know all about his shortcomings, having received a customary elbow whilst heading the goal.

Following the match, Sir Robert Kelly was hesitant about fulfilling the return leg. If his club had received that kind of treatment in Glasgow, then the thought of playing away from home didn't sound too convivial. Despite Kelly's concerns, the show had to go on, though his fears were realised before play had even begun in Argentina. Ronnie Simpson was wounded in the back of the head thanks to a missile that struck the goalkeeper during the warm up. Considering that there was huge netting in front of the crowd, many deduce that a photographer must have been responsible for the attack. John Fallon took Simpson's place – Scotland's player of the year being ordered to withdraw from the starting 11 by Jock Stein. Fallon was understandably cautious, spending most of the match on the penalty spot, whilst the fans behind him bayed for blood.

It would be forgivable to fold under such conditions, yet Celtic had immense mental strength, which Tommy Gemmell epitomised when he overcame 103,000 boos to dispatch a spot kick in the 22nd minute. The Celts were 2-0 ahead on aggregate but there was no away goal rule in those days. The tie was not yet beyond Racing and the necessity to attack (on the park) prompted the Argentinians to start playing football. They pegged one back within ten minutes, although the scorer (Raffo) appeared to be a long way offside.

True to Jock Stein's philosophy, Celtic regained their composure and continued to play attacking football. However, their play became increasingly tentative, which ensured that chances were few and far between. Celtic would rue their lack of creativity as Cárdenas slotted home to level the tie just after half time. The match stayed that way and the Racing fans celebrated the securance of a play off in exuberant fashion.

With the game over, Celtic went from despair to desperation as focus switched firmly to escaping Buenos Aires. A large mob of Racing Club fans had surrounded the team bus and were rocking it from side to side. At this point, most players no longer wanted to compete for the trophy. A still unclaimed shout from the back seats: "Boss just give them the bloody cup and get us out of here," demonstrated the mood among the travelling party.

The board had contemplated the prospect of endangering their players again in the play off. Aside from Bobby Lennox, few were in favour of the notion. Nonetheless, Jock Stein wanted to see the job through. Such was Stein's stature at the club, his wish was granted. Of the board members, Desmond White had been most keen for the decider, thus he led the way when it came to negotiating special requests surrounding security and a change of referee. When both demands were met, the club agreed to play the game in a neutral country. Farcically, Uruguay was the neutral country suggested. The geographical location of the chosen city (Montevideo) enabled some 30,000 Argentinians to travel over for the game - hundreds of whom visited Celtic's team hotel on the eve of the match at 2am.

The day of reckoning had arrived: 4th November 1967. Predictably it was violent, but nobody could have known that the game would forever be referred to as 'The Battle of Montevideo'. Celtic lost the first battle before a ball was even kicked, when the team attempted to win over the crowd by flying the Uruguayan flag on the pitch. Unbeknown to the Bhoys, Racing had already done likewise, to a rapturous reception.

After all the intimidation, spitting, elbows, headbutts, missiles and disturbances – Celtic were determined to fight back. Such resistance manifest itself in catastrophic fashion as Bobby Lennox was sent off midway through the first half. It was a case of mistaken identity after John Clark had squared up to an opponent following a scathing foul. Alfio Basile of Racing was also ordered off for his part in the incident. Next to leave the field was Jimmy Johnstone, who had been brutally hacked several times before lashing out with a right hook after one assault too many. In the melee that ensued, Humberto Maschio ran across the Celtic back four and spat at each of them before hiding in the fracas around Johnstone. Gemmell identified the offender and evaded the sight of the match officials, to exact revenge in the form of a kick to Maschio's family jewel region. The Argentine hit the deck and howled as Gemmell escaped undetected.

Soon after play resumed, Racing Club scored a long-range strike to take the lead. Just as quick, football took a back seat again and the street fighting continued. John Hughes let his temper complete the trilogy of red cards for Celtic, when he punched the goalkeeper in the ribs with a sharp jab in the 74th minute and then kicked him in the stomach as he fell to the turf. Hilariously, it emerged that Hughes thought he wouldn't be seen, despite the 60,000 crowd, television cameras and match officials zoning in on the play. When in the dressing room, Jock Stein questioned Hughes. The striker had the absence of mind to relay his thoughts to the Manager. One can only imagine how that comment was received.

A further red card was awarded to Juan Carlos Rulli of Racing, for a tackle out of the rugby textbook, whilst Bertie

Auld threw a right cross after being fouled in the 88th minute. He followed it up in traditional Glaswegian style… by chasing his victim, manoeuvring for a 'Glasgow kiss' and putting him in a headlock when the desired strike couldn't be made. Auld was to be the fourth sending off for Celtic. His refusal to leave the field prompted armed police to intervene - a sad scene, symbolic of the footballing travesty that the World Club Championship of 1967 had become.

Racing had displayed a sinisterly cold and calculated method to their fouling, coupled with an ability to cause a fracas and confuse officials when a brutal challenge was made. The Argentine's became world champions with a 1-0 win: an absolute insult to football.

The Battle of Montevideo may have been lost but worse was to come for the Celtic squad when they arrived back in Scotland. Bob Kelly had been furious at the violence that his club's players had resorted to in the play-off game. He showed little consideration for the provocation that the players experienced and wanted to be seen to condemn his club's role in the controversy. As such, he fined each of the team £250. Given that the average wage at Celtic was £30 per week at the time, such a huge fine was a startling punishment.

The Battle of Montevideo may not have been a positive moment in the history of Celtic Football Club, yet thanks to the wonderful ability of the Glasgow-Irish to turn physical defeat into spiritual victory, this infamous war has been remembered in song by Celtic fans throughout the years.

Way down in Uruguay, in the land of sun
A football feast was to be seen
Between the Glasgow Celtic, the champions of Europe
And Racing from Argentine

Well, nearly everyone came to this land of sun
A football feast, just to see
There was TV camera's from every nation,
But none from the BBC

One, two and then kick! cha cha cha
It was the dirtiest game I've ever seen
Between the Glasgow Celtic, the champions of Europe
And Racing from Argentine

Well the referee, he came from Paraguay
A South American state
Oh well the Glasgow Celtic, didn't think much of him
Racing thought he was great

Oh well he sent off Bobby Lennox, Bobby Murdoch too
He sent off Yogi Bear as well
But when he sent off Bertie, and told him he was dirty
Bertie told him to go to hell

One, two and then kick! cha cha cha
It was the dirtiest game I've ever seen
Between the Glasgow Celtic, the champions of Europe
And Racing from Argentine

Well you may have heard, or even read somewhere
That a racing player was attacked
By big Tam Gemmell, the gentle giant
The Glasgow Celtic's full back

Oh well, we asked big Tam, who's as gentle as a lamb
If there's anything he'd like to say
He says, I saw the action replay, I know it looks like me
But I swear it was Danny Kaye

One, two and then kick! cha cha cha
It was the dirtiest game I've ever seen
Between the Glasgow Celtic, the champions of Europe
And Racing from Argentine

Well it's a sad reflection, on a game of football
When a team like Racing won the cup
But the next time we meet them, we're surely going to beat them
Because the Celtic will be toughened up

Oh well the news today, from down Parkhead way
Mr Stein won't let it get him down
He said to make Celtic super we're signing Henry Cooper
And we're working on Walter McGowan

One, two and then kick! cha cha cha
It was the dirtiest game I've ever seen
Between the Glasgow Celtic, the champions of Europe
And Racing from Argentine

FROM CELEBRATION CAME DESPERATION

It is a little-known fact that during Celtic's run of nine consecutive league championships under Jock Stein, not one title was secured in front of the home crowd at Celtic Park. The Hoops had lifted their first title in 12 years on the final day of the 1965/66 season, by beating Motherwell at Fir Park, and they confirmed two in a row with a 2-2 draw at Ibrox on the penultimate week of the following league campaign.

As the curtain was coming down on the 1967/68 season, the league championship hung in the balance for a third successive time. All had appeared lost for Celtic in mid-April, until Bobby Lennox scored a last-minute goal at Celtic Park to hand the Bhoys a 2-1 victory against Morton, which then ensured that Celtic and Rangers remained level on 61 points going into the final game of the season.

Rangers played their last game at Ibrox on Saturday 27th April, where Aberdeen handed the Govan club their first defeat of the campaign, beating them 3-2. This meant that Celtic had all but won three in a row, considering that the Bhoys had scored 104 and conceded 23, giving a goal average of 4.5 as compared to Rangers, who had scored 93 and conceded 34 – giving them a goal average of 2.7. Ibrox didn't take the result well. In apoplectic rage, one fan leapt on to the pitch and took out his frustration by booting Alex Ferguson, the club's top scorer that season with 23 goals, in the shin! Ferguson later said: "I can't blame him, we all felt sick."

Regardless of Rangers conceding the title, Celtic wanted to win the league outright, and to celebrate three in a row in style. The Parkhead men travelled to East End Park to play against Dunfermline on Tuesday 30th April 1968. The Pars confirm that this match was witness to the record attendance at the stadium, with local police estimating that 25,000 Celtic fans were locked outside of the ground, unable to party with the 31,000 people fortunate enough to make it through the turnstyles. The fact that only 6,000 of those spectators were Dunfermline fans is somewhat surprising as the club had just won the Scottish Cup against Hearts three days previously, in front of a crowd of 56,366.

Naturally, hundreds of the Celtic supporters, who had made the trip to Fife, wanted a glimpse of the champions. A huge group of fans charged at a gate outside the stadium and smashed it down to force entry, whilst dozens were scaling the walls and entering by any means possible. Consequentially, there was grave danger of a crush and those already inside the ground tried to escape by climbing the 80-foot-high floodlighting pylons. Several supporters also took refuge on the roof of each stand, at which point play had to be stopped in the 8th minute. Managers, Jock Stein and George Farm, took to the field to plea with supporters to get down from the roof, whilst the Grandstand was cleared to become a makeshift casualty area for those injured in the overcrowding.

The injured were treated by Dr Yellowley, who was a Director on the Dunfermline board, and a local surgeon named Dr Wardlaw. An ambulance shuttle service was hastily organised, transporting those in need to West Fife Hospital. Among the reported injuries were broken legs, fractured ribs and head wounds. Furthermore, the ambulance controller, David Morris, was caught up in the crush and needed treatment himself.

191

Play restarted after a long delay. Ten minutes later, the referee, Tom 'Tiny' Wharton, had to adjourn proceedings again. This time 190 police officers managed to restore order within nine minutes, by clearing areas of terracing to allow more fans to disembark from the roof of the enclosure. Normal order prevailed thereafter, and Celtic got back to celebrating the day with two second half goals from Bobby Lennox earning a 2-1 win. Astonishingly, Lennox's brace meant that he had racked up 20 goals in the final 12 games of the season.

There was further cause for celebration as a product from the youth team, George Connelly, made his debut after coming on as a substitute. The youngster impressed and looked assured on the ball in midfield, which is no surprise given that he went on to become one of the main players in the Quality Street Gang.

In total, 49 fans were injured at Dunfermline that day, 16 of whom were treated locally, whilst one fan was taken to Edinburgh Infirmary. The players of both teams deserved enormous credit for producing an excellent spectacle amid potentially disastrous scenes. Equally, on the terraces, good will was maintained as the huge Celtic support gave a great ovation to the Dunfermline squad when they paraded the Scottish Cup trophy around the pitch. It was also fitting that Celtic's victory should take them to 63 points, from a possible 68 – the record total amassed in Scottish football history at the time (2 points for a win back then).

PRINCIPLED FOOTBALL

There's an age-old argument concerning sport and its association with politics. We often see football clubs disassociate themselves from political causes, and governing bodies of the game are quick to punish clubs if they refrain from doing so. However, the notion that football and politics should be mutually exclusive is not a view to which Celtic's board have always subscribed. Indeed, Bob Kelly spoke enthusiastically on the matter in 1971 when he remarked: "I wish I had a pound for every time it has been said or written that politics and sport do not mix – or should not mix. But with the emergence of sport, especially football, as an important aid to enhancing a country's prestige in the world it is much harder to keep politics and sport apart."

It was only three years before Kelly uttered those words, that he had used his role as Celtic Chairman to take a powerful political stance on behalf of the club. On that occasion, Celtic had been paired against Hungarian champions, Ferencvaros, in the European Cup. Political problems had been brewing in Eastern Europe since the end of World War II. A metaphorical 'Iron Curtain', termed by Winston Churchill, had split Europe in half. On the west side one would find the USA's NATO allies living in capitalist free market economies, whereas the east side was home to communist, totalitarian dominions such as the Soviet Union.

Many of Europe's Communist states formed a military alliance, known as the Warsaw Pact, which was dominated by the Soviet Union. One should not assume that everything went smoothly between the aligned nations. It goes without saying that there were issues and no example better demonstrates this fact than the Hungarian Uprising of October 1956. The nationwide revolt against the government of the Hungarian People's Republic and its Soviet-imposed policies had seen Hungary's population gain temporary freedom from what they viewed to be red oppression. The Hungarian revolutionaries went further, stunning communism's strongest supporters by forming a new government, which vowed to withdraw from the Warsaw Pact, re-stablish free elections and seek priority on the United Nations' agenda. However, those freedoms were sharply revoked as Soviet tanks re-entered the nation and descended on the east of the country in early November. As Soviet troops amassed, communication with the west was cut off once again and over 4,000 people were to die in the resulting re-invasion.

12 years later, the Soviet Union had become concerned about the actions of another nation. This time Czechoslovakia would receive the full wrath of Soviet forces because the Czech's Communist Party leader, Alexander Dubcek, had introduced reforms under the banner of 'socialism with a human face'. These reforms, which liberated the media and lifted travel restrictions for its citizens, frightened Leonid Brehznev, who was the figurehead of communism in Moscow. As an influential presence at the epicentre of the ideology, Brehznev was wary of maintaining Moscow's influence over the Communist states of central Europe. His doctrine regarding the Warsaw Pact stated that 'Nobody will ever be allowed to wrest a single link from the community of socialist States.'

Czechoslovakia's refusal to undo the reforms did little to ease the paranoia in communist circles. That the Czechs might do as Hungary attempted and withdraw from the Warsaw Pact, led Brehznev to ensure that communism's grip would not be loosened again. Therefore, the invasion of Czechoslovakia was ordered with immediate effect.

Regardless of fierce criticism of the invasion, tangible opposition in Western Europe was limited. A United Nations' formal legislature of opposing the action was vetoed by the Soviet's themselves. Whilst, opposition from the USA and western nations was mocked as hypocritical due to the Vietnam War and similar misdemeanours. As a combination of forces within the Warsaw Pact alliance occupied Prague, it became apparent that organisational and military intervention from the west was never going to happen.

One may wonder where Celtic comes in to all this. Up step Bob Kelly, who found another medium to take a stance against the invasion, when Celtic were paired with Ferencvaros in the European Cup first round, on 18th September 1968. The imperialist events unfolding in Prague, coupled with the restrictive conditions of travelling behind the Iron Curtain, were not something that a progressive institution such as Celtic Football Club felt comfortable with. Of course, the Soviet Football Federation insisting that Celtic travel on a Soviet plane and take a 1000-mile detour when the club faced Dynamo Kiev a year earlier, was also fresh in the memory.

Bob Kelly implied that there would be a protest from the club, when he claimed that it would be "One way of putting on record our moral support for the Czechs." Celtic confirmed those actions when they sent a telegram to the UEFA Secretary. It read: *In view of the illegal and treacherous invasion of Czechoslovakia by Russian, Polish and Hungarian forces and in support of the Czech nation, we, the Celtic Football Club, do not think that any Western European Football Club should be forced to fulfil any football commitment in any of these countries.*

The protest was not warmly received by UEFA, who were more intent on appeasing its Soviet members than supporting human justice. However, the move by Kelly and Celtic had an incredible rippling effect. A conglomeration of clubs moved to join the Celts in demanding not to be asked to play football in Eastern Europe. Switzerland then called off an international friendly against Poland in protest at the Polish aspect of the Czech invasion.

In Scotland, the support Celtic received over the move, from their domestic competitors, was of a scale seldom seen before. The position taken by the club even gained public support from two opposite ends of the spectrum. Rivals, Rangers, praised the action of the Celtic board, whilst Aberdeen sent a telegram of their own to the committee of the International Trade Fairs Cup. Not everyone fell in line with Celtic's altruistic approach though, and despite Aberdeen's request, the organisers refused to allow the deplorable actions behind the Iron Curtain to divide the competition.

Perhaps the committee's decision was influenced by the fact that it was primarily English led, and Aberdeen's telegram had not been received until the final stage of the tournament; a Final which included English club, Leeds United.

Leeds were, ironically, scheduled to play the second of a two-legged Final against Ferencvaros, the very team that Celtic were paired with in the first round of the European Cup that season. Ferencvaros were permitted to compete in both the European Cup and the Fairs Cup competitions as the latter was initially open to teams from cities which hosted trade fairs, whilst national champion status, allowing clubs to enter the European Cup, bore no relevance. Following a revamp of the competition after 1968, teams only competed in the tournament if they finished as runners up in the league, meaning this was the final time that national champions such as Ferencvaros were eligible to partake in the Fairs Cup, alongside its premier counterpart (European Cup), in the same season.

Leeds had won the first leg against the Hungarian champions by a goal to nil. At that halfway point in the Final, the Yorkshire club's Manager, Don Revie, said to The Yorkshire Evening Post: "We will be condemned by many people for not refusing to play the Hungarian champions in view of what has happened recently in Czechoslovakia. Much has been written and said about the ways in which the western world can show its disapproval. Sadly, soccer is being used as a weapon in the political arena." Revie continued with a verbal attack on Celtic: "Celtic, who were due to meet Ferencvaros in the first round of the European Cup this season, threatened to boycott the match because of the Czech crisis. Politics? I prefer to leave this to the politicians. This does not mean I do not feel strongly about what has happened in Czechoslovakia – but I feel that political opinion should not be allowed to interfere in any way with sport."

Danish teams were among those, who didn't share Revie's view, stating that they would withdraw from the Fairs Cup tournament if they were drawn against teams from Eastern Europe during the next season. Momentum was building in favour of Celtic's position when the stakes were heightened, as the Swedish Government suggested that UEFA competitions were re-drawn to exclude countries behind the Iron Curtain.

UEFA were now forced into action. It was the moment they feared most, which is reflected in their attempt to appease both jurisdictions of their membership. The governing body had decided that representatives from the east and west would be kept apart in the first round of the European Cup and the European Cup Winners' Cup. It was a measure to buy time, but Celtic and clubs of similar persuasion, accepted the decision as the first progressive blow to Soviet aggression. Predictably, the Polish and Soviet football federations responded tempestuously. Both organisations highlighted the fact that the ruling was in breach of UEFA constitution, which vowed not to discriminate along regional or political lines. The Soviet Federation went further, threatening to involve FIFA if Europe's footballing committee did not revoke its decision.

UEFA didn't flex to any demands, but they experienced a chain reaction of withdrawal from their competitions by Eastern European nations. Only Romanian, Yugoslavian and Hungarian teams remained.

The redrawing of the tie saw Celtic paired against St Etienne instead of Ferencvaros. Yet as fate would have it, the Bhoys would then go on to be drawn against

Yugoslavian giants, Partisan Belgrade, in the second round, who they determinedly thrashed 6-2 on aggregate.

Celtic's point of principle may not have greatly improved the lives of the Czechoslovakian people. However, it raised public awareness for their plight. It sparked the flames of justice amongst the western public and showed a more determined effort to speak for the oppressed than the United Nations', NATO and multiple national governments combined.

Bob Kelly's words leave a stirring synopsis of the affair: "Celtic will hold their heads high for what they did. If UEFA had ruled against us, we would almost certainly have competed under the strongest type of protest. We might well in the circumstances have withdrawn from the competition. There are things for Celtic more important than money."

WAR & PEACE

January 2nd 1971 is a day that permanently haunts Scottish football. Celtic travelled to Ibrox that afternoon and conceded a late goal in a 1-1 draw with Rangers. Colin Stein struck the equaliser for the 'Gers, but football quickly took a backseat as stairway 13 gave way during the celebrations. A terrible crush occurred, in what was to become the third Ibrox stadium disaster, which claimed the lives of 66 Rangers fans and injured over 200 more. The tragedy represented the biggest loss of life at a British football game at the time, only to be surpassed by the horrific events at Hillsborough in 1989.

Almost four weeks after Scottish football's darkest hour, a charity game was arranged between a Scotland XI and the two competing teams of the tragic day – Celtic and Rangers, in a combined select side. The match, which was played at Hampden Park on 27th January, was in aide of the Ibrox Disaster Fund; an initiative established to help support the relatives of the fans that were killed at Ibrox earlier that month.

There had been hopes that the extenuating circumstances would forge a temporary unity between the two sets of supporters. Indeed, the image of Jock Stein helping Willie Waddell to lift victims on to a stretcher had already become synonymous with the disaster. Whilst Stein himself said: "This terrible tragedy must help to curb the bigotry and bitterness of Old Firm matches. When human life is at stake this kind of hatred seems sordid and little. Fans of both sides will never forget this disaster." If anything could break the age-old polarity between Glasgow's giants, then sadly it would require a horrific tribulation to do it.

In terms of the charity match, attractive guest players, George Best, Bobby Charlton and Peter Bonetti were invited to play for the Celtic/Rangers select side. This boosted the crowd and gave fans some neutral players to cheer. The trio more than served their purpose in that regard, as a bolstered attendance of 81,405 was achieved. Other stars such as Archie Gemmill and Peter Lorimer turned out for the Scotland squad, which was teeming with quality.

The respective line ups were as follows:

Scotland XI: Cruikshank (Hearts), Hay (Celtic), Gemmell (Celtic), Stanton (Hibernian), McKinnon (Rangers), Moncur (Newcastle Utd), Lorimer (Leeds Utd), McLean (Kilmarnock), Gemmill (Derby Co.), Stein (Rangers), O'Hare (Derby Co.), Cooke (Chelsea)

Celtic/Rangers Select: Bonetti (Chelsea), Jardine (Rangers), Greig (Rangers), Murdoch (Celtic), McNeill (Celtic), Smith (Rangers), Henderson (Rangers), Hughes (Celtic), Charlton (Man Utd) Johnston (Rangers), Best (Man Utd)

In keeping with the high hopes of the organisers, Celtic and Rangers fans mixed respectfully in the main, upholding an admirable level of decorum. There was just a minority fragment of each support, who stayed at opposite ends of the stadium, chanting their own respective songs. Though overall, it was an enjoyable atmosphere, enhanced by the exceptional football on show.

Charity and mourning was naturally at the forefront of the fixture, but both teams certainly approached the match with a positive spirit. Jock Stein and Willie Waddell, the

201

respective Managers of Celtic and Rangers, shared command of the select side. The pair had been roaring with laughter before kick-off, whilst Tommy Gemmell and Ron McKinnon appeared to do likewise.

The select side's approach to the game was one of relaxation, with just 45 minutes of training having been undertaken earlier that day. On the flip side, Scotland's Manager, Bobby Brown, had been putting his team through their paces at the Inverclyde Centre in Largs before the match. Brown's more drilled and methodical approach to the game was perhaps a reflection of the fact that he was using the match to prepare for the looming European Nations Cup game against Belgium.

The varying styles collided in an enthralling encounter, dubbed 'A Real Hampden Classic' by The Evening Times. The newspaper gave a glowing report of the game, which enthused about the performances of Peter Lorimer and Willie Henderson in particular.

For some years Sir Robert Kelly, Chairman of Celtic, has advocated that there should be a Great Britain team. At Hampden last night, for the very first time, I agreed with him.

This Scotland-Old Firm Select proved that Irishmen can play alongside Scots; that Englishmen can knit in as everybody did during the war. Last night's match, which Scotland won 2-1 by a late goal from Peter Lorimer of Leeds, was the best game I have seen since Real Madrid beat Eintracht 7-3 in this same stadium.

The report continued by discussing Scottish optimism ahead of their clash in Liege, versus Belgium, before returning to recounting the charity game in question.

At one stage the Select played the head off Scotland. Bobby Charlton was spraying passes all over the field with the finesse and accuracy of Robin Hood. His long passing was fantastic. This man makes football look easy.

Wee Willie Henderson had obviously taken a liking to Ireland's George Best and he wanted to be upsides with the hairy one. He wanted to show the world, in the nicest way, that he could as much with a ball as Best. This was the pattern for the night: "Anything you can do pal, I can do better." It was all there – no daft big kicking and no stupid petty fouling. It was all first class competitive football.

For the book there wasn't a bad player on the field. When Scotland were chasing the white ghosts they did so with composure. I never saw John Greig play a better game since I saw him break through in Russia. A wonderful left back. But so was Tommy Gemmell. Sandy Jardine was brilliant. I went home wondering if he was as good as David Hay, who was immaculate.

That's the kind of game it was. McKinnon? The Rock of Gibraltar. But how about the guy in the other No. 5 jersey, Billy McNeill? Never put a foot wrong...

(Malcom Munro's report in The Evening Times - 28th January 1971)

As the above section of Malcom Munro's report suggests, the preponderance of international quality made for a great occasion. The game opened frantically, with the Select side being marshalled from the midfield by Murdoch and Charlton. The pair combined in the first minute to put Scotland on the back foot. However, it was the national team who took the lead in the tenth minute, thanks to Colin Stein's cross being thundered into the back of the net by the right foot of Archie Gemmill. The goal sprung Scotland into life but they couldn't help being stunned by the mesmerising skill of George Best. The Belfast superstar had the crowd in raptures at times and drew the teams level with a free kick, which almost shattered the net. Moments later, the Ulsterman embarked on a sensational dribble, nutmegging no fewer than four Scottish players within a distance of about ten yards, before having the cheek to woefully miss from close range.

Scotland took the initiative after the break, with some deadly attacks of their own. Despite the pendulum swinging in Scotland's favour, Charlton played a swift one-two with Hughes before rifling into the stanchion from the edge of the area. The Manchester United maestro quickly retracted his celebratory fist pump though, as he realised that the linesman had raised his flag to signal an infringement by Hughes on Stanton in the Scotland defence.

The best chance of the game fell to Lorimer in the 70th minute, when he headed wide from six yards. He soon atoned for this blooper, when he toe-poked a low finish beyond Bonetti to win the game six minutes from time. However, the Leeds United midfielder was taken off as a precaution, having picked up a minor knock as he converted his chance.

The game finished 2-1 to Scotland, whilst the night raised more than £40,000 for the benefit of the Ibrox Disaster Fund. It was a night of peace, which finally brought some positive press to the Glasgow derby.

Match programme from the charity game

STEIN'S SONGBOOK LAMBAST

A 3-0 win against lowly Stirling Albion of the second division may sound like a routine curtain raiser. Yet Celtic's League Cup clash with the Binos, on the opening day of the 1972/73 season, was anything but conventional. The Bhoys had been drawn in a favourable section of the competition and were also joined by East Fife and Arbroath. Celtic were boosted by the return of Kenny Dalglish ahead of the match, who shook off a pre-season thigh injury and replaced Dixie Deans in the squad, the latter having been dropped due to his poor performance during the 3-2 defeat by Hamilton Academicals in a practise match four days earlier.

The emphatic win over Stirling Albion at Annfield Park, courtesy of a brace from Lou Macari and a trademark Dalglish lob, put Celtic top of the group. Despite the ease with which Celtic broke in the new campaign, the mood at Parkhead was marred by action off the pitch stealing the headlines. The Sunday Mail reported that Celtic fans had been repetitively chanting 'IRA', whilst surrounding a small band of police officers, who had moved in amongst the Celtic support to address a separate minor incident. Stein had noticed the scene as it unfolded and acted to dissipate the tension by jumping into the crowd. Joined by trainer, Bob Rooney, the respected Celtic Manager acted like a superintendent and began to remonstrate with his supporters. After a short-impassioned tirade, he returned pitch side with the sound of applause ringing in his ears. No further rebel songs were sung throughout the match.

Undoubtedly, the acceptance and will to listen to Big Jock was a mark of respect from the Celtic faithful, for a legend whom they held in the highest regard. However, due to the worsening of the Troubles in Ireland, a Republican – Loyalist chanting epidemic was soon spreading throughout the terraces of Easter Road, Celtic Park, Tynecastle and Ibrox. Stein knew that his paroxysm of anger at the Stirling Albion match would not be enough to curb the situation. Therefore, he reaffirmed his stance when he moved to address the wider support in the next edition of the Celtic View:

I don't like criticising Celtic fans. But I have to take odds with at least a section of them. What I did on Saturday was something I've felt like doing for quite a while.

It's my sincere wish that it will have a lasting effect, as I'm sure that the vast majority of our fans do. Celtic supporters have enjoyed a lot of good times during the past few years and all of it was due to hard work – by the players, the backroom boys and the directors.

The fans too have played a major role and we don't want to see it all ruined now by the bad element who have recently emerged. Nor do we want to see the fans of long standing who followed us through the lean years discouraged from watching us play.

This bad element – or the wreckers as the View called them last week – are singing and chanting about things which have nothing to do with football.

Surely there are enough Celtic songs without introducing religion or politics or anything else.

OFFERS

These offensive songs and chants could damage Celtic's hard-won reputation built up by good football and sportsmanship.

Offers to play all over the world keep arriving at Celtic Park. Last year we took part in the Bobby Moore testimonial. Next month we play in Bobby Charlton's benefit match.

This is an indication of our high standing in world football. The club don't want to lose all this. Neither, I'm sure do any of our real supporters.

It is important to note that Jock Stein's tough action was not an act in isolation. Hooliganism was rising throughout British football and, even worse than later years when organised firms emerged, its sporadic mayhem threatened to spiral out of control. Social factors such as alcohol, high rates of inflation and unemployment were all key contributors to fostering this growing problem. Given that the Conservative government oversaw unemployment figures rising to 1.3 million and inflation creeping up to 7.10% in this period, it is likely Jock Stein noticed that Scottish football could ill afford a contentious subject such as Ulster's political troubles being thrown into the mix. This theory would explain his quotes surrounding the incident, printed in The Sunday Mail, on 13th August 1972. Stein said: "I just told the fans what they were. It's only the start of the season and look at the trouble we've had already. We'll have to do something."

By the time Celtic hosted East Fife in the League Cup the following week, Glasgow Magistrates had vowed to introduce a plan to control violence at football matches in the city. In their infinite wisdom, the Magistrates came up with unenforceable proposals, which ignored the social aspects of football violence.

Stein didn't take matters further. He had made his point, much like his counterpart, Willie Waddell, did at the start of the season when the Rangers manager addressed the crowd on the PA system at Ibrox and reminded a section of fans to behave appropriately. The Celtic boss would have been well aware of the history, culture and politics that surrounded Celtic in the early 1970s. These were different times from the modern era, and indeed the club had released two LPs during his tenure - one titled The Holy Ground of Glasgow Celtic, at the end of the 1966/67 season, and the other named Glasgow Celtic The Champions, at the end of the 1970/71 season. Both commemorative records, the former celebrating the club's European Cup success and the latter dedicated to the Hoops' domestic double, included Irish rebel songs such as A Nation Once Again, Sean South of Garryowen and We're All Off to Dublin In the Green.

It is one of the great oxymorons of the man, that Stein is also thought to have requested Sean South of Garryowen to be played before European matches because it "Lifted the Parkhead crowd." Readers of a certain age will recall the song being echoed across the old Celtic Park, alongside The Holy Ground on nights such as the 1970 European Cup Quarter Final against Benfica. Perhaps this could be explained by the foreign opposition, whose small travelling support would not react negatively towards such a song. We can only but speculate.

*Jock Stein returns to the pitch side, having jumped the
barrier to have a stern word with the Celtic support at
Stirling Albion – 12th August 1972*

POISONED FRUIT

Only three of the starting Lisbon Lions remained at the club when Celtic undertook another European adventure in the 1973/74 season. The Celts had maintained their success in the six intervening years, thanks to a new look team known as The Quality Street Gang, who guided the club to two Quarter Finals, a Semi-Final and a Final of the European Cup.

Celtic found themselves in the European Cup Semi-Final again in April 1974. This time the club was paired with Atletico Madrid. The Spaniards were then under the guidance of Juan Carlos Lorenzo, who had been the Manager of the Argentina national team that disgraced themselves against England during the World Cup eight years previously. Jock Stein knew what to expect and issued a stern warning to his players, they would have to be prepared for battle.

Celtic approached the game with a team that was teeming with talent. From the imperious stalwarts of the side such as McNeill and Johnstone, to the tremendous Dalglish and Deans; this star-studded Celtic team were heavy favourites to advance to the club's third European Final in seven years. On the other hand, Atletico had one predictable answer – kick Celtic off the park.

Under the stewardship of the Argentinian, who had been inspired by Racing Club's brutal theft of the World Club Championship in 1967, Atletico ensured that they would dish out the worst possible kind of treatment to their opponents. Some say that the violent tactics of the Madrid men even surpassed those of Racing Club, whilst Dixie

Deans remarked that he'll "Never forget the pre-meditated, waist-high intimidatory tactics that went on."

Following the shocking first match, which saw Atletico receive three red cards and seven yellows, in a 0-0 draw at Parkhead - UEFA stepped in and fined the Spanish club £14,000 (approx. £141,000 in today's money). The European governing body also ensured that no fewer than six Atletico players were banned ahead of the return fixture.

Celtic fans were advised not to travel to Madrid due to the inevitable hostility that would await them. Meanwhile, the team were given a police and army combined escort throughout their short stay in Spain. In the build up to the match, Celtic trained under heavily armed guard, surrounded by police riot trucks and Spanish security forces. Following the training session, the squad were told that the Atletico fans would be ferocious because the club had been supplying relentless propaganda to the local media. The Madrid press had acted with complicity, behaving like succulent lambs to the slaughter, and dispersing horrendous untruths across Spain. Despite the fine, the bans, the red cards, the travel warning and the huge security operation; it was claimed that Celtic were the aggressors!

Although the first leg had been shown live on Spanish TV, the fascist press managed to convince fans that Atletico Madrid were the victims of an orchestrated campaign of abuse at the hands of Celtic, the referee and Glasgow Police. Indeed, the Spanish media claimed that the police had entered their dressing room to assault players, whilst there were also unfounded assertions that Celtic had bribed the referee.

One would forgive Celtic for throwing in the towel at this point. The scenario was a carbon copy of the World Club Championship disaster and surely the same mistake couldn't happen again. Wrong. The board, in line with public outcry, had considered withdrawing from the fixture. However, just like in Uruguay, the decision was made to press ahead – this time because the club were afraid of retribution from UEFA. This position was understandable, for Benfica had threatened not to take part in the 1965 European Cup Final against Inter Milan, unless the match was switched away from the San Siro stadium (the home of their opponents). UEFA claimed that they would fine the Portuguese club a sum approximating to £40,000 if they didn't reconsider. This figure comprised of a punishment, plus compensation for lost gate receipts.

UEFA clearly viewed any threat to their bank balance with greater importance than a club tarnishing the game, as had been the case with Atletico at Celtic Park. Celtic estimated the financial punishment of withdrawal would be in the region of £100,000 - a gargantuan sum. The club also had to consider the possibility that they may be banned from Europe. After all, it was only two years earlier that rivals, Rangers, were denied the chance to defend the European Cup Winners' Cup as their supporters had invaded the pitch at the Final in Barcelona.

A dejected Celtic squad returned to their hotel rooms in Madrid, dreading what may lay in store at the European Cup Semi-Final the next day. Jimmy Johnstone was room sharing with Bobby Lennox. The pair were chatting when

Johnstone took a phone call and learned that he had been issued with a death threat! The club's Manager, Jock Stein, had also received a phone call of similar nature. According to Bobby Lennox, speaking at the Celtic Supporter's Association Rally in 2017, 'Jinky' put the phone down and began pacing around the room. He told Bobby the worrying news and reached for an apple from the fruit bowl. Lennox leapt up from the bed to stop his colleague: "Wow! What are you doing? They didn't say they were going to shoot you, they just said you have a death threat. What if they've poisoned the fruit?" 'Jinky' immediately dropped the apple, a quite comical scene on reflection. Certainly, the tale raised a smile on the face of Lennox as he retold it almost 50 years after the event. Nevertheless, there was nothing funny about the lengths to which Atletico were prepared to go in order to prevail in April 1974.

Morning broke and the team was greeted by the sight of 1,000 mounted police officers circumnavigating the stadium. Home supporters welcomed the Hoops with stones, flung through a wire-mesh fence. Hate filled the air. This expected reception prompted Jock Stein to pull Jim Brogan aside. In a Scotsman newspaper interview, Brogan said: "The death threats against Jimmy Johnstone and Jock Stein were taken very seriously, but looking back now I can laugh because I always remember as we were heading out Jock said to me quietly 'you get in front of wee Jimmy and keep him as close as you possibly can'. What? I was trying to get as far away from him as I humanly could!"

Just three minutes into a warm-up, the Celtic players had to evacuate the playing field for their own safety. Whilst water cannons and tear gas were used to keep the crowd at bay, it was abundantly clear that regardless of the various pompous statements, sanctions and warnings that had been issued by UEFA, this was never going to be a game played under normal sporting conditions. The Celtic team was hesitant. They were afraid to attack, and the referee was equally petrified of officiating in anything other than a partial manner in favour of the Spaniards.

Atletico Madrid ran out 2-0 winners to deny Celtic a place in another European Final. Stein and his players didn't strike as crestfallen figures though as Celtic had not truly lost as far as they and their supporters were concerned. The word "Scum," used by Billy McNeill to describe Atletico Madrid in the wake of the tie, is probably all that needs said in summary of the emotion felt throughout this horrific escapade. Thankfully, Bayern Munich won the European Cup Final after a replay and Atletico remained in the shadow of their neighbours, who by contrast epitomised footballing aristocracy.

FOGGY DEW RESCUE

The latest connotation of fog affecting Celtic is the 2014 Europa League group stage match against Astra Giurgiu. On that occasion the tv cameras could scarcely follow the ball, whilst the Celtic support, housed at one side of the pitch, couldn't see any of the action either.

The club are not strangers to playing in foggy conditions and counted on a reduction in visibility to save them from defeat against Hibernian in the mid-70s. Glasgow was buried beneath a blanket of mist for two days prior to 18th October 1975, yet the game at Celtic Park went ahead. The Hoops would have been glad to play, considering that they were unbeaten in their last ten matches in all competitions. Sean Fallon had really got his Celtic side on song, after initially struggling when he took over the reigns from Jock Stein, who sat out the season due to a serious car crash in early July.

Ten minutes into the match, Celtic probably wished that the game was in fact called off. A Pat Stanton inspired Hibs team dominated proceedings and were making things difficult for the Bhoys. The dominance of the Edinburgh side was reflected on the scoreboard in the 26th minute, when Des Bremner put the visitors in front after capitalising on a poor back pass by Johannes Edvaldsson. The Hibernian attacker couldn't believe his luck as the ball fell at his feet; he rounded Peter Latchford and slotted into an empty net.

Thick fog quickly descended, prompting fans at either end of the stadium to chant to one another, so as to inform fellow supporters of the unfolding action. One need not imagine the polite nature in which the Jungle described a missed opportunity to supporters housed at the opposite end of the stand.

Play continued and the visitor's lead was deservedly doubled by Joe Harper in the 76th minute. The goal was reportedly an absolute peach, which silenced Celtic Park. Along with the silence, increasing mist fell across the stadium. Fans began to wonder, 'could the conditions save Celtic at this late stage?' To their shame, some frustrated supporters in the Jungle took the opportunity to force things in the Hoops' favour. Unbeknown to the referee (Bobby Davidson), behind the thickening layers of fog, several Celtic fans had leapt the barrier and entered the field of play. Davidson was preparing for the restart when he looked to his horror as faint silhouettes revealed themselves in his peripheral vision. The police immediately pursued the pitch invaders, whilst Sean Fallon also left his dugout to assist in clearing the field.

Alarm bells were ringing in the mind of the referee, but play did eventually continue. A further nine minutes elapsed without Celtic posing any threat to the Hibernian defence. It was looking like two points dropped for the Hoops, which would put a dent in their quest for the title. Although, Rangers would remain level on 11 points due to their 2-1 loss v Motherwell at Fir Park that day, victory would send Hibernian top with 12 points.

In the 85th minute, the unthinkable happened. Bobby Davidson put the whistle to his mouth and abandoned the match due to the worsening fog. The Celtic support cheered the great escape as if they had scored a last-minute winner. By contrast, the incensed Hibees' winger, Alex Edwards,

217

headed to the Jungle as a matter of priority. When faced with the vociferous Celtic support, he presented them with a less than warmly received V-sign gesture!

In the wake of the abandonment, Hibs launched a protest, demanding that the Scottish League Management Committee convene a meeting to discuss the issue. Their wish was granted a day later, on October 19th 1975, when Hibs directors voiced their complaints to the Scottish football authorities. The Capital club's Chairman, Tom Hart, is noted as saying: "We are most concerned about the invasion of the field after we scored our second goal. We feel that our players and the referee were intimidated at a time when the game was running away from Celtic." The Hibernian delegation went on to demand that the points be awarded their club's way. However, it wasn't to be. The view taken by the Scottish League was that awarding the points would be an entirely presumptuous position to take, as Celtic could theoretically have equalised in the short time that remained.

Few could have complained in the Celtic camp if the points were taken, though they were certainly not going to decline the opportunity to replay the match at Celtic Park seven weeks later. The replay took place on Wednesday 10th December. By this time, Celtic were joint top of the table with Motherwell on 20 points, and two points in front of third placed Hibernian. It comes as no surprise that Hibernian were out to reclaim the points taken in October, particularly as victory would move them into pole position. The Hibees' started fast, forcing Peter Latchford to make a number of saves in the Celtic goal. Twice Latchford denied Pat Stanton, before clutching a Des Bremner header, which was bound for the top corner. However, the shot-stopper was eventually beaten in the 45th minute, when Ian Munro chipped a pass out wide to Arthur Duncan. The winger caught the Celtic keeper by surprise when he shot from the by-line, but Parkhead breathed a collective sigh of relief as the linesman correctly raised his flag to signal for offside.

Celtic dusted themselves down during the break and Fallon's men returned to the field a different proposition. On the stroke of 60 minutes, Harry Hood played a driven pass into the feet of Dixie Deans at the edge of the box. Just when it appeared that the forward would be tackled, he stabbed a low shot passed Jim McArthur in the Hibernian net. The majority of the 33,000 crowd were sent into delirium.

Celtic's joy was short lived, as in the 72nd minute, Tom Callaghan clashed with Alex Edwards, resulting in a Hibernian free kick. Eric Schaedlar looped the set play into the penalty area and Latchford came to claim the ball. Unfortunately, Edvaldsson in the Celtic defence, ignored the call of his keeper and thrust his head into the mix. A goalmouth scramble followed, with Joe Harper getting the telling touch to equalise. The balance of play was very even thereafter, and the two teams remained locked at 1-1. The point was enough to put Celtic clear at the top of the table, overtaking Motherwell by the most-slender of margins. They could thank their lucky stars, or perhaps the foggy dew for that.

RIDICULOUS RED

Johnny Doyle was no stranger to red cards. The combative midfielder could be described as the embodiment of Celtic and naturally his commitment to the cause landed him in hot water with referees up and down the country. He was famously ordered off for his role in an incident with Alex MacDonald during the 4-2 game against Rangers when the Ten Men Won The League chant was born. However, Doyle is equally famed for receiving one of the most ridiculous red cards in the history of Scottish football.

On 20th August 1977, Celtic made a 31-mile journey to Somerset Park, where Ayr United lay in wait. Despite the absences of Stanton, Conn and Lynch, Celtic would have expected nothing less than a victory to kick start their league campaign. For Johnny Doyle, the game had an extra edge as the hosts had formerly employed his services for six years, prior to his £90,000 move to Parkhead in March 1976.

Confident as Doyle and his Celtic teammates may have been, they soon found themselves 2-1 behind and staring defeat in the face. It was Doyle, who Manager, Jock Stein turned to in the hope that the winger could spring from the bench to salvage a point for the Hoops. Never lacking enthusiasm in a Celtic shirt, it didn't take long for the read-headed wide man to get in to the thick of the action.

Six minutes from time, the ball was lofted into the Ayr United penalty area. A starmash ensued, with three Celtic players battling to get a defining strike ahead of the Ayrshire defence. Johannes Edvaldsson thought he had scored when he shot from five yards, but his effort was blocked by a mass of men in red shirts. The ball broke out to McCulloch on the edge of the area, who miscued his desperate clearance under the close attention of Joe Craig, cannoning it awkwardly towards Johnny Doyle on the left wing. As Doyle sought to bring the ball under control, he accidentally handled. The referee, Bob Cuthill, blew his whistle for handball, just as the Celt was about to drive a cross back into the danger area. It was too late to abort the action... BANG! The ball struck the referee's face, sending him staggering as if he'd been hit by a spherical missile. The match official went down in stages.

A combination of laughter and concern rung around the stadium as the referee was checked over. He returned to his feet, regained his bearings and duly pulled out his notebook. Doyle was called over, a wry smile etched across his face, as if to suggest he couldn't believe that he was about to be booked for a clear accident. Suddenly, the smile turned to red faced rage as it became clear that the referee was sending him off for unsporting conduct. Doyle threw his arms in the direction of the match official, sprinted towards the tunnel and evaded the clutches of Jock Stein, who was trying to return him to the pitch. The decision was an absolute embarrassment to Scottish football, adding insult to injury in the sense that Celtic ultimately lost the game in disappointing fashion. The only silver lining was that common sense prevailed on the Monday morning and the SFA quickly overturned the red card decision.

Johnny Doyle returned to the starting line-up for the 1-0 loss against Motherwell a week later - another disappointing result, in what was a miserable month for the club. Indeed, Celtic went through the entirety of August 1977 without winning a single match and would have to wait until 24th September to achieve their first domestic win of the campaign.

It wasn't always doom and gloom for Johnny Doyle at his boyhood club though. Perhaps his most iconic moment was scoring a brilliant header during a 2-0 win against Real Madrid in the 1980 European Cup Quarter Final. He would also win two Scottish cups and four league championships (one clinched after his death) at the club, earning the acclaim of his beloved Celtic faithful along the way. Yet as oft times the case, success was marred by tragedy in October 1981, when Doyle was electrocuted as he attempted to rewire the lighting in his attic. The loss of one of the club's most loved sons struck at the heart of everybody connected with Celtic. The Hoops went on to secure the league title that season, amid of echoes of "Won the league for Doyle, we've went and won the league for Doyle."

Termed "The epitome of a true Celt," by Billy McNeill, Johnny Doyle is immortalised in song and as part of a mural in Bar 67 on the Gallowgate.

JOHNNY DOYLE SONG – BY CHARLIE AND THE BHOYS

I've travelled round these islands, from shore to shining shore
I've met so many heroes from the team that I adore
I followed Glasgow Celtic, from Lisbon to Aberdeen
But I always remember Johnny Doyle in the Green.

He came from Ayr United, to join his favourite team
To play for Glasgow Celtic, would fulfil his dream
Around about St. Patrick's Day, signed by Big Jock Stein
He played only for the jersey, Johnny Doyle in the Green.

(chorus)
And Johnny Doyle told me, not long before he died
He said I love my Glasgow Celtic
Because I'm just a Celtic boy.

In Europe 1980, we all know what Johnny did
He capped a great performance, against Real Madrid
He rose with two defenders, to win the ball so clean
With Sabido and Camacho, was John Doyle in the Green.

(chorus)
So in your prayers remember, a gallant Celtic son
His young life cut so cruelly, in 1981
The nineteenth of October, turned a grey and rainy day
And then I heard John Doyle, had sadly passed away.

A PIPE FOR BRITAIN'S RECORD GOALSCORER

The name of James McGrory sent shivers down the spine of defenders all over Britain. The greatest goal scorer these islands have ever seen racked up 550 goals in 547 first class games. Even the great Pele once remarked that if he could do half as well as Jimmy McGrory then he would have had a magnificent career.

Of the 550 goals scored in his illustrious career, McGrory netted 522 in a Celtic shirt, in just 501 appearances for the club. This remarkable feat comes as no surprise when you consider that Jimmy had the ability to net eight goals in a single match, as he did for Celtic against Dunfermline Athletic in 1928. Britain's greatest striker also won no fewer than 15 honours in as many years as a player for the club, before becoming Celtic Manager in mid-1945.

During his managerial post, the Garngad man guided the Hoops to six honours, including the Coronation Cup, throughout a 20 year stay in the position. It was under McGrory's stewardship that Celtic also defeated Rangers 7-1 in the 1957 League Cup Final.

Officially ranked as the 8th highest goal scorer in the history of world football, McGrory provoked the first ever 'Hampden roar', when he scored a late winner against England in 1933. The goal was one of six netted in international matches by McGrory, from just seven caps. Clearly, his religion and ethnic background played a far greater role in the decision-making process of Scotland's selectors than his world class ability.

Sadly, it was not only the SFA, who underappreciated McGrory. After his role as Manager came to an end at Celtic and he was replaced by Jock Stein, Jimmy found himself taking a seat in the boardroom as PR officer. He held this post for 14 years, until retirement in 1979. Throughout such incredibly loyal service to Celtic, McGrory was only publicly appreciated on one occasion. That recognition came on 1st September 1971, when the Hoops legend was invited to officially open the reconstructed Grand Stand, ahead of Celtic's clash with FC Nacional. 60,000 people applauded him that day and a plaque was nailed to the stand, bearing the words:

This reconstructed grandstand was opened by Jimmy McGrory on 1st September 1971 and on this date Celtic played Nacional of Uruguay, the Champions of South America.

McGrory could have been forgiven for viewing the moment as bittersweet, considering that the club had wanted to sell him to Arsenal in order to fund the construction of the original (then 5,000 seater) Grand Stand in 1929, which was built to replace the similarly named Grant Stand. In the summer of 1928, Celtic accepted an offer of £10,000 from Arsenal to boost the bank account and finance said plans. McGrory turned down the move and the chance to become the highest paid footballer in Britain because he could not bear to leave Parkhead. He is famously quoted as saying: "McGrory of Arsenal doesn't have quite the same ring to it as McGrory of the Celtic." Upon hearing of his rejecting the move, Celtic secretly paid him less than his team mates for the rest of his career. His pay was docked from £9 per week to £8 per week, and when McGrory later discovered this, he simply said: "Well it was worth it just to pull on those green and white hoops."

When McGrory did finally retire from his final role at Celtic in early 1979, he was invited to attend a mass in New York by Father Coleman. The invitation was said to be "In thanksgiving for being such a wonderful Celt." By contrast, Celtic could only offer the immortal man a new pipe.

One group of people connected with the club saw to it that McGrory would receive the appropriate appreciation for a service to Celtic Football Club, which few could argue ranked him as the greatest Celt of all time. The Celtic Supporter's Association dedicated their 34th annual Rally to his honour, inviting him to be special guest for the evening on Sunday 4th March 1979 at Kelvin Hall.

It comes as no surprise that the event was an immediate sell-out. Perhaps a mark of the underappreciation he experienced, or his genuine modesty, Jimmy McGrory was reportedly moved to tears, exclaiming "Goodness," as he walked in to see the huge number of guests that had turned up to pay tribute to him. The official programme for the evening waxed lyrical about 'a giant of the game'. Whilst, Desmond White sought to make amends on the board's behalf, when he opened the evening by presenting a silver salver to the Celtic legend. The salver bore the inscription: 'To the one and only Jimmy McGrory'. It was also fitting that Billy McNeill, then Manager of the club, led the entire Celtic backroom staff, along with players from the past and present squads, up to join McGrory on stage.

When the meal had been devoured and the formalities concluded, there was an interval, which afforded President of the Association, Peter Murray, an opportunity to address the audience with some words of his own.

Peter called Jimmy McGrory to the stage again. This time the great Celt was to be awarded with a commemorative clock and a much-needed cheque. It had saddened the Celtic support that a factor in McGrory's decision to step down after 50 years of service to the club was partly financial. His wages of £70 per month did not bequeath the McGrory family with tremendous riches, considering the service that he had dedicated, on and off the field, to making Celtic a worldwide institution. His wife, Barbara, had continued to work as a private nurse and the family had to maintain their hard work. This was never something that Jimmy complained about, for as far as he was concerned, his life had been enriched by things more important than money.

The Rally concluded with some music and the sincerest thanks was directed towards Jimmy McGrory for the joy he brought to many Celtic fans, his incredible loyalty to the club and his remarkable character as a man. Finally, he had been given a fitting show of appreciation. Although, there is no doubting that he understood how loved he was by the supporters as opposed to the old boardrooms of Celtic Park and Hampden.

It is fantastic that Celtic fans remember him beyond this event, with a weekly chorus: *And they gave us James McGrory and Paul McStay. They gave us Johnstone, Tully, Murdoch, Auld and Hay. Most of the football greats, have passed through Parkhead's gates for to play football the Glasgow Celtic way.*

James McGrory pictured on a Mitchell's cigarette card in the 1930s

RIOT CUP FINAL

1980 represented a temporary shift in the balance of power within Scottish Football as Alex Ferguson's Aberdeen had won the league, whilst Dundee United had won the League Cup. The pair, then known as 'the new firm', had left just one trophy for the nation's traditionally dominant clubs to clinch.

The day of reckoning fell on 10th May. Temperatures were forecast to peak at 27.5oc in Western Scotland and 70,303 people packed into Hampden Park beneath the blazing sun. Celtic fans may have felt the heat more than their Rangers counterparts, when they noticed that the team sheet had omitted the names of Tom McAdam and Roddie MacDonald due to injury. Instead, Roy Aitken and Mike Conroy were drafted into the side to form a makeshift central defensive partnership. Any fears the Celtic faithful may have had were soon allayed as Conroy stamped his authority on the game from the heart of Celtic's defence. The Johnstone born Bhoy, one of 21 Scotsmen on the pitch, had linked up well with Alan Sneddon, in his secondary position. Equally assured, was the Rangers backline, with Sandy Jardine and Colin Jackson showing robust defence.

The anxiety of each side to win some silverware for their supporters ensured that the match was a tentative affair. Unsurprisingly, the match was 0-0 after 90 minutes, though the only non-scot on the park, Peter Latchford, did have to make a reaction save when Davie Cooper had a free header inside the Celtic penalty area.

Celtic came in to their own during extra time and Peter McCloy was forced to make a couple of smart saves from

229

Davie Provan. However, the Rangers goalkeeper was helpless to stop Celtic taking the lead in the 108th minute, when Danny McGrain scuffed a long range shot across the floor; George McCluskey stretched out his right foot and diverted the ball fortuitously past the wrong-footed McCloy. One half of Hampden erupted, prompting an ash cloud to rise like a volcanic eruption, thanks to the dilapidated terracing at the Celtic end.

Rangers had to go on the offensive to salvage the cup. In doing so, they were left exposed and were almost made to pay when Tommy Burns broke on the counter. As he closed in on goal, Peter McCloy dived at the feet of the Hoops' favourite and snatched the ball away. It mattered little though, as the full-time whistle was blown seconds later.

That famous 'Hampden Roar' bellowed around half of the national stadium again. The Celtic team sprinted to their fans to join in the celebrations, where some young supporters scaled the ten-foot fence, which was installed around the perimeter of the pitch to prevent a repeat of the scenes after the 1965 League Cup and 1969 Scottish Cup, Finals. On those occasions, Rangers fans had invaded the pitch after their team had lost against Celtic.

Celtic fans were enjoying their moment in the sun, but for the remaining supporters at the opposite end of the stadium, it was a provocative step too far. Unlike the situation at Easter Road a week earlier, when Aberdeen fans ran on the pitch to celebrate winning the league championship, the Rangers contingent weren't as patient as the Hibernian faithful had been that day.

In a drunken rage, hundreds of angry Rangers fans ran on to the pitch to confront the Celtic support. This emptied the Celtic end as several concerned Celts sprung to retaliate, especially as so many youngsters were on the field. Only a dozen policemen stood between the rival mobs. All other officers were manning the surrounding streets, where trouble was expected to occur, since as the ten-foot fence was supposed to stop fans battling inside the ground.

Chief Inspector, Iain McKie spoke to The Scotsman newspaper after the day: "They say there was 400-500 officers on duty that day. Well, I can tell you that the majority of them were outside the stadium by the time the match was over. There was nothing unusual about that. It was standard procedure. Most of the trouble at Old Firm matches took place outside the ground; fighting, urinating in gardens, all sorts." The decision proved disastrous. Cans and bricks were thrown by each support, whilst a photographer for The Daily Record was bottled. Things turned even more sinister when iron bars and wooden staves, extracted from terracing frames, were used as make shift batons. Rangers fans charged like a pack of wolfs. Celtic supporters regrouped, steadied themselves and burst on their own offensive, in the manner of a group of hungry hyenas. It was a scene akin to the Siege of Alesia.

The bedlam of the riot was best described by the incredible commentary of Archie McPherson: "They're spilling right on to the pitch. And where are the police? Where the hell are the police? This is like a scene out of Apocalypse Now... We've got the equivalent of Passchendaele and that says nothing for Scottish football. At the end of the day, let's not kid ourselves. These supporters hate each other."

Eventually the constabulary did arrive. Mounted on horseback, batons to boot, they could do little to quell the violence. Only as more and more officers were deployed to the stadium, did order slowly begin to be restored.

Four policemen were injured, along with 100 fans, many of whom were hospitalised. 160 people were arrested inside the stadium, whilst a further 50 were jailed on the streets. It was a battle to end all battles... Scotland hoped.

An investigation by the SFA executive committee found that the initial invasion of the pitch by Celtic fans was "A spontaneous, if misguided, expression of joy." However, due to what followed, both clubs were fined £20,000. The matter was taken further, reaching the highest echelons of the British government. The police had blamed Celtic fans. Rangers directors concurred with the constabulary. Desmond White, however, had spoken up on the Parkhead club's behalf. He claimed that sectarianism was the cause of the riot and went on to say: "I can tell you that Celtic's Cup Final side featured six Catholic players and five Protestants, who include our captain, Danny McGrain." His remarks left little to be deduced. There was danger of the case becoming one with lots of blame, but little progressive discussion. George Younger, the Secretary of State for Scotland, put paid to that issue. He ultimately blamed alcohol and the actions of the Celtic players for the riot. An Act of Parliament was then passed, banning the sale of alcoholic beverages within Scottish sports grounds. The legislation remains in place, except for Scottish International rugby matches, as the ban was amended by Cabinet Secretary for Justice, Kenny MacAskill. He decided to permit rugby supporters of the national team a drink, as of 2007. It should also be noted that the law can be escaped at Scottish football matches for those within hospitality suites, as alcohol sales can be made in those areas, where there is no view of the pitch.

BOXER WITNESSES BOXING

Celtic Park has a long history with boxing. The stadium was first used to host an official boxing bout on 2nd June 1937, when 20,000 fans saw the legendary Gorbals character, Benny Lynch, suffer a rare points defeat to Jimmy Warnock. The match was made at 8st 4oz that night, but Lynch came in at 8st 2lbs, which resulted in a £200 purse increase for his Belfast born opponent.

Paradise had to wait until 18th May 1949 to host its first title fight. Harry Hughes of Wishaw topped the bill in a bout against Billy Thompson from Hickleton Main that night. The main event drew a crowd of 15,000 people, who saw the English fighter become British Lightweight Champion, by way of technical knockout in the fifth round.

Celtic Park has been visited by multiple boxing legends: Jim Corbett, the immortal Muhammed Ali, Pat Clinton, Sugar Ray Robinson and Sean O'Grady. The latter visited Paradise in the most unusual and chaotic of circumstances. O'Grady was due to fight Scottish hero, Jim Watt, for the WBC Lightweight belt at Kelvin Hall in November 1980. A week prior to the event, the Oklahoma cowboy approached Celtic to ask for assistance in promoting the fight. The club were willing to oblige, inviting the 'Bubble Gum Bomber' to make an appearance on the pitch during the half time interval of Celtic's upcoming clash with Kilmarnock on 25th October.

The 21-year-old arrived at Celtic Park in full country and western apparel. He was treated to a thrilling first half of football as Frank McGarvey scored in the 44th minute to put the Hoops 2-1 in front, having trailed early on. The noise had barely abated by the time Sean O'Grady took to the field, in front of the Celtic support. He had clearly been well advised, as the American boxer circulated the field before removing his denim jacket to reveal a Celtic jersey. Suddenly, the dynamics were changed, and polite applause turned into a rapturous cry of "One Sean O'Grady, there's only one Sean O'Grady." Kilmarnock fans had taken exception to Celtic cheering for the opponent of a Scottish national boxing hero like Jim Watt. Before a second loop of the chant was made, a scrap suitable for the undercard broke out at the unsegregated, traditional 'Rangers End' of the stadium. O'Grady looked on, cutting a perplexed figure, whilst the Jungle serenaded him with a rendition of The Soldier's Song as the crowd trouble fizzled out.

Much was made in the media about O'Grady having an Irish-Catholic background. It was claimed that Celtic had only given him a platform to promote himself for this reason. However, the press were made to look foolish when it transpired that O'Grady had no such heritage, despite the connotations associated with his surname. Nevertheless, many newspaper reports hadn't found out this fact until after the fight, which they had attempted to build up as a Catholic v Protestant affair. The fact that Jim Watt was a Rangers fan was also thrown into the mix, in an attempt to fan the flames of fire. Though, Watt soon extinguished any controversy when he made it known that his son was a Celtic supporter.

Ironically, the fight took place the day before a Glasgow derby game. The bout needed no sectarian or football supporting element to inspire the crowd, as Sean O'Grady performed a boxing masterclass in the ring. The non Irish-American, wearing green shorts emblazoned with a shamrock (his father, Pat O'Grady said this was done for "Cosmetic reasons") came forward and threw a right hook, which Jim Watt anticipated, ducked beneath and countered with a left hook over the top. In doing so, the Glaswegian accidentally headbutted O'Grady, resulting in a horrendous cut. The fight had to be stopped in round 12 and the Scot could relax, having retained his title by a stroke of good fortune after being dominated.

Sean O'Grady demanded a rematch, but his plea fell on deaf ears. He regathered himself to become a world champion in his next fight and went on to have an incredible career, which saw him inducted into the World Boxing Hall of Fame in 1992. He retired at the age of 24, having amassed remarkable stats of: 81 wins (70 by knockout) and 5 defeats.

Muhammed Ali is joined by some familiar faces as he visits Celtic Park in August 1965

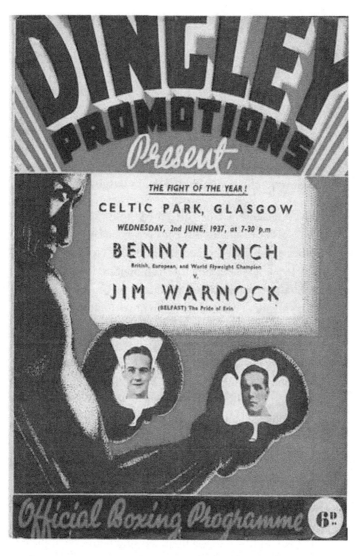

*The official programme for the first major boxing bout
hosted at Celtic Park, in 1937*

SOLITUDE AGAINST CLIFTONVILLE

Celtic Football Club has always been intrinsically connected to Ireland, but no city on the Emerald Isle is it more tied to than Belfast. Ever since Belfast Celtic (see page 358), a carbon copy of the Glasgow club, was formed in 1891, the Bhoys became frequent visitors to Antrim. The tragic demise of the most successful Irish club, Celtic's greatest friend, ensured that the devotion of Nationalists in Belfast was fully committed to their Glasgow counterpart.

Whilst (Glasgow) Celtic filled the void for many Catholics in the North of Ireland, it wasn't always easy to travel to matches at Parkhead, especially after the Troubles broke out in 1969. It was during this turbulent period that community boundaries were redrawn as Unionists sought to gerrymander electoral areas, in order to dominate the newly formed Northern Ireland state. The population changes as a result of gerrymandering meant that some Nationalists in North Belfast began to attend Cliftonville FC matches. In time, these new fans generated a political association with the club, though The Reds were far from sympathetic to the Irish cause, prior to the demographic shift.

Celtic were invited to travel to Solitude Stadium for a friendly fixture against Cliftonville on 14th August 1984. The hesitant acceptance by the Celtic board produced great joy in Belfast Nationalist circles, this being the first time that they would get to see their sporting heroes visit the city since the since they paraded the European Cup on the Falls Road in 1967. 8,000 people filled Solitude on a boiling hot day. Tri-colours and green and white hoops filled all quarters of the unsegregated stadium. The atmosphere was electric, with jubilant fans climbing The Cage at one end of the stadium and drinking on the roof of the stand. On the field, the action was just as scintillating, with Celtic going 2-0 ahead inside 25 minutes.

The positive mood at the match served as welcome relief from the horrors of the violence that had plagued two thirds of Ulster at the time. There had been a cloud of apprehension hanging over the friendly because Sean Downes had been killed by the RUC a week earlier. Downes was a local Nationalist, who had been attending an anti-internment rally, which was headed by Martin Galvin (publicity director of the New York-based Northern Irish Aid Committee). Galvin was banned from the United Kingdom by British authorities due to his outspoken political allegiances, and the police moved in to arrest him at the rally. In doing so, they fired plastic bullets at the crowd, two of which struck Sean Downes in the chest and mouth from close range. As Galvin escaped in the distance, Downes lay lifeless on the ground.

Against such a sinister backdrop, Celtic and Cliftonville had come to an agreement with the RUC that the police would remain outside of the stadium to avoid tensions with both sets of supporters. The fact that fans of both clubs were so close meant that a police presence was hardly necessary anyway.

75 minutes were on the clock when two goals in as many minutes from Graeme Sinclair put Celtic in to an unassailable 4-0 lead. Little did anyone know that the match was soon to be abandoned.

The RUC had already renounced their word in the first half, when they patrolled one side of The Cage behind the goal (the area where the noisiest supporters congregated). The unexpected presence of the constabulary was about as welcome as a hole in a lifeboat. Fighting between the crowd and armed police soon broke out, before reinforcements in armoured vehicles were deployed to the scene. In no time, bricks and bottles flew across the stand, darkening the sun filled sky. Celtic's worst disaster was unfolding. Nevertheless, the trouble did cease at half time and many fans moved to other sections of the stadium.

When supporters cheered the fourth Celtic goal, the RUC burst towards The Cage again, withdrawing their weapons and firing plastic bullets at the remaining occupants of the stand. Hundreds fled and cowered, whilst some battle-hardened supporters resisted the onslaught with makeshift missiles. 24 people were reportedly wounded, whilst hundreds more were belted with batons and dragged along the terracing by an almost exclusively Unionist police force.

In the aftermath of the disorder, it was claimed that the RUC had moved in to dissipate crowd trouble. The Glasgow Herald followed this line of reporting, whilst Desmond White (Celtic Chairman) strongly denied the claims and set the record straight in a television interview with the BBC, as soon as he arrived back in Scotland:

"Cliftonville had been promised early on that there would only be a shadow police presence. There were riot squads there. Celtic were playing Cliftonville – half the Cliftonville supporters are Celtic supporters. There could have been no trouble at the match at all because it was between two

friendly sets of supporters. The violence was artificially created in my opinion. Neither Cliftonville nor Celtic are part of that violence."

So harrowed were Celtic by the events of that day, the club did not return to Belfast until 23rd July 2008, long after The Troubles had finished. On that occasion the Glasgow side beat Donegal Celtic, a phoenix club of Belfast Celtic, courtesy of a goal from Derek Riordan. The match passed without issue, much like Celtic's return to Solitude in October 2009, when Cliftonville triumphed 3-0 during a match to mark the 130th anniversary of the Belfast club.

Celtic faced Cliftonville in a competitive match, for the first time, on 17th July 2013, as part of the Champion's League qualifiers. The build up to the game was slightly reminiscent of the infamous friendly in August 1984, as there had been rioting in the city five days earlier due to the orange marches on 12th July. However, the match went ahead without any problems and Celtic ran out 3-0 winners, amid a phenomenal atmosphere.

Proceedings were less peaceful on Celtic's most recent visit to Belfast, when the Hoops were paired with Linfield in another Champion's League qualifier. Linfield had been the team blamed for the disbandment of Belfast Celtic. The bulk of their support is drawn from the loyalist heartlands of East Belfast, and the match was scheduled to go ahead on that day of days – 12th July (2017). The game had to be moved to Friday 14th July, due to obvious safety concerns, especially as there had been effigies depicting Celtic players being burnt on some 12th July bonfires, alongside racist depictions of Celtic staff, accompanied by sectarian banners. The change in date was sensible but did little to quell the animosity inside Windsor Park.

Celtic had taken the step of refusing an away allocation for the match, though it was decided at the last minute, to allow a small section of supporters to enter the away end. There was a quite bizarre scene in the second half, when Lee Griffiths went to take a corner, making a '5-1' gesture (Celtic had beaten Rangers 5-1, twice, in the previous season), and he was pelted with coins, whilst a Buckfast bottle whizzed past his head. The referee deemed this a bookable offence and Griffiths was cautioned. At full time, Lee Griffiths tied a Celtic scarf to the goalpost, which is his trademark action. Linfield fans reacted by attempting to invade the pitch, such was their incredulous rage. Therefore, UEFA fined Celtic €4,500 and hit Griffiths with a one match ban. The governing body also fined Linfield €10,000 and gave the club a partial stadium closure.

There is never a dull moment for the Bhoys in Belfast. It is a city that has seen much change over the years but remains a stronghold of Celtic support.

Celtic & Cliftonville fans at The Cage end of Solitude stadium

Celtic mural – The Markets area, Belfast

RAPID DECLINE

The mere mention of the name Rapid Vienna makes the blood boil for many Celtic fans. The Bhoys were paired against the Austrian side in the second round of the 1984 European Cup Winners' Cup. The tie posed a tricky proposition for the Celts, something the faithful became acutely aware of when Celtic fell to a 3-1 defeat at the Gerhard Hannapi Stadion, in the first leg. Hans Krankl almost broke the net with a left foot thrash from just inside the box in the 87th minute that night. The goal, many Austrians felt, had guaranteed Rapid qualification for the Quarter Finals.

Close to 49,000 people attended the return leg at Celtic Park. First half goals from McClair and MacLeod had them rocking the terracing as the tie was now level on aggregate, with Celtic set to progress on away goals. Work still needed to be done and Tommy Burns ensured it would be, when he slide tackled the goalkeeper, who was scrambling to pick up an over hit pass. Burns took the ball and passed into an empty net, then he turned with one arm aloft and a beaming smile, making headway for the Jungle. Celtic were 3-0 up and cruising.

Dynamo Dresden would await in the Quarter Final, but it was Rapid Vienna, who played against them! This shock twist came as a result of one of the most controversial events in football history. Celtic did indeed see out the second leg to win 3-0. However, the Rapid players had been very unhappy with Tommy Burns' goal. Reinhard Kienast, of the Austrian's defence, ran towards the Celtic man and struck him on the back of the head. He was sent off, but incredibly the Rapid goalkeeper kicked Burns on the floor and the Vienna club contemplated leaving the field in protest. The Celtic support was riled by this and in the 78th minute, a fan in the Jungle launched a bottle on to the pitch. It landed acres from any player, but Rudi Weinhofer took the opportunity to hit the deck.

Television cameras, the linesman and the Celtic first aider all testified that the player had not been injured. Yet the Rapid midfielder got bandaged up and left the field on a stretcher. His embarrassing antics were replicated by the club themselves, when they refused to accept a £5,000 fine from UEFA and appealed for a replay. The European governing body for football astonishingly overlooked all available evidence and ordered the match to be replayed... at Old Trafford! The verdict was made even more baffling, when the committee also decided to double Rapid Vienna's £5,000 fine.

The replayed match at Old Trafford was one of the most poisonous games involving Celtic. Rapid officials complained that their Celtic counterparts refused to shake hands in Glasgow airport. Meanwhile, 40,000 Celtic fans headed to Manchester, creating an extremely tempestuous atmosphere. It was war without the bullets.

Locals and some away fans added to the Celtic contingent to produce a crowd of 51,500 - a larger attendance than the original second leg at Celtic Park. As the aggregate score had reverted to 3-1 in Rapid Vienna's favour, the Hoops required another healthy victory to progress. Celtic went on the attack from the outset. Roy Aitken squandered two early chances, one of which struck the woodwork. As the ball rebounded off the post, Rapid broke up field. A sensational counter attack was rounded off by the

Austrians, when the ball was played out wide to Peter Pacult, who skinned Danny McGrain and gave Rapid the lead. The goal dealt a crushing blow, with Celtic now needing to score three without reply.

Lingering hope began to be lost when Celtic were denied a clear penalty. Sadly, anger got the better of one fan, who attacked Herbert Feurer in the Rapid goal, before being tackled by no fewer than six policemen. Exasperation then spilled to the opposite end of the stadium when Peter Pacult was attacked by another Celtic supporting madman.

The only cheers on the night came at full time, when a pocket of Manchester United fans revelled in the news that their team had beaten Dundee United 3-2 at Tannadice, to advance to the UEFA Cup Quarter Final by way of a 5-4 aggregate win.

Celtic had unjustly bowed out of the European Cup Winners' Cup. However, the poor behaviour of the support that night gave the club a further problem in the form of a £17,000 fine, alongside a ruling to play their next European match behind closed doors. As for Rapid, they advanced as far as the Final, before being beaten 3-1 by Everton.

Green Brigade banner during the Europa League group stage match between Celtic and Rapid Vienna – 1st October 2009. The match ended 1-1.

JANEFIELD STREET RIOT

A strangely indifferent build up preceded the final Glasgow derby of the season. Sir Alex Ferguson's Aberdeen had taken the league by storm and were back to back champions elect with a six-point advantage at the top of the table. Despite a low crowd of 40,079 at Celtic Park, the Glasgow derby wasn't lacking the excitement that invariably accompanies the fixture. It was barely two minutes past 3pm, on 1st May 1985, before Celtic were awarded a penalty after Dave McPherson pushed Mo Johnston in the back. Roy Aitken stepped up, aiming to slot home his fourth spot kick in three matches. The Celtic defender planted his standing foot in the turf and swung his right leg back, only for the wind to blow the ball off the penalty spot. Aitken smashed his shot home after returning the ball to its proper position, but the referee felt that the ball had moved off the spot again and ordered the penalty to be retaken. Inevitably, the stand in skipper missed at the third time of asking, thanks to a great save by Peter McCloy.

The half time talk of the penalty fiasco was quickly forgotten, as attention was switched to Davie Cooper who was sent off for a retaliatory tackle on Peter Grant early in the second half. Alan McInally then made Celtic's numerical advantage show on the scoreboard in the 60th minute, whilst Ally Dawson was sent off following a clash with Mo Johnston, ten minutes later. Nevertheless, nine-man Rangers rallied to get an equaliser in the 77th minute, when Ally McCoist scored a penalty, awarded for a handball by Roy Aitken. To top things off, Davie Provan struck a volley against the post in the closing minutes, which denied Celtic all three points.

Despite all the drama of the match, the main talking point came after full time as fans exited via Janefield Street. All was as normal until, out of nowhere, five mounted police horses charged down the road. They turned at the end of the narrow street, Celtic Park on one side and the cemetery wall on the other. The startled crowd regathered and pelted the police with coins. Some ripped aerials off cars and whipped policemen with them, whilst others were lifted over the graveyard wall and seen scampering to safety through the headstones.

Charge followed charge, as the police made four attempts to overcome the crowd. During the mayhem, the brick cemetery wall and its steel railings toppled on the people below. 39 fans were injured, ten of whom went to hospital. Nine police officers were also hurt, with one sporting a broken nose.

The Strathclyde Police Constable, Sir Patrick Hamill, called for an immediate inquiry. Concurrently, Kevin Kelly (Celtic Director) asked for witness reports to be sent into the Celtic View from residents of Janefield Street and those in the crowd itself. In the following two editions of the magazine, Celtic stated that they felt the crowd had been making a peaceful exit until the police decided to charge:

Celtic Football Club have always cooperated with the police in every way and it is recognised that sometimes the constabulary have a difficult job to perform to keep law and order.

Regrettably however it would appear that some policemen put many innocent people at risk as the crowds streamed out of Celtic Park last Wednesday night.

An overwhelming consensus of opinion among people who witnessed the scene clearly indicates that the action of the mounted police in Janefield Street after the game must be called into question.

When scattering, panic-ridden fans caused the collapse of 100 yards of an iron fence topped wall without as much as a broken window in any of the closely adjacent houses it can only be assumed that the debris was caused by a stampede.

Our many callers, letter writers and even the residents of Janefeld Street all indicate that, whatever precipitated the charge of the mounted policemen, it was nothing to do with fighting fans as reported in the press the next day.

Reports indicate that the police are instituting a full enquiry. It is to be hoped that the Chairman and Directors of Celtic Football Club will be given full access to their findings.

One thing is certain - this must never be allowed to happen again.

The outcome of the police inquiry absolved the force of any wrongdoing. The matter was escalated to the House of Commons where it was noted that of 1,093 complaints against the police that year, the procurator fiscal had only taken action on 21 cases, none of which included Strathclyde Police. The question was raised by MSP Dennis Canavan, as to why the police were not punished for their actions at Janefield Street on 1st May 1985, which he said were "Worse than any football hooliganism." The Solicitor General for Scotland retorted: "The honourable gentleman and I must use words differently if he can describe the events of that afternoon as peaceful. Not only were 21 police officers injured, but 12 civilians were injured, one police officer was rendered unconscious and required plastic surgery, and a teacher who assisted a police sergeant was seriously injured and required intensive hospital treatment. In those circumstances, and against the background of the fact that about 62 people are yet to be prosecuted and brought before the courts in relation to the events of that afternoon, it is inappropriate for me to make any further comment on the matter. However, I inform the honourable gentleman that only two specific complaints were made to the procurator fiscal about police conduct that afternoon. I am aware that a broader and more general criticism has been made of the use of police horses that afternoon, but Crown counsel has said that no proceedings will be taken in respect of that."

Some action was eventually brought against the Chief Constable of Strathclyde Police, by Easterhouse Solicitors, who led an independent case on behalf of a young girl that had been injured in the melee.

It is unclear as to what sparked the riot and clearly both sides differed on the events and number of injuries that day. Celtic knew that something further had to be done and so the club moved to establish a police liaison committee in January 1986.

ON OR OFF?

Celtic and Rangers were again competing during the scene of this next incident. This time the chaos was on the pitch. It was the League Cup Final at Hampden Park on 26th October 1986. Every one of the 74,219 people in attendance were gripped for the right reasons.

Rangers started the game exceptionally well. The Ibrox club's dominance continued in to the second half when they took the lead on 62 minutes thanks to a clever free kick, which saw Ian Durrant dispatch from close range. Celtic then finally showed they could play a bit themselves, when they were forced to chase the game. Brian McClair hit a volley against the crossbar and Paul McStay stung the gloves of Chris Woods in the Rangers goal. The Hoops then drew level - McClair latched on to a long ball from Aitken, who had combined with Mo Johnston, and he took the shot early. Half of Hampden erupted as McClair's strike sailed over Chris Woods and into the far corner of the net.

The equaliser shifted momentum and it seemed that Celtic were most likely to prevail, but as extra time loomed a penalty was controversially awarded to Rangers. Terry Butcher and Roy Aitken had competed for a high ball when the pair fell in a heap. Both were shocked to see the referee award a spot kick. Tony Sheppard, playing in Celtic's midfield that day, told The Herald newspaper: "I wouldn't say it was soft, I would say it was extremely soft. It was a tough one to take in a cup Final." Be that as it may, Davie Cooper showed little hesitation in accepting the gift, putting Rangers 2-1 in front from the spot.

The key flashpoint of the afternoon took place in the 87th minute though, when Mo Johnston received a second yellow card for an off the ball incident. As he left the field, blessing himself, Tony Sheppard ran from midfield to remonstrate with the referee. David Syme, the man in the middle, turned away to shun Sheppard's complaints, when he was struck by a 50 pence coin thrown from the crowd. Upon feeling the blow, the referee immediately turned and sent off Sheppard.

Tony Sheppard spoke of the event in a reflective piece by The Herald newspaper, on 27th November 2016:

"Mo Johnston got sent off for an off-the-ball thing, a head butt on Stuart Munro I think it was," he said. "I ran over to the referee to protest his innocence. Mr Syme said: 'Get yourself away or you'll be joining him'.

As I went to walk away a coin came over from the crowd and hit him right on the back of the head. He must've thought I had flicked my hand at him and hit him. He turned around and showed me a red card. I can remember the look to total bewilderment in everybody's faces.

(Davie) Hay ran out of his dugout to confront the match official over the blatant injustice and had to be escorted away by police officers as bedlam broke out among the fans inside the stadium.

Derek Whyte came over to me. He told me: 'Tony, just go off! There's going to be a riot!' I was just 19, but, even at that age, I had enough courage in my convictions to say: 'No, I'm not doing it'.

I went over to the linesman. He was the proverbial rabbit in the headlights. I said: 'Gonna tell him what happened there?' He consulted with the referee. Mr Syme came over to me and said: 'Mr Shepherd, please carry on'."

In the eyes of Davie Hay, the mix up wasn't rectified by allowing Tony Sheppard to continue. Indeed, the then Celtic Manager said after the match: "If it was up to me our application to join the English League would be made tomorrow. When Celtic play top teams there are always controversial decisions against us." Despite Hay's comments, covering the game as a whole, the individual decision to dismiss Tony Sheppard was one occasion when the term 'honest mistake' could be used accurately.

COURT CASE

"I used to say to the wide men, if you get a chance launch the ball in at the goalkeeper, and I used to go in and hit them. I used to put them in the net just to let them know that I'm there, keep them on their toes. It didn't matter who it was, and I done that with Chris (Woods). Chris knocked the ball round the post and it was a foul, but the referee gave a corner and I couldn't stop laughing because Chris was all tied up in the net. He didn't take too kindly to that." Frank McAvennie said those words to The Celtic Star podcast in February 2018. He may look back on the events that led to him standing before the courts with a degree of laughter now, but it was no joke back in late 1987.

Celtic travelled to Ibrox on 17th October 1987 to compete against their age-old foe. Just like so many other games between the clubs at that time the match was laced with negative talking points. An altercation occurred in the 19th minute, preceded by the clash which McAvennie's comments above allude to. Chris Morris broke down the right wing and played a low cross along the six-yard box. Rather than take it cleanly, Woods collected the ball and waited to exact revenge on McAvennie half a second later. He thrust out an elbow, which failed to connect. McAvennie returned fire with a cuff round each ear of the Rangers goalkeeper, who aimed a jab towards the striker. Terry Butcher arrived on the scene with a firm shove in the chest of McAvennie, before Graham Roberts aimed a half-hearted punch towards the Celt, who promptly hit the deck. The relatively small Ibrox crowd (43,486) went berserk as the scuffle unfolded before their eyes.

Chris Woods and Frank McAvennie were sent off for their part in the incident. Terry Butcher got a booking, whilst Graham Roberts escaped Scot free. It was the latter who took over as goalkeeper for the remainder of the game. Roberts showed himself to be capable between the sticks when Peter Grant broke through on goal and he stood up well to save the one on one opportunity. However, the stand in keeper was beaten in the 33rd minute, when Andy Walker controlled a clearance by Aitken and passed the ball under the diving Roberts. Celtic's lead was then doubled two minutes later, as Terry Butcher looped a desperate clearance into his own net. Butcher's afternoon got even worse in the second half, when he thundered into Allen McKnight in the Celtic goal as a free kick was hoisted deep into the penalty area. As McKnight tried to get off the floor, Butcher dug him with a not so sly jab, resulting in a red card.

Unbelievably, Celtic surrendered their 2-0 lead despite a ten v nine advantage. Ally McCoist finished a wonderful move, which featured some excellent skill by Ferguson in midfield. Billy Stark then rued hitting the woodwork for Celtic, as Rangers struck level through Richard Gough in the final minute. Having got back on terms, Rangers survived one final scare when Owen Archdeacon chased down a through ball, which Roberts just got to first. The stand in goalkeeper then proceeded to dive on the floor, following minimal contact. When he got to his feet, the Englishman disgraced himself by cheerleading the Ibrox crowd in a sectarian rendition of The Billy Boys.

The full-time whistle did not bring an end to the saga. The Procurator Fiscal ordered a police enquiry into the incidents at the match. The findings were unforgiving, as Frank

McAvennie explained to The Scotsman newspaper: "I had been at a party on the drink all night, then the Sunday morning Billy McNeill phoned and said 'you need to go to Bellahouston Park Station, you're getting charged in relation to the game. Get Allen McKnight to drive you.' I thought I had murdered about 20 people when I saw the amount of press there."

McAvennie wasn't alone in his punishment. Chris Woods, Terry Butcher and Graham Roberts were also charged. All four individuals had been accused of 'behaviour likely to cause a breach of the peace' and were to appear in court the following April (12th April 1988). McAvennie explains how the commotion unravelled: "I know the boys, we're all pals. We kicked lumps out of each other in a game but off the pitch we're alright. We couldn't leave the court because of the world press."

The trial opened with a day of Assistant Chief Constable, John Dickson, talking in the witness stand. The senior officer for Strathclyde Police suggested that a pitch invasion could have been caused, similar to the Hampden Riot in 1980. McAvennie was found not guilty and Roberts avoided further punishment as he was found not proven. Butcher and Woods were less fortunate, as both were found guilty, whilst Woods was hit heaviest, with a £500 fine, compared to Butcher's financial penalty of exactly half that amount. Sheriff Archibald McKay also added that Wood's involvement was the most serious of the quartet, who had been dubbed 'Goldilocks and the three bears' by the press. McKay stated to Woods: "Video clearly establishes that you jabbed McAvennie on the chin with your left forearm. It was an assault which constituted breach of the peace." The Sherriff then addressed Butcher and said: "You performed a violent push, which might reasonably have been expected to upset other Celtic players and their support." The case was finally closed with a dressing down of all four individuals by the Sherrif: "A large percentage of supporters are readily converted by breaches of the peace into two rival mobs. That they were not so transformed is no credit to you. You must have been aware of your wider responsibilities and you failed to discharge them."

So cheeky was McAvennie, that upon completing the Centenary double a month later, he reflected on the campaign as "The season they couldn't even beat us in court." Despite this tongue in cheek remark, he did stand by his former competitors in an interview with The Scotsman newspaper on 14th October 2007. McAvennie said: "Chris and Terry were given criminal records because we four players were exploited to further the ambitions of others in legal circles. We were a test case. No actions have been brought against players in similar fashion since 1987 because the test failed." The Celtic hero's opinion is matched by Terry Butcher, who, as part of the same report, reflected: "Because Rangers felt we had been victimised, they said they wouldn't stand in our way if we wanted to go back down south, but I told Souness I wanted to stay." Souness himself claimed the Procurator Fiscal had no place getting involved in football, the former Rangers Player-Manager gave his assessment in Clash of the Titans documentary: "I'm sure he (Procurator Fiscal) is embarrassed when he looks back now, because he had no place, it didn't warrant it. Football can manage its own business."

CS GAS

The 1980s was a crazy time on the terraces in British football. In Scotland, Aberdeen became the first club to have a firm as the casual scene took hold across the country. The raucous era had already seen full scale pitch riots at Hampden Park and Aberdeen casuals beating a Hibs fan to a comatose state, yet the violence reached new heights in 1985 when Hibernian's mobs, The Capital City Service and Hibs Baby Crew, ambushed Aberdeen with Molotov cocktails on Princes Street (Edinburgh), to knock the Aberdeen Soccer Casuals off their perch as the leading hooligan group in the country.

The casuals scene never took off in the same way at Celtic Park and though there was a hooligan group named the Celtic Soccer Crew, they regularly found themselves ran off the terraces by the wider support and were often subject to chants of 'Casuals get to f**k, casuals, casuals get to f**k'. However, the Celtic Soccer Crew did leave an indelible mark on the Scottish game in 1987 with one of the worst incidents in the decade.

Celtic were playing Hibernian at Easter Road on 28th November and were just a point behind Hearts in the race for the title. A massive away support of over 10,000 travelled to the capital, which meant that the crowd far exceeded the 23,500 capacity attendance quoted, and kick off was delayed by 13 minutes. Once everybody had safely taken to their spot on the terraces, Celtic turned on the style with a sublime performance. Their phenomenal start to the game was rewarded in the 21st minute as Paul McStay and Frank McAvennie combined brilliantly, with the latter shooting past Andy Goram from 12 yards.

Andy Walker had a great opportunity to double Celtic's advantage before the break, but Celtic headed into the half time interval with a solitary goal advantage and a huge roar of approval from their adoring fans. During the break, according to Celtic Soccer Crew leader (John O'Kane), there was discussion among some Celtic hooligans about when they would deploy a weapon on the unsuspecting Hibs fans. The story goes that a CS gas cannister had been acquired by a member of the firm during a recent trip to watch Celtic against Borussia Dortmund in the UEFA Cup. The said member had supplied the hooligan group with the missile that morning and the Celtic Soccer Crew would have seen an opportunity to earn a major coup against one of Britain's most feared hooligan outfits.

The second half begun without incident. Pat Bonner made a string of superb saves to keep Hibernian's Paul Kane at bay, but proceedings were about to be adjourned in the 62nd minute. A loud boom rang out and gas swept along the East terrace of Easter Road. Suddenly, people started spilling on to the pitch to take refuge and eyes began to burn and stream throughout the ground. The Celtic Soccer Crew had fired a CS gas cannister, which they later claimed was a smoke bomb, into the Hibs support housed closest to the away end. A cloud of panic hung over the stadium as supporters were treated on the field and 45 fans were taken to hospital. Fortunately, there were no serious injuries and the worst of the casualties was a 77-year old man, who had broken his ribs in the chaos that followed the explosion of the cannister.

The match was delayed for almost 20 minutes and upon the restart, the flow of the game had gone. The contest simmered out to a vital 1-0 victory for the Celts, which put them back to the top of the table as Hearts had lost 3-2 at Ibrox that afternoon.

Riotous scenes broke out outside of the stadium, as the Capital City Service sought revenge on the away support. The vast majority of the Celtic contingent had been disgusted by what had happened, but ultimately became victims in the crossfire of a brawl between the Capital City Service and the Celtic Soccer Crew on Easter Road.

Half a dozen people were arrested over the incident, with one man being held in prison on remand for 16 weeks prior to a high court appearance. By the time of the trial in February 1988, two twin brothers, who had been at the scene, were also arrested and due to stand before the judges. The trial lasted a few days before the supplier and thrower of the gas cannister received substantial sentences, whilst the other six accused were allowed to walk free.

The incident remains something that most Celtic fans look back on with a sense of embarrassment.

Hibs fans treated on the pitch after the CS gas attack

JUDAS JOHNSTON

Nobody unites the Celtic support like Mo Johnston, or 'Judas' as he is simply known today. Once a darling of Parkhead, Johnston scored 52 goals in 99 games, whilst wearing a hooped shirt. He was enshrined into the hearts of the Celtic faithful in 1986 when he finished off one of the best team goals ever scored by the club at Love Street against St Mirren. The fact that Celtic snatched the title from Hearts in dramatic fashion that day only added to the value of his goal.

Johnston's talent earned him a move to French side, Nantes, in the summer of 1987. Two years later, after Celtic had finished in third place (20 points behind champions, Rangers), Billy McNeill sought to bolster his squad. He had masterminded a deal with Nantes for the return of Johnston, subject to a fee of £1.2m. A boyhood Celt, Johnston was keen to re-join his beloved club, despite once claiming that he would never return to Scotland.

By 1st July 1989, the deal was all but done. Celtic Chairman, Jack McGinn, and Director, Chris White, flew to France to make payment of a £400,000 deposit to Nantes on the deal. The club also checked with officials at FIFA to ensure that the paperwork was correct and posed no legal qualms. FIFA assured Celtic that everything was in order and this assurance, coupled with Johnston's letter of intent to sign, meant that Celtic decided to publicly announce the deal.

Johnston appeared at a press conference to announce that he would sign for Celtic, despite his signature not being on the dotted line of a contract yet. After a disappointing season, it was a transfer that could give the club a real lift. However, something was being plotted across the city, which would stun the football world. Speaking on Clash of the Titans documentary, Graeme Souness said: "My children were Catholics, my wife was a Catholic and my supporters were singing songs about killing Catholics. It didn't sit comfortable with me. I think every Rangers Manager had been asked 'would you sign a Catholic?' and when I was asked I felt I would. I said 'I go home and have dinner with Catholics, you ask me to come to work as a bigot and go home a normal person, I say no. If there's a good Catholic player that comes along and I feel it's right for this club then I'll do it.'"

Rangers had come under increasing pressure from European bodies to drop a decades old sectarian recruitment policy. David Murray described the issue as "A monkey on the club's back." It was thought that if a Catholic had to be signed by Rangers then it would need to be a player from outside of Glasgow to appease the fans. Anyhow, it surely couldn't be Mo Johnston, considering that during the aforementioned press conference, the striker had stated "I'll finish my career here (at Celtic), I don't want to play for anybody else."

Celtic had dealt directly with Mo Johnston throughout negotiations. However, the player's agent's (Bill McMurdo) company owned his contract as opposed to Nantes. This was a fact that Johnston had withheld from Celtic and it posed a stumbling block to the immediate go ahead of the deal. Celtic publicly acknowledged that there were some issues, which needed ironing out. The club contacted FIFA again, who confirmed that Johnston's written agreement to sign a four-year deal with Celtic was legally binding, thus rumours that Graeme Souness had met with Bill McMurdo did little to unease the Parkhead board.

It is thought that Billy McNeill felt FIFA's assurances meant that Celtic should pay the remainder of the agreed fee with Nantes. This would allow the club to acquire the registration of the player and put a stop to the possibility of him possibly doing the unthinkable. It was McNeill's view that contractual issues could then be negotiated from that position of strength. In the Manager's absence, due to a family holiday in Florida, the Celtic board made the decision to withdraw from the deal. Chairman, Jack McGinn confirmed that this action came after Johnston failed to turn up at Celtic Park the following week. Meanwhile, Johnston's agent, an avid Rangers fan, feels that Celtic were in the wrong throughout because they spoke to the player and Nantes Football Club rather than dealing with McMurdo himself, whose company owned the contract.

Within days of holding aloft a Celtic shirt and pledging his allegiance to the club he grew up supporting, Mo Johnston appeared at another press conference in Glasgow. Souness had indeed spoken to his agent and Johnston had stunned the world by opting to join Rangers! The signature of the first Roman Catholic employee since the Govan club realigned their position to become a sectarian institution in the World War I era was too much for many people to handle. Rangers fans burned scarves and returned season tickets in mourning. Yet opposition to the move wasn't just felt by supporters. The club's kit man, Jimmy Bell, allegedly protested in his own personal way by making Johnston arrange his own kit. Graeme Souness told The Sunday Times newspaper: "We unveiled Maurice at Ibrox and I dealt firmly with players in the squad who refused to welcome him, making it clear they wouldn't be staying." Before the start of the 1989/90 season, Davie Cooper, Jimmy Nicholl and Davie Kirkwood had all left Ibrox.

Back at Celtic Park, the club had more than humiliation to overcome. Indeed, whilst fans labelled Johnston: 'Judas' and vented their anger in the form graffiti across the city, the board needed to support Billy McNeill by signing another striker. The club had allowed talisman, Frank McAvennie to return to West Ham in March 1989 following a dip in form, bust ups with the Manager and a longing for London. Johnston had been the intended replacement, just as McAvennie was brought in for the former, when the roles were reversed in 1987. However, Johnston's shock betrayal left Celtic in the mire.

Days later, on 14th July, the club officially signed 'the disco king' Dariusz Dziekanowski from Legia Warsaw for a fee of £600,000. The centre forward came with a respectable reputation, having amassed 44 goals in 95 games for the Polish side. As for Johnston, he had to wait until 4th November 1989 to win over many Rangers fans, doing so when he scored an injury time winner for his new club against Celtic at Ibrox! In the aftermath of the game, a wall in Bellgrove Station bore the words 'collaborators will be kneecapped', which tells one all they need to know about the esteem in which he was held by the Hoops faithful.

Celtic fans have never forgiven Johnston for his antics, and for most, he will always remain 'Judas'.

Mo Johnston pictured with Billy McNeill at the press conference, in which he announced that he would sign for Celtic, just days before he joined Rangers

BLOWING AWAY THE BLUES

The publication of the Taylor Report in 1990 created an unstoppable momentum against the notion of standing at football matches in the UK. The new safety measures were the perquisite to the death sentence cast upon the North Enclosure of Celtic Park, famously known as 'the Jungle'. The stand was famous for being one of the loudest and most wild in world football, only crowds in South America ever coming close to reaching similar decibel levels to the Jungle in full flow. Yet beyond the noise and passion, the Jungle was also full of great characters with fantastic stories, camaraderie and tradition. The Celtic shrine was consigned to the history books in June 1993, when years of memories and footballing folklore crashed around the ears of devastated Celtic fans.

Ironically, the stand was last occupied in a competitive match by Rangers supporters. Due to the redevelopment of Hampden Park that year, the cup finals were moved to Celtic Park, and fans of the Govan club stood on the famous terracing as they witnessed their side beat Aberdeen 2-1 to complete a domestic treble on 29th May 1993.

There had been 16,000 certificates printed by The Evening Times newspaper and handed out to Celtic fans in the Jungle, alongside cans of Jungle Juice, during a match against Dundee two weeks previously. Yet the scene of the Rangers supporters enjoying a treble from the sacred terracing was something that needed banished from Celtic Park and a proper commemoration for the enclosure was organised.

The Jungle, which had housed the most fanatic of the Celtic support for several decades, vanished with a proper farewell on 1st June 1993. On that date, the Celtic team of 1967 hosted some of the Manchester United squad of 1968, with both European Cup winning outfits being joined by celebrity guest players for the evening. The occasion was billed by Celtic directors as The Blowing Away of The Blues'.

The blues were more washed than blown away, as rain lashed down throughout proceedings. The deluge dampened everything but the passion of the Celtic support, who turned up in their droves to bid farewell to the standing area. The Peatdiggers folk band kicked things off by performing at pitch side, as members of eight lucky supporter's clubs were given the opportunity to play in a five-a-side competition. Next on the field were Dukla Pumpherston, a charity team in Scotland, named after the fictional team Dukla Pumpherston Sawmill and Tannery – created by Tony Roper during the 1980s comedy programme: Naked Radio. The squad was made up of former professional players and television personalities, who fulfilled exhibition fixtures to raise money for charity. The Dukla team included Tony Roper, Pat Clinton (former world champion boxer) and a host of former professional footballers such as former Rangers man, Robert Russell, and Celtic supporters: Gerry Collins and John McCormack. A number of ex-Celts also represented Dukla, these included: Danny McGrain, Peter Latchford, Jackie McNamara Snr, Roddie MacDonald and Ally Hunter. The opposition was a celebrity select, which included Michael Turner, who played Kevin Webster in Coronation Street, and Bill Tarmey, who played Jack Duckworth in the same soap - fitting nicely with the Manchester v Glasgow theme of the evening. The former was serenaded in unique Jungle style, with a chant of "There's only one Kevin Webster," a moment he subsequently described as "One of the greatest in his life." Another notable celebrity on the park was Patrick Robinson, who is better known as a consultant named Martin Ashford in the TV programme: Casualty.

Dukla ran out 3-1 winners but the win was far from routine as Bill Tarmey, who led the celebrity select, contested: "Dukla's third goal was suspiciously offside and we were denied two stone wall penalties. Despite all that though, it was a wonderful night."

The main event of the evening was then finally upon the near 20,000 crowd. Sean Fallon led out the two teams, as Billy McNeill and Pat Crerand held aloft the European Cup trophy, just behind. The Celtic team featured all of the Lisbon Lions, apart from Willie Wallace, who was in Australia (at this time every Lisbon Lion was still alive). The Lions were also accompanied by Joe Craig, Frank McGarvey, Murdo MacLeod and various other familiar football names. Meanwhile, the Manchester United select included the aforementioned former Celt, Pat Crerand, who lined up beside Bill Foulkes, Nobby Stiles and David Sadler from the European Cup winning team of 1968. The English squad's numbers were bolstered by some ex professionals, many of whom were once Celtic players: Jim Brogan, John Fallon and Tommy Callaghan; whilst Roddie MacDonald and Jackie McNamara Snr also stayed on to play for Manchester United in this centrepiece match of the event.

Play commenced with Bobby Murdoch, declining in health at the time, strolling up the field. He was graciously left unmarked as Celtic advanced in to the final third before he received the ball and crossed into the box. The Jungle went wild in an emotional show of support for their hero, who gave a wave in acknowledgement, before being substituted a short while later. Nevertheless, it was Jimmy Johnstone who stole the show and got the Jungle roaring at its loudest for a final time. The wing wizard reminded the Celtic faithful of how much they missed his magic as he turned back the clock, showing no signs of being past it at the age of 48. The man, who would go on to be voted 'the greatest ever Celt' in 2002, jinked and weaved past defenders at will, before bringing the house down with a stunning chip over the goalkeeper into the back of the net from 35 yards. Johnstone wheeled away with a clenched fist aloft, before giving a wink to the Jungle as he strolled back in to position for the restart.

At half time there was a cracking fancy dress competition, which didn't quite reach the same level of excitement as The Jungle's Last Stand on 15th May, during the last competitive match of the season for Celtic. On that occasion, a fan had come dressed in an elaborate parrot costume, but his superb efforts looked to be in vain as he arrived too late to partake. As hundreds of entrants lined up by the tunnel, this colourful bird was being pushed to the front of the Jungle, in a flap. The parrot was stopped trackside thanks to his poor punctuality. However, the Jungle was uproarious in its defence of the hopeful contestant. Indeed, a sustained chant of "We want the parrot," went up along the touchline, but it wasn't to be as a fellow fan dressed as a clown was invited on to the pitch and presented with a plaque for his fancy dress victory. Though sick as a parrot, the fan who missed out on the competition was eventually tracked down by The Celtic

View, who offered him a free season ticket for the following season.

The second half of The Blowing Away of the Blues was played in front of an electric atmosphere, the like of which Frank Worthington (then an Arsenal defender) "Couldn't believe." Celtic ultimately ran out 3-1 winners, but the night belonged to local charities as the Jungleites raised £30,000 through a share of the ticket sales.

The event was well synopsised by Andrew Smith, then of the Celtic View:

For 19,316 fans to turn up at Celtic Park in absolutely dreadful weather for what was a couple of charity matches and a sing-song is nothing short of astonishing. It was yet another remarkable demonstration of the depth of feeling that Celtic supporters have for their club and proof that such passion and commitment remains as powerful as ever, despite recent years without success. It was an evening to say farewell to the Jungle as a standing area and pay one last tribute to the Lisbon Lions at the end of their testimonial year. Fittingly, these two institutions which have become such an important part of the fabric of being a Celtic fan were given a superb send off.

Celtic

B448

THIS CERTIFICATE WAS PRESENTED TO
THE HOLDER TO COMMEMORATE

"The Jungle's Last Stand"

CELTIC V DUNDEE
SATURDAY, 15TH MAY 1993
CELTIC PARK

*Certificates handed out to people in the Jungle on 15th May
1993 – The Jungle's Last Stand*

*The parrot costume during The Jungle's Last Stand fancy
dress competition*

*Vince the parrot – Celtic mascot after the parrot was so
popular in the fancy dress contest*

THE END OF TIGER TIM

DJ 'Tiger' Tim Stevens was best known for his work on Radio Clyde, where he would play comical songs. He was a crazy character from Easterhouse and was rumoured to have hosted his radio show in the nude at times in the 1970s. His fondness for a laugh earnt him the gig as Celtic PA announcer, but it was also to be his downfall.

On 29th September 1993, Celtic hosted Young Boys Berne in the second leg of the UEFA Cup first round. The Hoops had drawn 0-0 in Switzerland two weeks earlier, meanwhile Rangers had beaten Levski Sofia 3-2, in the first round of the Champions League. It was typical of the time. Rangers were winning in Europe's premier competition, whilst Celtic were struggling in what was then the third best tournament on the continent.

Celtic eliminated the Swiss side in 105th minute of extra-time, when a dangerous reverse pass by Charlie Nicholas resulted in an Alain Baumann own goal. The goal ended a 195-minute stalemate and ensured that Celtic were in the hat in Zurich the next day, where they were paired with Sporting Lisbon.

Rangers had been playing the second leg of their Champions Leg clash with Levski Sofia that same day. Due to the time difference in Bulgaria, the match was a late afternoon kick off. At half time in the Bulgarian capital, the score was locked at 1-1 and Rangers looked good to progress. Little had changed by the 90th minute, when up stepped Nikolay Todorov with an injury time winner to stun the 'Gers and take Levski Sofia through on away goals.

Back at Celtic Park, with the Hoops' evening match about to get underway, 'Tiger Tim' surprised the crowd when he deviated from the script and called a minute's silence. Confusion was replaced by laughter moments later as he elaborated: "In memory of Rangers' European Cup campaign, which was declared dead earlier today in Bulgaria." Parkhead let out a collective chuckle as the crowd enjoyed a rare opportunity to poke fun at their city rivals in those days.

Tiger Tim's voice did not return to the PA system at half time – nor did it ever return again. His gag saw him sacked by the old board, which was a decision none too popular with the Celtic support.

KILMARNOCK BOYCOTT

Formed in September 1993, after the Save Our Celts group's demise; Celts For Change battled to oust the old board and seek a brighter future for the football club. Their initial committee comprised of five key men: Matt McGlone, who was the face of the organisation and Editor of Once a Tim fanzine, Brendan Sweeney, Colin Duncan, David Cunningham and John Thompson.

The group's predecessor, Save Our Celts, had served as a good example to the committee. Save Our Celts was founded by Willie Wilson in 1991. They held an opening meeting with an attendance of just over 300 and further meetings attracted more. A host of high profile speakers such as overthrown board member, Brian Dempsey, and Lisbon Lion, Jim Craig, got involved. Despite its early success, an ever-decreasing morale amongst the support led to the organisation suffering an irreversible decline.

Willie Wilson was invited to join Celts For Change but he decided not to do so. However, it was he who pointed Brendan Sweeney in the direction of the group. Having learned from the previous effort, Celts For Change aimed to present the frustrations of the support as one. These frustrations would be of relevance to the overhaul of the board and ultimately the removal of the practise that was coined 'the biscuit tin' (lack of spending).

The group set about their aims with quite radical action, something that caught the attention of the media and bolstered efforts immensely. A protest outside the Royal Bank of Scotland, when supporters gathered holding aloft signs asking the bank to put the squeeze on the board and thus force a takeover by Fergus McCann, was perhaps the first real poignant breakthrough in terms of press coverage. Consequentially, the Celtic support started to recognise Celts For Change as the group to champion their concerns and bring about genuine transformation.

Matt McGlone's influence at Once a Tim fanzine ensured that a flow of information was maintained, and the exposure given to their 'back the team, sack the board' mantra seemed to generate an unstoppable momentum. By the time BBC News gave coverage to a scene from a Celts For Change Rally, meetings at City Halls were being filled to the brim. With that said, the organisers weren't without opposition. There was in fact quite a clamorous minority who supported the Kelly's and White's. They were never more than a minority but to drive change they needed to be curtailed.

The committee and its members worked with a relentless enthusiasm. Their finest hour is the focus of this piece, which came on 1st March 1994. The group organised a boycott for a Tuesday night league match against Kilmarnock. Whilst small sections of the support chose not to give up their enjoyment of watching Celtic and felt that to do so would deviate from the 'back the team, sack the board' ideal – most fans placed their trust in the group's guidance.

Celtic beat Kilmarnock by a goal to nil. The official club attendance was given as 10,055. Little did the board know that Celts For Change had employed an outside agency to stand at the turnstyles and count the genuine attendance on the night. The figure of the agency: 8,225. The key fact with these figures is that the break-even requirement stood at 10,000 paying fans.

A matter of two days passed before the board, red faced by Celts For Change, called a press conference which they claimed would be the most momentous in Celtic's history. The conference covered plans for a new Celtic village in Cambuslang and claimed financial backing of the project by a Swiss bank. These astonishing claims were quickly found to be untrue and the reputation of the board plummeted to horrendous levels. Less than 24 hours later, on 4th March 1994, the board gave way at the last-minute to allow Fergus McCann to takeover. Brian Dempsey then emerged at the steps outside Celtic Park, proclaiming the immortal words: "The battle is over. The rebels have won."

Celts For Change Rally fills the hall

Matt McGlone (front, centre) leads the protests outside the Royal Bank of Scotland

HE'S PORTUGUESE AND CAN'T PLAY WITH EASE

The mere mention of 'the three amigos' is enough to etch a nostalgic smile across the face of Celtic supporters of a certain age. Pierre Van Hooijdonk, Jorge Cadete and Paulo Di Canio terrorised Scottish defences in the 1996/97 season and many speculate that Scottish football history could have taken a very different course had illegal intervention not prevented Cadete from playing for the club sooner.

Celtic fans had every right to feel optimistic when the signing of Jorge Cadete was announced in February 1996. It was less than three years prior that the Portuguese striker had bagged a brace to take Sporting Lisbon to the third round of the UEFA Cup at the Bhoys' expense. At £400,000 Cadete was a snip, his tally of 33 goals in his first full season paying testimony to that claim.

In late February 1996, Celtic submitted legitimate registration documents to the SFA and awaited international clearance for the player to officially be permitted to join the club. That clearance duly arrived on March 7th when, in keeping with FIFA rules, the Portuguese FA faxed an International Transfer Certificate to their Scottish counterparts at Hampden Park. Days later, the Portuguese FA also sent a hard copy of the original certificate in the post, as instructed by FIFA officials. All appeared in order until the SFA failed to process Cadete's registration and in Sunday league style, the striker was not yet allowed to play.

Over the course of the next two weeks it became clear that Jim Farry of the SFA had deemed the International

Transfer Certificate invalid. Although, this was only something that the Celtic board could deduce, as the SFA failed to notify the club of any problems. Concurrent to the processing of this administration, Celtic were negotiating a compensation fee with Sporting Lisbon over the transfer, which seemed to be the crux of the issue that the SFA silently held when it came to certain clauses within the transfer certification. Nevertheless, Celtic had reached an agreement with Sporting Lisbon and Jorge Cadete had also made a private settlement that he was happy with, on March 23rd. Having been left in the dark by the national football authority, Fergus McCann ensured that further player registration documents were submitted to the SFA, this time incorporating a full professional application form and a new player agreement.

The unease felt by the Celtic board was soon realised when a fax was received from the SFA, explaining that the registration forms concerning Jorge Cadete had been rejected on the grounds of a disagreeable clause within the new player agreement file. This clause was present in the initial documentation, submitted on February 26th, which was of no concern to the governing body at that time. Therefore, Fergus McCann and his board members tended to feel that something underhand was going on within the offices at Hampden Park.

FIFA waded into the debate at the end of March 1996. The global organisation had their say by faxing the SFA with notification that any clauses relating to contractual agreements between Sporting Lisbon and Celtic, are not sufficient grounds upon which to deny the validity of the International Transfer Certificate. With their hand forced by FIFA, the SFA almost immediately deemed international clearance to have been granted, but further delayed the transfer by demanding that player agreement forms again be submitted, with the objectionable clause and two further clauses removed. Having been given no opportunity to contest the case, Celtic submitted a third and final set of documentation on 30th March 1996.

Jim Farry ran the rule over the paperwork once more. Importantly, it is thought that during a phone call, Farry had come to a verbal agreement with members of the Celtic secretarial team, that the registration would be listed as taking effect from 22nd March. This date was crucial, as in order for Cadete to play against Rangers in the upcoming Scottish Cup Semi-Final, the Portuguese man had to have been registered by no later than 23rd March.

The files hit Farry's desk and this time there was nothing he could claim to be disagreeable. However, that didn't mean that Cadete would simply don a Celtic shirt with immediate effect. Instead, Farry claimed no knowledge of ever reaching a verbal agreement with Celtic and saw to it that the registration would not be noted as coming into effect from 22nd March. Rather iniquitously, Farry ensured that Cadete was registered with effect from 30th March 1996. Celtic had little choice but to accept the outcome because the Scottish Football League registration deadline expired on March 31st and therefore any further delays would have ruled Cadete out of all remaining league matches that season.

Upon examining Jim Farry's historical behaviour it becomes clear that he operated in a partial manner against Celtic. He started his involvement in football as an administrative assistant at the offices of the Scottish

Football Association in 1972. As an excellent administrator, Farry was quickly promoted through the ranks of the organisation, and when Willie Allan left the Scottish Football League in the late 1970s, Farry was chosen to replace him as the SFL's youngest ever secretary. This was a position that he held for ten years.

What is peculiar about Jim Farry is that prior to his involvement in the sport, he was not a football fan. Instead, Jim Farry was a prominent member of Cambuslang Rugby Club, where he made the most of his passion with his hometown team. However, other passions of the Cambuslang man included writing, administration and reciting constitutions, laws and rules. Given this background information, it seems bizarre that three days before Dundee played Hearts in the final game of the 1985/86 league season, Farry decided to switch the referee for the match to appoint a well-known Edinburgh gentleman and Heart's supporter (WNB Crombie) as the man in the middle. Within any other governing body this decision would have set alarm bells ringing, considering that Hearts only needed a point to assure the league title, in the event of a win for second place Celtic, against St. Mirren. The move backfired as Hoops fan, Albert Kidd, struck a double to give Dundee victory over Hearts at Dens Park. Meanwhile, Celtic scored five goals without reply to snatch the title on goal difference at Love Street.

Four years later, in 1990, the same secretarial role that Mr. Farry held with the Scottish Football League, became available at the SFA as Ernie Walker vacated the role. Jim Farry applied and was awarded the job. From this position, he went on to become Chief Executive and masterminded the Jorge Cadete registration scandal.

In total, the registration saga meant that Cadete missed out on six matches. Four of those missed games were in the Scottish Premier Division, which included two wins and two draws, whilst Cadete also missed a victorious Scottish Cup Quarter-Final, as well as the aforementioned Scottish Cup Semi-Final defeat against Rangers:

February 24th - Celtic 4-0 Partick Thistle
March 2nd - Celtic 4-0 Heart of Midlothian
March 10th Celtic 2-1 Dundee United (Scottish Cup)
March 17th - Rangers 1-1 Celtic
March 23rd - Motherwell 0-0 Celtic
April 7th - Rangers 2-1 Celtic (Scottish Cup)

Fergus McCann immediately indulged in a bitter feud with Jim Farry after being incensed at losing the cup Semi-Final against Rangers. Like many Celtic stakeholders, McCann couldn't help but wonder what might have been if his star man was on the team sheet. The fact that Cadete scored over 30 goals the following season only reinforced this frustrating curiosity.

By January 1997, in an interview with Scotland On Sunday newspaper, Farry claimed: "Fergus McCann's arrival in Scotland was to the detriment of the well-being of Scottish Football." He went on to scathe of McCann further when he remarked that "There are already too many foreigners ruining our game." Meanwhile, the Canadian Celt had already been pursuing the man at the top of the SFA through legal avenues for almost a year.

Justice was finally done in March 1999, following the investigation of an independent commission, who examined the following allegations put forward by Celtic's majority shareholder:

On the basis of the first valid application for registration, submitted on 26th February 1996, Jorge Cadete should have been registered with effect from that date, when international clearance by way of the International Transfer Certificate was received by the SFA on 7th March.

On the basis of the second valid application form and a player agreement submitted on 23rd March 1996, Jorge Cadete should have been registered with effect from 23rd March as the SFA were in receipt of a valid set of player registration documents and the International Transfer Certificate was received on 7th March.

On submission of the third application and player agreement on 30th March, Jorge Cadete should have been registered with effect from 23rd March 1996.

McCann maintained a less than phlegmatic approach in dealing with the issue and the matter was finally settled after close to three years of legal struggle, as outlined in the following report by The Independent newspaper on 2nd March 1999:

JIM FARRY'S football career is effectively at an end after the Scottish Football Association chief executive was yesterday suspended over the Jorge Cadete affair. Celtic have claimed for three years that Farry delayed the processing of the transfer of the Portuguese player in time for the Scottish Cup semi-final against Rangers in 1996. Celtic lost the game 2-1, but yesterday they won the war against the most powerful figure in the Scottish game.

The SFA has offered Celtic a written apology as well as agreeing to pay compensation and meet Celtic's legal fees, and Fergus McCann, the Celtic chief executive, yesterday

*wasted little time in condemning the part played by Farry.
"It has taken Celtic and its supporters three years to
receive justice on the issue of the SFA's chief executive Jim
Farry's failure to properly register Jorge Cadete."*

*"It is deplorable that a prominent member club should be
disadvantaged in this way when on several occasions the
SFA's chief executive had the opportunity to make the
correct decision. Mr Farry's failure to properly and
timeously register Jorge Cadete leaves the club in no other
position than to ask for the office bearers of the SFA to
recognise that Mr Farry's position is untenable. This case
demonstrates clearly that Mr Farry cannot be allowed to
hold and exercise such powerful authority."*

*The issue recently went to arbitration with the SFA
admitting liability before proceedings could finish. Clearly
angered by the whole situation, Celtic are demanding the
dismissal of Farry, who has held the top job at the SFA
since 1990 following 10 years as secretary of the Scottish
League.*

*In the last nine years he has been frequently criticised for
his dictatorial attitude which at times appeared out of tune
with the ordinary supporter. He insisted on Scotland
playing a European Championship qualifier on the day of
the funeral of Princess Diana only to back down in the face
of severe pressure and criticism.*

*Farry's motives for delaying the Cadete transfer remain
unclear and although Celtic supporters will interpret his
actions as indicating a pro-Rangers stance, McCann
refused to be drawn on the topic. "I'm not claiming there
was malice but there was intent. There was a failure on his*

part despite the advice of FIFA and Celtic. This is a matter that goes beyond Celtic Football Club, it's a question of somebody who has failed to follow the rules of football. "

McCann intends to hold discussions with the other clubs in the Scottish Premier League and his frustration with the powerbrokers at the SFA could prove the motive towards a shift of power towards the new body who would effectively run the elite body of Scottish football. In the meantime, Farry has agreed to co-operate with an SFA investigation into his actions.

Days after the above report, on 8th March 1999, the SFA announced that Jim Farry had been sacked for gross misconduct. They brought the curtain down on the controversy with this statement:

THE Scottish Football Association advises that, following the suspension on full pay of its chief executive, Mr James Farry, the decision has been taken to dismiss Mr Farry immediately for gross misconduct.

Pending the appointment of a new chief executive/secretary, the president of the association, Mr Jack McGinn, has been appointed acting chief executive.

A detailed report from the SFA's external lawyers was received by the Association last Thursday, March 4th. The report related to matters arising from the recent arbitration with Celtic FC, relating to the registration of Jorge Cadete.

The Emergency Committee, comprising the SFA's office-bearers, considered the report on Friday, March 5th, and decided to request the views of the executive committee, given the policy issues involved.

The executive committee, after detailed consideration of the report and having received further legal advice, unanimously recommended that Mr Farry be dismissed from the SFA immediately.

The emergency committee effected the recommendation on Friday evening. Council was appraised today of the situation, viewed the report, and detailed discussion took place.

The reasons for Mr Farry's dismissal result from his acts and omissions during the Cadete affair, including his conduct during:

(i) the period of the investigation of the registration by an SFA sub-committee;

(ii) the preparation of the SFA's case for the arbitration;

(iii) his testimony during the arbitration; and

(iv) the period since his suspension on February 26th.

The SFA does not intend to make further comment on the reasons for Mr Farry's dismissal for reasons of confidentiality.

In relation to the Cadete affair itself, approximately 110 documents were produced by the SFA and Celtic, 13 witnesses in total would have given evidence, and there had already been five days of evidence, which was scheduled to last at least a further three days with legal submissions to follow.

The SFA has made the most strenuous efforts to keep matters confidential throughout, first to comply with the rules of confidentiality in the arbitration, and thereafter in fairness to Mr Farry.

The SFA wishes to make the following comments:

(i) The SFA decided to settle the arbitration prior to the conclusion of Mr Farry's evidence, following very strong advice and recommendations from its external legal team;

(ii) Mr Farry was immediately advised of the decision to settle and, indeed, agreed with the decision. He did not, however, agree with the terms of the letter of apology to Celtic;

(iii) Attempts were made by the SFA's legal team to have Mr Cadete himself testify on their behalf. However, Mr Cadete refused to come to Glasgow.

In light of recent events, the SFA will, of course, undertake a thorough review of its registration procedures.

For information, the SFA processes around 47,000 player registrations per year at all levels of football, and this has been an isolated case.

It has been a very difficult period for the association and the recent events should not be allowed to cloud the work which Mr Farry has undertaken on behalf of the association and, indeed, Scottish football.

There are many positive things which can be attributed to Mr Farry over these years which should not be forgotten.

I JUST SNAPPED

Tosh McKinlay is a boyhood Celtic fan, who lived his dream when he signed for the club in 1994. He spent five years in the hoops, winning a league title (which stopped Rangers achieving ten in a row), a Scottish Cup and a Scottish League Cup. The feisty full back racked up almost a century of competitive appearances in a Celtic jersey, but it wasn't all plain sailing throughout his time at the club.

In 1997 McKinlay found himself increasingly exiled from the starting 11, having been displaced by Stephane Mahe. He was desparate to make the Scotland World Cup squad for France '98 and thus remarked that the season was "The biggest of his life." Therefore, it was natural that McKinlay was anxious to win his place back in the Celtic team and impress Scotland's Manager – Craig Brown. Eventually this desperation saw McKinlay at the centre of a training ground bust up.

Celtic were travelling to Ibrox in an important derby game on 8th November 1997. The Hoops had the edge over Rangers in the league at that stage, having recovered from two defeats in their opening two games, to earn 24 points as opposed Rangers' 23. It was the type of high profile match that could put a player in the frame for national team selection. A week earlier, Tosh McKinlay had been left out of the squad for the first time during his spell at Celtic. The Hoops won 2-0 against Dunfermline at East End Park on that occasion, but the boyhood Celt was distraught at not even being included among the substitutes. Nevertheless, a welcome morale boost arrived on the Monday morning when Craig Brown announced his Scotland squad to play against France. Needless to say, McKinlay was included.

On Tuesday 4th November 1997, Celtic reserves played against Dunfermline Athletic reserves. It was a match that included Tosh McKinlay, who asked for a meeting with Wim Jansen afterwards. Speaking to The Daily Record that week, McKinlay revealed: "I asked to see Wim because I had been left out of Celtic's first team and that had never happened before. Wim told me that he didn't consider me to be among the top 16 players at Celtic Park. You can't be much more straightforward than that."

By the Wednesday, McKinlay had parted company with his agent and this provided the final spice to the perfect recipe for disaster, on Thursday 6th November. McKinlay was understandably at a low point, going through a difficult period of his career. He had been seething throughout training at Barrowfield Park that day and got into an altercation with Henrik Larsson, who was starting to win over the Celtic support after a shaky start to his very young Celtic career at the time. During a first 11 v non-starters practise match, which Simon Donnelly said: "Wim Jansen used to do to add to the intensity," McKinlay squared up to Larsson and proceeded to headbutt the Swede in the face. It was immediately feared that Larsson had suffered a broken nose, but when it appeared that there was no serious damage, the striker was quickly patched up and Celtic did their utmost to downplay the incident.

Tosh McKinlay was ordered to stay away from the training ground on Friday 7th November, until further notice. Meanwhile, Henrik Larsson himself wasn't at training as he had been given compassionate leave to fly back to Sweden for his Father in Law's funeral. Larsson was rushed back for the game against Rangers the next day, whilst McKinlay did not feature. The press got wind of a training ground bust up and circled like sharks when they saw the omission from the team sheet. The match itself was a miserable one for Celtic, as the Bhoys befell a 1-0 loss thanks to a first half Richard Gough goal for Rangers. Many felt this was a turning point and a guarantee that Rangers would now press ahead to win ten league titles in a row.

Despite the potentially devastating impact that McKinlay's headbutt could have had, the frustrated full back told The Daily Record: "I just snapped. I played in every qualifying tie for Scotland and I believe I can still make the World Cup if I can put this behind me and get back into Celtic's side before the end of the season." His incredible desire to play for Celtic and Scotland meant that McKinlay never lost hope of regaining his first-time place, regardless of the hole he had dug himself. Be that as it may, he was sent out on loan to Stoke for a month in January 1998. The temporary move away from Parkhead allowed him to get some game time and had likely been part of Jansen's plan to remove him from the dressing room, since the infamous training ground incident had taken place.

McKinlay did return and soon patched up his relationship with Henrik Larsson. The pair went on to make history as members of the squad who stopped the ten, even if McKinlay only made two starts and a handful of appearances. As for the World Cup, he achieved his dream by being selected in the squad for the tournament. He played the final six minutes during a 2-1 defeat against Brazil, was an unused substitute in a 1-1 draw with Norway and came on as a substitute in the 54th minute of the final group game against Morocco. Scotland lost the final match

3-0 and were eliminated, having finished bottom of the group.

DREADFUL DERBY

Celtic v Rangers. A Rangers win would earn them the title at Celtic Park. The kick-off was 6.05pm on a Saturday. The weather was scorching, and the referee was Hugh Dallas. These conditions sound impossible today, but it's exactly the backdrop to the derby match on 2nd May 1999.

The game had been subject to two weeks of marketing from Sky Sports, who were behind the irregular kick off time. Naturally, Celtic were desperate to delay Rangers' title party, whilst the latter were hoping to gloat at Parkhead. It all culminated in a packed Celtic Park, with a crowd as full of alcohol as the stadium itself. In other words, the ideal preparation for bedlam.

Celtic were plagued by injuries but did still have the reliable Stubbs, Lambert, Larsson and Viduka as four stand out names. Meanwhile, Rangers had a strong line up including Klos, Hendry, Amoruso and Van Bronckhorst. Paradise was a cauldron of animosity at kick off, with over 50,000 people hissing and booing every touch of the Rangers team from the outset. However, the insolence of the Celtic support did little to affect their rivals. 12 minutes were on the clock when Neil McCann reacted sharply to a cross by Wallace, putting Rangers into the lead. The tumultuous atmosphere had been momentarily subdued.

A few minutes after the restart, Stephane Mahe crashed into a tackle, in which he scarcely connected with Wallace. Dallas blew his whistle and Mahe immediately got in the face of the referee to remonstrate with him - a yellow card was shown. The full back was in the thick of it again when Celtic broke from the resulting free kick and Mahe stung the hands of Klos in the Rangers goal. Morten Wieghorst then burst through the midfield and was fed by Viduka, but the Dane could only flash wide from close range. Once more Celtic were on the attack with Mahe at the forefront. He latched on to the ball and was taken down for a clear penalty, only to see the offside flag incorrectly raised. Yet, in spite of this flurry of chances, Rangers were certainly the better side.

On 31 minutes, disaster struck. The man of the moment was cynically fouled by Neil McCann and he reacted with little more than a stern word in the Rangers man's direction. Incredibly, Dallas produced a second yellow card and ordered a disgusted Mahe to leave the field. It was an action that he refused to perform, and the Frenchman had to be dragged to the touchline by his teammates. He hid his face as he walked down the tunnel, evidently in tears at the blatant cheating he had fallen victim to.

In the 40th minute, Dallas awarded a legitimate free kick to Rangers, at the corner flag where the North Stand and Jock Stein Stand meet. A Celtic fan entered the field of play in protest at the officiating. He charged at Dallas, showing all the signs that he was going to belt him. Fortunately, Celtic players intervened at the final moment, but Dallas wasn't out of the woods yet. A hail of coins and lighters rained down on the pitch and a 50 pence piece connected with the left eyebrow of Hugh Dallas, who dropped to one knee. As blood poured from his forehead, it seems clear that the main match official was plotting retribution.
Consequentially, as the free kick was eventually swung into the box, Dallas awarded an indescribably soft penalty kick against Vidar Riseth for allegedly holding on to Tony Vidmar's shirt. Paradise was collectively seething. Another

fan entered the pitch and stewards tackled him to the ground before he could reach the referee.

Jorge Albertz coolly slotted home the spot kick, putting Rangers 2-0 up. As the half time whistle blew, a third Celtic fan was restrained whilst attempting to enter the pitch. Chaos didn't abate through the interval. Indeed, a Rangers fan fell from the top tier at half time and was seen singing and waving as he was taken to the ambulance on the stretcher!

The second half passed without incident for half an hour. McCann put paid to that with his second of the game, earning Rangers an unassailable 3-0 advantage. There was time for another two red cards yet, as Wallace was sent off for Rangers after reacting to an aggressive tackle by Riseth, before the latter party was sent off for clattering Vidmar into orbit, when the Rangers player held the ball at the corner flag moments from full time.

When the match ended, the Rangers team mocked the huddle in front of their supporters. It was a dark day for Scottish football, from the organisation to the officiating, and the behaviour of the supporters. The match was known as the shame game by the press and politicians, and the authorities subsequently ensured that matches between the clubs would generally take place at midday. There were also fixture plans put in place to guarantee that a Glasgow derby could never be a league title decider in the future.

At Celtic, the club itself was so incensed at the embarrassment caused by a minority of lunatics, that Chairman, Allan MacDonald, sent the following letter to the fans:

As the dust begins to settle on yesterday's events, it is a time for serious reflection and inspection for all of us.

Celtic is staging its own investigation into yesterday's events and will also co-operate fully with the SFA and the SPL.

I would like to thank the vast majority of Celtic supporters, for their exemplary behaviour at the recent minute of silence in memory of the people of Hillsborough, and the many thousands of Celtic and Rangers supporters who represented their clubs with pride and dignity at yesterday's Old Firm match. When you represent a football club as a supporter, player or official you have a responsibility in society; we all have a responsibility to conduct ourselves appropriately.

At Celtic if you wear the name, you wear the reputation in your words and actions. The good name of Celtic and its supporters was threatened yesterday by the conduct of a few irresponsible people. This behaviour cannot and will not be accepted.

I want to make it perfectly clear any supporter entering the field of play will automatically receive a life ban from Celtic Park.

Any individual identified throwing a missile of any kind will face an automatic life ban. The reputation of our club and our support is worth too much to tolerate this type of unacceptable behaviour. We have 5000 decent supporters on a waiting list wanting to come and watch Celtic. No-one should doubt our resolve in removing those who refuse to recognise the club's principle of respect for everyone in society.

I would urge decent supporters to report those who acted to bring shame upon Celtic's good name by contacting our security operation at Celtic Park.

In respect of our paid professionals you can have total confidence that I will be working with Jozef Venglos and Eric Black to ensure that all appropriate action is taken and that the players recognise their responsibilities to the supporters, their team-mates, the club, the media and the general public.

The price of fame is responsibility; Celtic will not accept anything less than the highest standards. This process will happen in privacy, but you can be assured no-one will be left in doubt that the Celtic standard has to be the highest level of conduct on and off the field.

Everyone at Celtic Football Club congratulates Rangers on winning the Championship. Last season the league was ours and this season Rangers have proved to be worthy Champions.

Plans are currently being formulated to re-establish Celtic as a footballing force in Europe; it is essential the behaviour of our players and supporters reflects the club's history, principles and aspirations.

Celtic would have to wait until 29th April 2018 to get a chance of revenge by winning the league against a team calling themselves Rangers. On that occasion, the match played at Celtic Park, went ahead as a result of poor fixture planning, which meant that Celtic's unexpected loss at Easter Road the week before, allowed the club to lift the trophy against their rivals. The Bhoys ran out 5-0 winners with goals from Odsonne Eduord (2), James Forrest, Tom

Rogic and Callum McGregor. In doing so, Celtic lifted their seventh title in a row. The match passed without incident.

BAIRDS BAR PRESS CONFERENCE

Celtic were at a low ebb when Kenny Dalglish took over the reigns from John Barnes in February 2000. The club had just exited the Scottish Cup after a 3-2 defeat to lowly Inverness Caledonian Thistle, and the press coverage of the new interim management was relentless. Dalglish took great exception to the nature of this reporting and ordered a press conference, on 24th March 2000, to be relocated to the working-class beacon of hardcore Celtic support that was Bairds Bar on the Gallowgate (Glasgow).

For a moment, the sound of Irish bands, the thunderous atmosphere and the wall to wall memorabilia within this Celtic shrine remained silent and still. Amidst this rather awkward setting, a journalist opened the press conference by asking "Why are we here?" to which Dalglish replied: "Because I'm comfortable here. We like to get out and show the fans how we get ready for the game, and they get to see a media conference." Dalglish seemed relaxed, if smug, considering that his team were due to travel to Ibrox at 1pm two days later, in a bid to reduce the 12-point gap at the top of the Scottish Premier League. The Govan born man dismissed further questions regarding the fitness of his team with remarks such as "He's got a sore leg," when asked how Henrik Larsson was recovering from his double leg break. Next, the Celtic stand-in Manager was quizzed about whether he would remain in the dugout, or return to the director's office: "I know you said that you won't make a decision until the end of March, but will Sunday's result affect your decision?" Dalglish adopted the lowest form of wit in his response: "I keep saying we'll discuss it at the end of March. Every time we come to a press conference we hear the same questions. It might be repetitive for you to hear the same answers, but not half as repetitive as it is for us to hear the same questions."

Dalglish then took the opportunity to impress the punters by waxing lyrical about Celtic's recent CIS Cup triumph, which he described as "A marvellous achievement, despite the negativity written about it." He went further to congratulate the fans who greeted the team back at Celtic Park and (incorrectly) claimed that it was the first silverware won at the new Hampden. In fact, Rangers earnt that accolade when they lifted the Scottish Cup.

It was soon Vidar Riseth's turn to answer questions. Riseth had accompanied his Manager on the short trip from Celtic Park and was asked if Celtic's appalling record against Rangers put them at a psychological disadvantage going into the derby game. Before Riseth could reply, Dalglish stepped in: "We prefer to be positive about things," he remarked. At this there was a heated exchange between the journalist and Kenny Dalglish, before a female member of the broadcasting team interrupted to ask about the managerial position again. Once more, Dalglish batted the question away: "I have said all along the club is bigger than Kenny Dalglish." At that the interview was brought to a halt and the Celtic legend looked in the direction of punters, at which point he is alleged to have stated that "There are people in the media who have an anti-Celtic agenda and don't like to see the club do well." When the tension finally subsided, Riseth and Dalglish signed autographs for fans in the pub and made a slow exit. It was a PR exercise which had been well received at the time but is reflected upon with a degree of embarrassment by most fans today. Perhaps the fact that Celtic lost 4-0 at Ibrox that weekend has something to do with that.

All FOUR NIL

Three quarters of the season had passed when Celtic hosted Kilmarnock in the Scottish Premier League on 2nd April 2000. Rangers had dropped points with a 1-1 draw at Pittodrie a day earlier, yet they remained 16 points clear of Celtic, on 66 points. The 'Gers had also just thumped Celtic 4-0 at Ibrox the week before, thus the lowest crowd of the season, 40,569, turned up for the match at Paradise.

The Bhoys were missing Henrik Larsson, Mark Viduka, Tom Boyd, Jackie McNamara, Alan Stubbs, Stephane Mahe and Morten Wieghorst. Yet in retrospect, Celtic still had a very strong line up with Mjallby, Petrov, Lambert, Moravcik and Berkovic all starting the game. It came as no surprise when Celtic raced into the lead on the stroke of ten minutes, as Tommy Johnson broke free to fire home from just inside the box, following a well-timed pass by Vider Riseth. Ten minutes later, Regi Blinker made it two after Berkovic played a neat one-two with Moravcik, and his shot rebounded to Blinker in acres of space by the penalty spot.

Celtic continued their domination in the second half, when Berkovic again linked with Lubo, who switched the play with a stunning first time pass into the path of Johnson. The confident forward dispatched emphatically, only to see his goal chalked off when Martin Doran raised his offside flag. The replay subsequently showed the sky sports viewers that Johnson had been a yard onside. Within a minute, the former Aston Villa attacker had the ball in the net again, but the offside flag was raised once more. This time it was the correct call.

302

Kilmarnock made the most of their good fortune with Christophe Cocard swinging a speculative cross in from the left wing, the Celtic defence was caught slumbering and Paul Wright nodded home the easiest of headers from six yards. The away side rode their luck again when Olivier Tebily struck the post, and it was he who was at fault in the 57th minute, when the Ayrshire outfit equalised. On this occasion, Ian Durrant chipped a corner to the edge of the box which was helped into the danger zone by Gary Holt, and fell to Tebily's man, Jim Lauchlan, at the back post. The Kilmarnock player made no mistake heading into an empty net to stun Paradise into silence.

Celtic looked to recompense for letting their lead slip. Within minutes, Colin Healy found the back of the net but again Doran disallowed the goal for offside. It was another contentious decision. In the 64th minute, Berkovic broke between the lines of the Kilmarnock midfield and defence. The £5.75m star played the ball out to the left, where Lubomir Moravcik cut inside and smashed a low right footed shot towards goal. The goalkeeper could only spill the ball out in front of him and Berkovic followed in as all good attackers do, feigning to shoot and firing home to put Celtic back in front, or so he thought. Extraordinarily, Martin Doran had the cheek to signal for offside again and the referee complied with his assistant's decision. It was the fourth goal that Celtic had seen disallowed in 17 minutes!

Sensing an injustice, the Bhoys ploughed forward as they asserted their superiority. Johan Mjallby broke forward into unchartered territory for the then holding midfielder, and just like his defensive counterpart, Tebily, the Swede smashed the frame of the goal with a stunning effort. Make no mistake, Celtic could have been 6-2 ahead at this stage.

The tenacity of the Celtic team finally paid dividends in the 73rd minute as Mjallby stole possession in the middle of the park, outmuscling his opponent and giving the ball to Berkovic. The Israeli was crowded out by three defenders and returned the ball square to Mjallby, who executed a casual flick over the Killie backline, and Berkovic lofted the ball over the head of stranded keeper, Gordon Marshall, with a cool first-time finish. Parkhead held its breath as they looked for an offside flag, but thankfully the right decision was made, and Celtic were indeed 3-2 ahead. Berkovic ran across the pitch, giving the Jock Stein Stand the 'bras d'honneur' or 'Iberian slap' gesture, the equivalent of presenting someone with a raised middle finger. The Israeli never did enjoy the greatest of friendships with the Celtic support! Nevertheless, it was Berkovic that was amongst the thick of the action again, when he sidestepped a challenge to receive the ball 30 yards from goal. The midfielder drove at two defenders, changing the ball from one foot to the other, weaving between the helpless pair before squaring for Mark Burchill to tap home. In keeping with the second half antics, Burchill rather humorously glanced towards the linesman, but the goal stood and Celtic ultimately cruised their way to a 4-2 victory.

PEPERABI

This story is perhaps the most jovial in the book and in the interests of accuracy, it is important to state that the subject matter was only reported in one tabloid newspaper: The Sun. Therefore, there is no strong basis upon which a historian should claim this to be fact. However, in 2005 it was reported that Rangers had banned the sale of Peperamis at Ibrox because of their green coloured wrapper. Regardless of whether this was actually confirmed as being true or not, the Celtic support mocked Rangers over the debacle during a 2-1 victory at Ibrox on 24th April 2005.

Celtic took an early lead through Stylian Petrov's header. The Bulgarian jumped the advertising boards into the Rangers support at the Copland Road end and received a cup of hot coffee to the back of the head for his troubles. Craig Bellamy then doubled the Hoops' advantage before half time with a wonderful curling finish into the far corner, having cut inside on to his favoured right foot, from the left corner of the penalty box. Celtic remained in control throughout, although a late Thompson goal for Rangers two minutes from time, did momentarily unease the Celtic faithful.

Notwithstanding the action on the field, the purpose of this story is to explain the jesting by Rab Douglas and the Celtic support at half time. The Broomloan Road stand was swaying in an orgy of green and white delight, as one might expect with Celtic being two goals to the good against their most bitter rivals. It seemed certain that the three points would return to Paradise and give the club a five-point lead in the title race with as many matches to play. What better opportunity to wind up Rangers fans?

A hail of Peperamis fell from one quarter of Ibrox, with one fan even blessing himself with the snack before eating it. Rab Douglas was the substitute goalkeeper that day and was warming up behind David Marshall's goal, when a Peperami inadvertently found its way towards him. As the half time whistle blew, Douglas took a seat next to the goal and ate the forbidden meaty snack in front of the Celtic support.

As previously stated, it is not confirmed whether the food was actually banned from Ibrox or simply removed for other reasons. Yet, what was evident that day was that the Celtic support and Rab Douglas have a good sense of humour, capable of mocking any small-minded ridiculousness that they are up against in Glasgow.

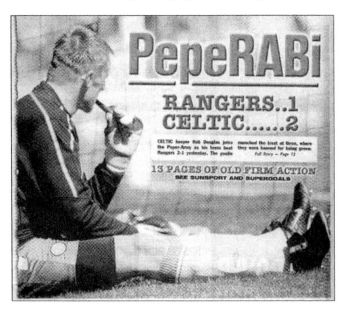

PENALTY PORKIES

In late 2010, Neil Lennon's Celtic team travelled to Tannadice looking to build on a run of 16 consecutive league victories. All the early signs suggested that it would be another routine win for the Celts when Gary Hooper smashed a Mark Wilson cross into the roof of the Dundee United net on 13 minutes. Celtic couldn't build on their early lead though and were made to rue their lack of clinical effectiveness in front of goal, when David Goodwillie hit a shot, which deflected off Glen Loovens and sailed past Fraser Forster.

Having drawn level, the home side came out for the second half with renewed enthusiasm. Bauben fizzed a shot, beaten away by Forster, as the Terrors sought to catch Celtic cold. Just like any title contending outfit, the Bhoys wouldn't be kept down and Giorgios Samaras broke free in the box as Mark Wilson squared a low cross in his direction. Only the last-ditch intervention of Garry Kenneth prevented a certain goal. As Celtic pressed again for a winner, the game exploded into life thanks to Dougie McDonald, the matchday referee. Samaras hared down the left touchline, cutting inside then out, leaving Garry Kenneth in his wake. Just as the long-haired winger sought to set up Gary Hooper for his second of the match, Scott Severin came sliding across his path and blocked the ball with his arm: no penalty. Minutes later the pair looked to combine again as Samaras fired a firm pass to the striker. Hooper took the ball in his path magnificently, shaking off a challenge from Kenneth, before being hauled down in the penalty area by Terror's goalkeeper – Dusan Pernis. This time McDonald pointed to the spot.

Within 31 seconds of awarding Celtic a penalty, Dougie McDonald overturned his decision, having spoken to his linesman – Steven Craven. A drop ball was awarded instead, leaving the Celtic fans incensed. Such a decision caused a huge reaction from the team, who went at Dundee United relentlessly. In the 81st minute, Ki found himself in a dangerous position. The South-Korean hesitated to allow Mark Wilson to overlap, before slipping the ball out wide to the onrushing full back. Wilson lashed the ball across the face of goal and an outstretched arm from Severin again had the Celtic faithful screaming for a penalty to no avail.

There was little time for Celtic to muster anything more. However, Paddy McCourt was always a man who the Hoops could rely on to produce a moment of magic when needed. With a minute left on the clock, the Derry man jigged past his marker and curled in a dangerous cross. Pernis could only flap the ball to Anthony Stokes, who blasted a volley on target and saw his effort extraordinarily diverted towards Joe Ledley. The Welsh midfielder wasted no time in passing the ball to Wilson on the right touchline, who in turn crossed to Samaras. The Greek attacker headed at goal, the ball deflected off the hand of a defender again and fell in the path of Gary Hooper, who frantically stabbed home from close range. Celtic had done it, they had taken maximum points for the 17th game in a row under Neil Lennon, with the derby clash against Rangers (who had also won every match so far that season) just around the corner.

What may sound like an exciting game of football with justice eventually prevailing, was in fact a disgrace. Indeed, it soon emerged that Dougie McDonald had not taken the advice of his linesman when deciding to overturn the penalty decision, rather he had withdrawn the spot kick on his own accord and instructed Steven Craven to go along with the lie that he had instructed the referee, himself, to reverse the call. This dishonesty became apparent with the fabrications in the match report and certain other members of the SFA became tangled in a web of lies surrounding the matter.

Mark Guidi from The Daily Record was among many journalists to lift the lid on the conspiracy, when he reported on the shocking news that Steven Craven had resigned. In an article for The Daily Record, published on 31st October 2010, the story was unravelled to the public. A remarkable headline read: *'Dougie McDonald told me to lie to Neil Lennon about Celtic penalty U-turn, says quit linesman Steven Craven'*. The piece continued as follows:

STEVEN CRAVEN today reveals the truth behind the lies of a controversial Tannadice cover-up.

In an explosive MailSport exclusive that will rock the SFA to its core, Craven lifts the lid on the spot-kick storm from Celtic's clash with Dundee United.

The linesman opens up about the lies and bullying that led to his resignation and reveals how: Ref Dougie McDonald lied to Hoops boss Neil Lennon about his sensational penalty U-turn.

Both he and McDonald came clean to refs chief Hugh Dallas. Dallas tried TWICE to get him to repeat what he knew to be a lie. Bullying, harassment and victimisation in the corridors of power will lead to refs quitting.

*Craven told MailSport: "Dougie ran towards me and said: 'I think I've f***** up.' After the game Dougie said we*

309

should tell the referee supervisor (Jim McBurnie) that I called him over to question the penalty award.

I went along with it because I wanted to be supportive of Dougie. But then Neil Lennon came in after the game and asked Dougie why he hadn't given the penalty kick. We told Neil the version that was a lie. It was wrong to lie. And I'm not proud that I went along with Dougie's suggestion. I decided to quit a few days later. I'd had enough of Hugh Dallas and John Fleming (the SFA referee development officer). For a while I felt I had been a victim of harassment and bullying from them. A lot of guys are not happy with it and are ready to walk away."

SFA chief executive Stewart Regan said: "Dougie hasn't accepted responsibility for Steven's resignation. His resignation covers other matters and we are looking at those."

STEVEN CRAVEN knew he was wrong to go along with Dougie McDonald's lies after the Dundee United v Celtic game. But he was stunned and shocked when refs supremo Hugh Dallas wouldn't listen to the TRUTH after the officials decided to come clean. Craven says in his resignation letter that Dallas twice tried to make him repeat a version of events he knew to be untrue. That was when the linesman realised he was going to be hung out to dry for McDonald's decision to overturn the penalty he had awarded the Hoops.

Inaccurate stories started to appear on a daily basis in an attempt to cover up the real version of events - and that's why Craven has decided to speak out.

The article continued with a more extensive interview, before uncovering the depth of involvement by Hugh Dallas, in the controversy:

Craven claims the refs supremo wasn't interested in the truth and wanted the linesman to keep taking the flak. That then kicked off a series of events that led to Craven handing in his resignation and the SFA starting an investigation. The first part of that probe led to McDonald receiving an official warning but the investigation is still ongoing.

Craven said: "On the Monday morning there was quite a reaction in the papers. I sent Dougie a text to ask what he thought of the fall-out. He called immediately and told me he had talked with Hugh the night before and decided to come clean. Dougie told Hugh lies were told to the supervisor. He then told Hugh the truth - that I had not shouted for him to come over. I was then urged to tell Hugh the truth when he called me. I was happy to do so and felt quite relieved.

When Hugh phoned he asked me to talk over the penalty. He said: 'So what happened after you called out for Dougie to come over? You called out Dougie, Dougie, Dougie?' My wife was in the room and I told him that was not the case. I told Hugh he now knew the truth. The truth was the version Dougie had told him over the phone. But Hugh repeated: 'What are you talking about, you said Dougie, Dougie, Dougie and called him over' but I told Dallas I did no such thing. Dougie came clean and so did I. But Hugh didn't seem to accept that.

I phoned Dougie back and told him Hugh tried to make out this wasn't true and denied having the conversation with Dougie on the Sunday night. Dougie's response was he thought Hugh was just trying to test me, that he wanted to see if I would tell the truth or stick to the previous story. My reading of the situation was Hugh wanted to protect Dougie and leave me to take the flak. It was wrong to lie and I'm not proud that I went along with Dougie's suggestion. Rewind the clock and I wouldn't do it. But it

311

was worse to continue the lie. I was really upset after that conversation with Hugh."

Craven then got even angrier when he checked his email and received the official match report. He was criticised for his performance at Tannadice and that convinced him it was time to get out of the game.

Craven said: "When I got my match report from the game emailed to me that proved to be the final straw. I was down-marked for getting an offside decision wrong. When I got the match report I phoned Drew Herbertson at the SFA and told him I'd had enough. I was going to quit at Christmas - but not because of my ankles, as has been reported elsewhere. It was because of all the nonsense with Hugh. I got my letter from the SFA on Friday morning to say my resignation had been formally accepted."

Whilst Celtic remained quiet on the issue, certain quarters of the Scottish game pointed the blame in the club's direction. Walter Smith (then Manager of Rangers) even remarked that Celtic had spoiled the season with their moaning about conspiracies involving match officials, however it was not Celtic who brought the scandal to light, nor would the club have been wrong to take such a position anyway, considering that the conspiracy was ultimately proven to be true. This was a fact that Celtic's Mark Wilson moved to point out in a post season press conference, aired on Sky Sports News. Yet prior to the end of the season and the reaching of that conclusive verdict, the story was understandably attracting a large degree of attention.

The Celtic support, led by the Green Brigade, mobilised to stand up against those perpetrating injustices against the club. On 6th November 2010, prior to Celtic's astonishing record 9-0 victory over Aberdeen at Celtic Park, the Green

312

Brigade Ultras led a march with the wider support. Hundreds of fans were striding to Hampden Park to protest against the SFA for acting in what most Celtic fans believed to be a partial manner against the club. After voicing their concerns with an array of chants throughout the protest, the crowd dissipated and headed to Paradise for the 3pm kick off.

It was the Green Brigade who led the way at the stadium again, displaying two protest banners in the North Curve of Celtic Park, as the teams took to the field.

As the pressure mounted on the SFA to provide answers, the organisation's grade one referees announced, on 21st November 2010, that they were going on strike over the debacle the following week. Astonishingly, the strike hadn't even come to fruition when Hugh Dallas and five of his colleagues were forced to resign within five days of the announcement. The dramatic story of the resignations broke in The Daily Record newspaper, a day after the departures took place. The tale revealed another misdemeanour by the nation's main football authority:

Hugh Dallas sacked and five other SFA staff forced out over Pope email

REFEREES chief Hugh Dallas was last night sacked by the SFA over the Popegate email scandal. Five other staff members were also booted out over the email, which contained a crude paedophile slur.

Dallas is understood to have offered to quit over the storm, which saw the Catholic Church make a public demand for his dismissal. But he was forced to stay in his post as head of referee development - so he could be fired by under-pressure chief executive Stewart Regan.

A source said last night: "Hugh was embarrassed and dismayed by the scandal. He was being vilified as some kind of bigot for forwarding an email which he believed satirical NOT sectarian, although it was undoubtedly in bad taste. But his primary concern was for his family. That is why he offered his resignation. Perhaps the SFA felt there was a need for them to be seen to take action. I would imagine he feels relieved now to be out of it."

Dallas was the only one of the staff under investigation over the email - sent on the day the Pope visited Scotland in September - to take a lawyer into his hearing. The others were targeted because their 'electronic fingerprints' were found on the email, sent from Dallas's account at the SFA. Last night, sources claimed one was dismissed simply for receiving the email.

One SFA insider said: "The other guys are members of the inner circle, very close to the coaching and support staff of the national team. They are all in a panic and are joining the union and looking for legal help."

Last night, there was nobody available for comment at the SFA, who are preparing to deal with a referees' strike this weekend.

Celtic hosted Inverness Caledonian Thistle on 27th November 2010, the day that the news broke. The Green Brigade turned up swaying and jumping together, whilst humming the theme tune to the American soap opera, Dallas. Yet the madness of the weekend was not yet done as Dougie McDonald became the final casualty when he resigned on Sunday 28th November. The man at the centre of the issue from the outset, finally exited the Scottish game after six weeks had passed since the original incident at Tannadice. The Guardian newspaper reported the story on the same day:

Dougie McDonald, the referee who lied about his reasons for reversing a penalty for Celtic, has announced his retirement.

McDonald had been under serious pressure to step down after the admission that he lied about the penalty in a game against Dundee United last month. Celtic's chairman John Reid had called directly for McDonald's removal after the club's recent annual general meeting; the referee's position was widely regarded as untenable.

McDonald's exit comes after a weekend in which Scotland's referees went on strike in protest at what they perceive as escalating abuse towards them and the questioning of their honesty.

Hugh Dallas, the Scottish Football Association's head of refereeing, also left his post on Friday. Dallas, who is known to be close to McDonald, had been under investigation for the alleged sending of an offensive email relating to the pope's visit to Scotland.

McDonald said: "My category one colleagues decided rightly to withdraw their services from matches this weekend in response to the outrageous way they have been treated by sections within Scottish football and, in my opinion, the lack of support they have received from the SFA general purposes committee in recent years. However, their united stand, and the position of strength they have established this weekend, has been clouded by one issue, namely the aftermath of the Dundee United v Celtic match on 17 October. I apologised for my role in that and want my previously unblemished 29-year career to move on. Now is the time for all of Scottish football to move on.

My decision will therefore remove that issue from the debate and ensure that the next day of action — which, in my opinion, will undoubtedly come if the football community does not have a massive change of heart — will result in media coverage being concentrated on those who engage in referee bashing and those who condone it."

Celtic refused comment on McDonald's decision.

McDonald's departure signalled the end of the whole 'penalty porkies' saga. From one small decision, a network of bigotry fuelled cheating was exposed to Scottish football supporters. The whole ignominious fiasco looked appalling for the credibility of the nation's game and is one of the most high-profile incidents in modern Celtic history.

BOMBS & BULLETS

To document the challenges that Neil Lennon has faced when it comes to sectarianism during his professional career would require a book of its own. However, as a follow on from all the controversy with the Scottish game's governing body in season 2010/11, there were a string of incidents involving bombs and bullets that took place during the latter stages of that same campaign.

As is sadly all too commonplace, Neil Lennon was the first recipient of a package containing bullets. A package was also sent to fellow Irishman, Niall McGinn. The incident took place on 5th January 2011 when staff at the Royal Mail sorting office in Mallusk, County Antrim, alerted police to two suspicious items. The pair had been targeted by bigots in their home province and by the time the news broke on 9th January 2011, a third suspicious parcel was en route to Celtic Park. This time the intended target was Derry man, Paddy McCourt, and the parcel was intercepted at a Glasgow sorting office. The Celtic trio kept a low profile and allowed the police to conduct their investigations.

It should be the height of scandalous shame when no less than three members of a football club are sent death threats. Disgusting it was then, on Wednesday 20th April 2011, when worse news was to hit the television screens ahead of Celtic's trip to Kilmarnock that evening. The United Kingdom was left dumbfounded at the harrowing thought that Neil Lennon had been the target of nail bombs "Designed to maim and kill," alongside prominent Celtic fans (QC Paul McBride and MSP Trish Godman).

The BBC broke the story with a chilling article that appeared on their website. It provides a timeline of the events in the second half of the season, which all fed into this disgusting bigoted attack. The piece read:

"Viable" parcel bombs have been sent to Celtic manager Neil Lennon and two high-profile fans of the Glasgow club, sources have told the BBC. Sources said the liquid-based devices, sent in the past month, appear to have been intended to "kill or maim."

Mr Lennon's lawyer, Paul McBride QC, and former deputy presiding officer of the Scottish Parliament, Trish Godman, were the other two people targeted.

The devices were found at various locations in the west of Scotland. Sources close to the investigation indicated they were rudimentary and did not appear to have been made by someone with paramilitary training in bomb-making.

Earlier this week, media organisations, including the BBC, had agreed to a police request not to broadcast details of the bomb incidents while officers carried out inquires.

Scotland's First Minister Alex Salmond said: "Let us be quite clear - there is a major police investigation under way to ensure that the individual or individuals concerned are identified and apprehended, and then brought to book with the full force of the law. We will not tolerate this sort of criminality in Scotland, and as an indication of the seriousness with which we view these developments the Cabinet sub-committee met last Saturday to ensure that the police investigation has every possible support to come to a successful conclusion."

The first suspect package was intercepted by the Royal Mail in Kirkintilloch, East Dunbartonshire, on 26 March and was addressed to Mr Lennon at Celtic's training ground in nearby Lennoxtown. Two days later a device was delivered to Labour politician Ms Godman's constituency office in Bridge of Weir, Renfrewshire. Her staff were suspicious of the package and contacted Strathclyde Police.

Detectives initially treated the two parcels as "elaborate hoaxes" designed to cause distress rather than serious injury but further analysis has led to them being reclassified as "viable explosive devices."

The third package was addressed to Mr McBride at the Faculty of Advocates in Edinburgh. It is believed to have been posted in Ayrshire before being found in a letter box by a postal worker on Friday and taken to a Royal Mail sorting office in Kilwinning, where police were contacted.

Explosive device

Detectives are also investigating another package addressed to Neil Lennon which was found at a sorting office in Saltcoats, North Ayrshire, on 4 March but this has not been confirmed as an explosive device.

It is understood that specialist anti-terrorist officers are involved in the investigation but a source close to the inquiry said they were "not linking this to any terrorist organisation."

Henry McDonald, Ireland correspondent for the Guardian newspaper, said that made sense. "I think in terms of the main loyalist terror organisations that are now on ceasefire and say they've decommissioned, I think they'd be frankly embarrassed by this kind of thing," he said.

"They would regard it as a thing of the past and rather as an irritant and an embarrassment to loyalism so I suspect it's an individual or individuals who maybe had bomb-making experience in the past who are disgruntled and looking for hate figures."

For the past decade Neil Lennon has been such a figure. The 39-year-old Catholic from Lurgan, County Armagh, has endured threats, abuse and violence. He stopped playing international football for Northern Ireland in 2002 after a death threat, said to be from loyalist paramilitaries. Lennon has also been the victim of a street attack in Glasgow and several other death threats since joining Celtic in 2000.

In January this year bullets addressed to the Celtic manager were intercepted at a sorting office in Glasgow. They appeared to have been sent from an address in Northern Ireland.

Media coverage

The BBC has been told that the three individuals appear to have been targeted after they featured, on separate occasions, in media coverage. Mr McBride is one of the highest-profile QCs in Scotland and a well-known Celtic fan. He has acted for the club and Mr Lennon on several occasions during disputes with the Scottish Football Association (SFA). The advocate has also been highly critical of the SFA in its dealings with Mr Lennon and Celtic.

Ms Godman has a lower public profile than Mr Lennon or Mr McBride but is well known in political circles as an avid Celtic fan. Until dissolution of the Scottish Parliament last month, she was deputy presiding officer and the Labour MSP for West Renfrewshire. On her last day as an MSP she was pictured in the Holyrood chamber wearing a Celtic football top.

Rangers and Celtic meet for the final time this season at Ibrox this weekend in a match which could prove crucial in deciding the Scottish Premier League title. It is understood that senior police officers are concerned about a potential rise in tension ahead of the game on Easter Sunday.

The rivalry between the two Glasgow clubs - known collectively as the Old Firm - is historically tied up in religion. Celtic were formed in 1888 by Irish Catholic immigrants to raise funds to alleviate poverty in the city's East End. To this day, most Celtic fans come from a Catholic background, while the majority of Rangers fans are Protestants.

Controversial match

Last month an ill-tempered Scottish Cup clash between the two sides led to political intervention. The match saw three red cards, several touch-line and tunnel confrontations and 34 arrests inside Celtic Park and 187 outside. After the final whistle, Mr Lennon and Rangers assistant manager Ally McCoist were involved in a confrontation.

Strathclyde Police requested a Scottish government-led summit after describing scenes at the game, which Celtic won 1-0, as "shameful."

Both clubs subsequently agreed to an action plan to tackle Old Firm-related disorder. The fallout from the controversial match continued, however, when the Celtic manager subsequently received a ban for his actions. McCoist had an initial two-match ban overturned, while two of his players, El-Hadji Diouf and Madjid Bougherra, were fined over their actions after the sendings off. This prompted highly-critical comments from Mr McBride towards the SFA. The advocate accused the organisation of being "dysfunctional," "dishonest" and "biased."

In response the governing body described the QC's remarks as "wild" and "inaccurate" and threatened to sue for defamation. The BBC understands there have since been moves by both sides to resolve the matter out of court.

Neil Lennon showed immense courage to remain in his role at Celtic and despite reports of the attempt on his life dispersing around the British media, the match against Kilmarnock went ahead at Rugby Park. Lennon's players responded terrifically, demonstrating extraordinary panache as they strolled to a 4-0 win. There was a touching moment in the 18th minute, when the Celtic fans at both ends of the ground gave a two-minute applause. As a player for the club, Lennon's squad number was 18 and the gesture was a fitting show of support for him.

The Hoops seemed galvanised by the adversity and followed up their performance at Rugby Park with a strong display at Ibrox, where only a fine save by Allan McGregor prevented Giorgios Samaras' penalty giving Celtic a 1-0 victory. The Bhoys then thumped Dundee United 4-1 at Celtic Park before disaster struck in the highlands as the Hoops befell a 3-2 defeat against Inverness Caledonian

Thistle. The result meant that Celtic surrendered their lead at the top of the table, handing Rangers the initiative in the title race. Nevertheless, Lennon's team returned to Rugby Park where they earned a comfortable 2-0 victory to stay hot on the heels of their rivals, ahead of a tough midweek trip to Tynecastle on 11th May.

There had been yet more unease in the lead up to the match against Hearts as a group of seven people had been arrested by armed police following a gun alert at Celtic's Lennoxtown Training Centre. Yet unbowed and unshakable, Neil Lennon and his team stayed focused on achieving the win in Edinburgh and potentially overtaking Rangers, should they offer a chance to erode their one-point advantage.

The match was packed full of drama, beginning when Gary Hooper gave Celtic an early lead in the 12th minute before David Obua, Hearts' Ugandan midfielder, was red carded on 32 minutes for an innocuous slap aimed at Charlie Mulgrew. Hooper took advantage of the additional space provided by the sending off and doubled Celtic's lead after the interval with a powerful toe-poke in the 49th minute. Joy turned to despair during the celebrations as attention was turned to a fracas at the Celtic dugout. A Heart's fan had leapt the advertising board and charged towards Neil Lennon to attack him. The Celtic Manager hadn't seen his attacker approaching but fortunately his assistant, Alan Thompson, managed to restrain the fan as he was about to strike the Irishman. A police officer quickly moved in and ejected the pitch invader from the stadium. The unseemly scene was described by Barry Anderson of The Scotsman newspaper in the following way:

After refereeing cover-ups, conspiracy theories and parliamentary summits to discuss Old Firm matches, season 2010/11 added another chapter to its book of infamy last night. In the 49th minute of play, Celtic's celebrations following Gary Hooper's second goal were cut short. A man leapt from Tynecastle's main stand to sprint down the track and assault Lennon. The surprised Celtic manager barely had time to react before stewards pounced on his assailant, but that did not stop Lennon swinging his boot at the flattened thug several times. In fact, twice he mistakenly connected with one of the grounded stewards as his rage took over.

Few could blame him given the letter bombs, death threats, 24-hour security and everything else he has tolerated of late. No-one should be subjected to physical abuse for simply doing their job, especially when that job is managing a football team. Where was his protection? Lennon hurled a few expletives at his attacker as he was marched down the tunnel by police and the Irishman was later described as "shaken but fine" by his assistant, Johann Mjallby.

Incidentally this was not the first time that a red-headed Irish Catholic had been attacked by supporters at Tynecastle. Indeed, the Cork born Celtic goalkeeper, James Foley, was set upon by several Hearts fans during a reserve match on 28th November 1936! Under intense provocation, Foley drop-kicked a ball, point-blank, towards the Hearts fans behind the goal. His actions prompted a pitch invasion, in which Foley was head-butted, then arrested and charged with assault. At the trial in Edinburgh on 1st February 1937, left back, Jack Doyle, and left half, Bertie Duffy, both denied that the ball had hit a spectator. Instead, Foley's teammates testified that it had hit the surrounding wall. Nevertheless, Foley was fined £2 with the option of 20 days imprisonment should he refuse to make payment. Foley, who was by then playing for Portsmouth, had to return to Scotland for this trial and paid the fine.

Jumping back to the case of Neil Lennon at Tynecastle in 2011, the Manager sharply switched his focus back to the football. Kris Commons netted a neat curling finish in the closing stages of the match. Though the Englishman strolled into the crowd to celebrate, oblivious to the fact that he had already been booked and was thus ordered off for a second bookable offence. It was a foolish action, which topped off a dreadful day in Scottish football.

The Celtic team had just one more fixture to fulfil, in the hope that they could yet become champions. The squad could have been forgiven for wanting the season to end after the Hearts match, especially when another package containing bullets was found at Celtic Park at 10.30am the following morning. The matter was becoming horrendous, both for the club and for Neil Lennon himself. Regardless, the club was united in trying to get the job done, which they set about doing with a 4-0 demolition of Motherwell inside a raucous Celtic Park. Be that as it may, their efforts were in vein as Rangers won 5-1 at Rugby Park to snatch the league championship by a solitary point. The Hoops did take some consolation from winning the Scottish Cup a week later, with a fine 3-0 victory over Motherwell. By this time, t-shirts bearing the words that Neil Lennon had uttered to his fans on the Parkhead pitch a week earlier, had already covered the terraces: "This isn't the end, this is just the beginning." How right he was as season 2011/12 saw

Celtic win the first of what is, at the time of writing, eight league titles in a row.

As for the offenders outlined throughout this chapter, Paul Wilson (the Hearts fan who attempted to assault Lennon in the dugout) was sent to prison for eight months for breach of the peace, whilst he was found unproven when it came to the accusation that his motive had been sectarian in nature. Meanwhile, Trevor Muirhead and Neil McKenzie were jailed for conspiring to assault Lennon, former MSP Trish Godman and the late QC Paul McBride, as well as staff at the Irish Republican organisation, Cairde na hÉireann, by sending devices they believed were capable of exploding and causing severe injury. McKenzie was also sentenced to 18 months for a separate charge of posting a hoax bomb to Lennon at Celtic Park, which ran concurrently with his five-year sentence.

The following timeline of offences were read out in the courtroom:

'A device sent to Lennon at Celtic's training ground in Lennoxtown, East Dunbartonshire, was intercepted at a sorting office in Kirkintilloch on 26 March last year when a postman spotted a nail protruding from it. It tested positive for peroxide, which can be used to make explosives. Two days later a package delivered to Godman's constituency office in Bridge of Weir, Renfrewshire, caused the evacuation of the building. Liquid inside a plastic bottle within the package tested positive for a small amount of the primary explosive triacetone triperoxide. Before the incident, Godman, who was Labour MSP for West Renfrewshire, had been filmed wearing a Celtic strip to the Scottish Parliament, which she claimed was meant to be a

private matter. Also, on 28 March, a postman tried to deliver a package to Cairde na hÉireann in Glasgow's Gallowgate. After two failed attempts, it was sent to the Royal Mail's national returns centre in Belfast, where it was found to contain potentially explosive peroxide. The final package, found on 15 April in a postbox on Montgomerie Terrace, Kilwinning, was addressed to the late McBride.'

Both men were originally accused of a more serious charge of conspiring to murder their targets, but it was thrown out a day before the trial concluded due to insufficient evidence. Muirhead was then ultimately cleared of the charge with a not proven verdict.

EUROPEAN LIFELINES

After the extreme difficulties faced the season before, Neil Lennon and his Celtic team escaped to Australia for three matches during pre-season in July 2011. Kris Commons was still relatively new to the club at the time and if he had any doubts about the magnitude of Celtic, they were soon quashed when a combined total of 55,144 fans turned up to watch the Hoops take on Central Coast Mariners, Melbourne Victory and Perth Glory. The popular attacker moved to say how "Overwhelmed," he was by the global reach of the club and the fervour with which the Scottish/Irish community down under supported the team. The tour was relatively successful with two wins from three, before Celtic returned to the UK to take on Partick Thistle (2-1 victory) and Cardiff City (1-0 loss).

The final week in July had not even been reached when the club found themselves opening the SPL season on a red-hot day at Easter Road. Ki Seung Yeung starred in central midfield that day, netting a goal from just outside the box in the 63rd minute, after Anthony Stokes had produced a stunning overhead finish early in the first half. Kelvin Wilson also put in a fine performance at the centre of defence on his competitive debut, which ensured that Celtic kept a clean sheet and returned from the capital with a 2-0 victory. The Celts then returned to friendly action with a 2-0 defeat at home to Wolves, before a double header in Dublin against Inter Milan (2-0 loss) and an Airtricity League XI (5-0 win). A scratch Celtic side completed friendly duties with another 2-0 defeat at the Liberty Stadium against Swansea, where a vocal away support witnessed Brendan Rodgers' newly promoted side control the play, with Scott Sinclair and Stephen Dobbie causing the Glasgow club's defence no end of problems.

The chaotic schedule had prepared the team for a return to league duty as Celtic edged past Aberdeen at Pittodrie, thanks to a solitary Anthony Stokes goal in the 74th minute, before the Bhoys thumped Dundee 5-1 at Celtic Park. It was then time to commence European exploits, with Swiss club FC Sion standing between Celtic and a place in the 2nd round of Europa League qualification. A depleted team, missing Hooper, Izzaguire, Kayal, Loovens and K.Wilson, took to the field at Celtic Park for the first leg. Despite being backed by 51,000 fans, the Bhoys put in a somewhat turgid display and certainly lost their rhythm in attack with so many key players ruled out. It was, however, still disappointing to come away from the match with the aggregate score level at 0-0.

Before the second leg could be played in the south of Switzerland, Celtic had a great opportunity to return to winning ways when they hosted St Johnstone at the weekend. The Celtic team could not atone for their midweek disappointment though, as a number of chances were squandered before St Johnstone snuck all three points curtesy of a solitary goal by Mackay, whose deflected shot found the back of the net in the 60th minute. It wasn't ideal form to take to the most sun blessed town in Switzerland, and matters were further worsened for Celtic when Dan Majstorovic made a ridiculous tackle in the third minute, earning himself a straight red card and handing Sion a penalty kick in the process. Immediately, the Swiss were ahead.

Midway through the second half, Sion doubled their advantage. Even the return of Kayal and Hooper made little difference as Celtic looked to be crashing out of Europe before August. Spirits were briefly lifted in the 78th minute as Charlie Mulgrew drilled home a free kick from just outside the box. However, any hope of an equaliser dwindled in the late stages as Celtic threw players forward, which allowed Giovanni Sio to break on the counter and finish the tie. The bulk of the 10,000 crowd at the Stade Tourbillon were sent into delirium. Full time: FC Sion 3-1 Celtic. Sinisterly, this meant that the Bhoys had now gone 30 matches without an away win in European competition.

The Celtic team had barely come to terms with the disappointment of being knocked out of Europe, when it emerged that FC Sion had fielded five ineligible players in both legs of the tie. In particular, Pascal Feindouno, one of the ineligible five, scored two goals in the second leg. Three days after defeat, on 28th August 2011, Celtic lodged a formal protest to UEFA over the matter. The core point centred on the fact that Sion fielded players who were signed during a transfer embargo, which was imposed on the club for breaching rules when signing the Egyptian goalkeeper, Essam El-Hadary, in February 2008. On that occasion, Sion announced that they had signed El-Hadary on a four-year contract, despite objections from his club, Al Ahly, due to the fact that he was still under contract with them. The consequence of this transfer resulted in a ban for FC Sion, by the FIFA Dispute Resolution Chamber, from registering any new players for two registration periods. No transfers were made in the summer of 2010 and an appeal by FC Sion to the Court of Arbitration for Sport (which was eventually unsuccessful) was in progress.

UEFA President, Michel Platini, commented immediately after the Celtic v Sion tie: "There are rules that have not been respected. FC Sion has not respected the rules of the transfer ban, they signed players and then played those players." As Platini's comments suggest, UEFA upheld Celtic's protest and ordered Sion to forfeit each match 3-0. Just eight days after exiting Europe, Celtic found themselves preparing for the group stages by way of a 6-0 aggregate victory!

In line with their right to appeal, Sion contested the ruling on the basis that they felt the transfer embargo had been lifted at the time of signing the players. On 13th September 2011, UEFA published the following statement on their website:

The UEFA Appeals Body today dealt with the appeal lodged by FC Sion against the decision of the UEFA Control and Disciplinary Body of 2 September to forfeit their two UEFA Europa League play-off games played against Celtic FC on 18 and 25 August.

The Appeals Body heard the parties and decided to reject the appeal lodged by Sion, confirming that the Swiss club had fielded ineligible players in both matches.

As a consequence, Celtic remain qualified for the UEFA Europa League group stage and will play against Club Atlético de Madrid on Thursday 15 September. An appeal against this decision can be lodged to the Court of Arbitration for Sport (CAS) within ten days of receipt of the written grounds for the decisions.

UEFA also received today on this matter a court decision from the Tribunal Cantonal de Vaud and will issue a statement in this respect at a later stage.

Sion were determined to pursue their appeal, taking their case to the civil courts (two of whom ruled in the club's favour). However, FIFA stepped in, appealing the ruling to higher court. The Valais cantonal court in Sion overturned the decision of the civil courts and sided in FIFA and UEFA's favour. At this stage, Celtic had already earned five points in four group matches of the competition, yet Sion persisted in submitting a dossier to the Court of Arbitration for Sport, who had the ultimate say on the matter. Should the entity favour FC Sion, UEFA would need to find some way of reintegrating the Swiss club into the group stage in place of Celtic.

In a statement released after the hearing on November 24th 2011, the Court of Arbitration for Sport (CAS) confirmed that they sided with UEFA in the debacle and Sion would not be reinstated to the Europa League. A spokesman for CAS said: "The request filed by UEFA, to confirm that FC Sion is not entitled to be reintegrated in the UEFA Europa League 2011/2012 is admissible and upheld." In addition, the organisation instructed Sion to pay 40,000 Swiss francs to UEFA as contribution towards its legal costs incurred in connection with this arbitration. In making this decision, CAS confirmed that UEFA was correct to enforce the FIFA regulations and that the UEFA disciplinary bodies were right in declaring the games of FC Sion in the UEFA Europa League lost by forfeit.

Celtic failed to build on the eventual security of their position in Europe and crashed out at the end of the group stage with just one win (3-1 v Rennes), three draws (including a superb performance away against Udinese) and two defeats (against Atletico Madrid).

EFE'S PASSPORT WOES

Having brushed aside HJK Helsinki and Helsingborgs to qualify for the Champions League, Celtic opened their group campaign with a 0-0 draw against Benfica at Celtic Park, and earnt their first ever away win at the group stage of the tournament thanks to a late goal against Spartak Moscow in the notoriously difficult Luzhniki Stadium. One could be forgiven for being a little overexcited ahead of Celtic's third match of the group, a trip to the Nou Camp on 23rd October 2012. Be that as it may, there can be little excuse for the absence of mind that Efe Ambrose displayed.

A day earlier, on 22nd October, the Celtic team checked in their luggage to fly out to Spain and prepare for the huge match against Barcelona. As his kitbag rested on the scales, Efe Ambrose looked to his horror upon opening his hand luggage. It was then that the central defender realised he had forgotten his passport and was about to experience a world of ignominy.

A contingency plan was put in place to ensure that the Nigerian international made it over to prepare for the match properly. Although, Efe's blushes were spared when he was able to retrieve the document and reunite with his teammates at Glasgow Airport with half an hour until boarding. He could finally relax, avoid the wrath of his Manager and set his sights on stopping Lionel Messi.

Little over 24 hours later, Celtic and Ambrose himself, performed terrifically against a star-studded Barcelona team. Samaras had actually given the Hoops a shock lead in the first half, a lead which Celtic held until Andres Iniesta rounded off an incredible passing move in stoppage time. Celtic held firm throughout the second half, owing enormous gratitude to Fraser Forster for producing an unreal performance to keep the score level. A monumental result looked on the cards, only for Jordi Alba to spoil the party in the 94th minute with a tap in at the far post. Celtic were heartbroken, but they would exact revenge on the Catalonians with one of the finest victories in the club's history two weeks later.

KILL THE BILL

2nd March 2011 will always be known as the date when the 'Shame Game' took place. However, there was a football match at Celtic Park that day, which Celtic won by a goal to nil, eliminating Rangers from the Scottish Cup in the process.

The match became infamous because of a string of incidents, which saw three Rangers players sent off and both managers square up to one another at full time. A summit was called by the First Minister, Alex Salmond, in the aftermath of the contest, whilst the head of Strathclyde Police contemplated the idea of playing the fixture behind closed doors in future. Concurrent to these top-level discussions, an SFA investigation was conducted in regard to the scenes at Celtic Park. Extraordinarily, the governing body decided to fine Bougherra and Diouf a measly £5,000 for offences ranging from manhandling the referee, to elbowing the Celtic physio. As for the Rangers Manager, Ally McCoist, he received a £2,500 fine, which was overturned on appeal. Amidst all of these misdemeanours, only Neil Lennon received a ban (four matches) for his role on the evening. QC Paul McBride subsequently commented: "The SFA are officially the laughing stock of world football." The lawyer went on to scathingly say: "They have been shown now to be not merely dysfunctional and not merely dishonest but biased, because McCoist, who undoubtedly said something that provoked a reaction from Neil Lennon that caused a four-match ban for him, received no punishment at all. We know that Bougherra, who manhandled the referee not once but twice doesn't get a ban. We know that El Hadj Diouf, who's involved in an altercation in the tunnel with a Celtic

337

physiotherapist, refuses to leave the park when given a red card and throws his top into the crowd against Police advice, isn't given a ban either. What is any sensible person to think of that set of affairs?"

Mindboggling as the decisions of the SFA were, there was much worse to follow from the Scottish government. The outcome of discussions surrounding the affair ultimately led to the creation of a draconian piece of legislation, known as The Offensive Behaviour at Football and Threatening Communications Act, by Kenny MacAskill on 19th January 2012. This reactionary, rushed, new bill enabled police to incriminate football supporters on the subjective basis of deeming them to be acting offensively within the context of a football match.

Given that the law flew in the face of free speech, civil liberties and absolutely failed to tackle sectarianism, (its cited purpose, for which laws already existed anyway) it was hardly surprising when Fans Against Criminalisation demonstrations began to garner huge support.

Fans Against Criminalisation (FAC) had been established in 2011 when the summit had been called. The organisation comprised of five key Celtic supporter groups, The Green Brigade, The Celtic Trust, The Celtic Supporter's Association, The Affiliation of Registered Celtic Supporters' Clubs and The Association of Irish Celtic Supporters Clubs. Although, FAC sought to branch out to the rest of Scottish football as fans from all clubs were inadvertently affected. Therefore, fans of Motherwell, Hamilton and Rangers were all involved in the planning of some FAC activities.

Despite the fact that the campaign by FAC was a long and hard fought one, the focus of this piece is an incident that occurred during a Green Brigade protest march in 2013. The ultras group had already staged a number of protests through banners, displays and sit down/silent demonstrations. However, their efforts were redoubled in accordance with FAC, when a spokesman for the group released the following statement just a week after Celtic beat Barcelona in November 2012: "Last Wednesday was a special night at Celtic Park. The display before the match was beyond our wildest expectations, the atmosphere was electric from start to finish and more importantly, Celtic beat arguably the best team in world football. It is a night that will live long in the memory of everyone connected to the club. However, while the rest of the support were still on cloud nine, our group was brought back down to earth with a bump as it transpired that Strathclyde Police had visited yet another two members' homes with a view to charging them. To put this into perspective, this means that just under 50% of the Green Brigade have either faced or are facing police charges/a ban from football." After revealing that shocking statistic, the statement continued: "It has come to a stage where we have to act and fight back. We can't continue to let the police have free reign to arrest and charge whoever they please. It is having an astronomical effect on people's livelihoods. Those members who are left without a charge can't even enjoy the football anymore in case it leads to a chap at the door that could change their lives forever. The grim reality is that if we don't act now, there may be no group left come the end of the season. As a result, we have no choice but to highlight this further in the form of a two-match boycott from Celtic Park. This will begin immediately and means that during the forthcoming league match v Inverness Caledonian Thistle and Scottish Cup match v Arbroath, The Green Brigade will not be present whatsoever. Our members live for going to watch and support the team we love, just like every other fan out there. Sadly, we aren't being treated like every other fan and in fact face victimisation and harassment on a scale that is unimaginable. We hope that this boycott will raise awareness of our situation and the end result will be that Strathclyde Police will relent."

The boycott was supported by all season book holders in section 111 (the area where The Green Brigade stood) both within and outside of the group. The matches saw possibly the worst two atmospheres of the season. Still the situation did not improve. After becoming sick of being filmed throughout every match, some members of The Green Brigade spontaneously decided to return the favour and flash their phone cameras back at the police. More joined in. Amazingly, the full stadium was awash with flashing camera lights and a chant of "All Celtic fans against the bill."

In contempt of the creative efforts, little improved by way of incrimination within section 111. Having worked with wider Scottish football fans through FAC, The Green Brigade publicised their ongoing plight with their own protest march, in March 2013. Joined by a healthy number of supporters, marchers gathered at Chrystal Bells pub and then headed further along the Gallowgate in a peaceful manner en route to Celtic Park. Suddenly things turned ugly. Around 200 police officers were deployed to the scene to prevent the march from going ahead. The walk was technically illegal as it had not been applied for, but the response of the police was viewed by many as disproportionate. Peaceful protesters were kettled beneath a railway bridge a few hundred yards from Glasgow Cross, which prompted a chant of "Supporting your team is not a crime." Amid a very tense atmosphere, people began to stray from the area as there was a feeling of intimidation. Yet it was then that the scene worsened. Supporters as young as 15, walking away from the crowd, were slammed to the ground and handcuffed. Men and women were struck with batons and most haunting of all, a little girl stood crying, terrified as she looked to her horror at the mayhem before her eyes. A lot of Celtic supporters caught the violence on camera, which led to international outcry from certain media outlets and showed thousands of people what the group had endured that day, through the medium of Youtube.

Following the incident, the campaign went from strength to strength. A month later, FAC held a demonstration at George Square in Glasgow, which drew huge numbers from supporters of many clubs. Jeanette Findlay, Joe O'Rourke and a strong presence from The Green Brigade gave a voice to the voiceless. It was clear - criminalisation of the Celtic support and of any other support in the country, would no longer be tolerated.

There would be innumerable challenges ahead for FAC, but their hard work ultimately paid off when Labour MSP, James Kelly, introduced The Offensive Behaviour at Football and Threatening Communications Repeal Bill on 21st June 2017. Kelly had described the 2012 legislation as having "Completely failed to tackle sectarianism," and as "Illiberal," which "Unfairly targets football fans." The politician also reported that the legislation had been

"Condemned by legal experts, human rights organisations and equality groups." Professor Sir Tom Devine was one such man, who previously spoke of the Act as "The most illiberal and counterproductive act passed by our young Parliament to date," and described it as a "Stain on the reputation of the Scottish legal system for fair dealing."

After passing the first stage of repeal on 25th January 2018 and the second stage on 27th February, the Scottish Parliament broke the news on 15th March 2018, that the act would be repealed. Royal Assent was secured, confirming the motion on 19th April 2018. The end of the Act was a cause of great celebration for many Scottish football fans, Fans Against Criminalisation and Celtic Football Club themselves.

FAC announce that the Act has ended

COMMONWEALTH GAMES

Following a successful bid, Glasgow was the city of choice when it came to hosting the 2014 Commonwealth Games. As the largest stadium in the city, Celtic Park was elected to stage the opening ceremony, which meant that the club would benefit enormously from the refurbishments made on Kerrydale Street and the surrounding area. The derelict London Road Primary School building that was a familiar landmark outside Celtic Park was demolished. Whilst, The Celtic Way was constructed from London Road, up to the Main Stand. The new look walkway provided a superb approach to the cities' premier stadium and was enhanced when the Sir Chris Hoy cycling velodrome was erected on the opposite side of the road.

Outside of the immediate area surrounding Celtic Park, there were major modernisations made to Dalmarnock Railway Station. Meanwhile, a new road named the Eastern Regeneration Route was opened for the games in mid-2012, connecting Celtic Park to the M74 from the area behind the Jock Stein Stand. The completion of these redevelopments concluded preparations in the Stadium District and the city was ready to put Celtic Park under the microscope of the world.

The 23rd July 2014 saw the curtain raised on the Commonwealth Games in impressive fashion. An extravagant ceremony was put on and the largest TV screen in Europe was in place, spanning the full length and height of the Main Stand. 40,000 people tasted the occasion in person, whilst an estimated billion people viewed the event on television.

As is customary for such events, many celebrities were present. Although, the night needed no person to raise the excitement levels, for there was a firework display, flybys by the Red Arrows and light shows. That said, many in attendance would have been impressed by the official rendition of God Save The Queen and were sent in to orbit when her majesty appeared. However, for most Celtic fans who watched the event, the Tongan boxer Lomalito Moala, provided the highlight of the evening. Moala had spoken of his love for Celtic on social media and was given six tickets to Celtic's Champions League qualifier against KR Reykjavik at Murray Park in Edinburgh a few days earlier. The match had been moved to the national rugby stadium in order to accommodate Celtic Park and indeed Glasgow's preparations for the Commonwealth Games. Moala appeared with his fellow Tongan athletes at the opening ceremony, wearing the new Celtic hooped shirt and kissing the badge as he took to the stage.

The whole event was a huge success, which showed Celtic Park as a world class arena for elite sporting competition.

Red Arrows Fly Above Celtic Park

NO LEGIA TO STAND ON

Ronny Deila took over the reigns at Celtic Park with a new blueprint for the club and lofty modern ideas when it came to fitness. The new Celtic Manager had a positive pre-season and skipped past Icelandic side, KR Reykjavic, by way of a 5-0 aggregate scoreline in the opening round of Champions League qualification.

A man known for putting his faith in youth and working wonders on a shoestring budget, Deila drafted Callum McGregor into the team after a reasonably successful loan spell at League 2 club, Notts County. The young Celt was on the scoresheet in Iceland and seized his opportunity in the second round of qualification against Legia Warsaw. McGregor started the first leg in Poland, on 30th July 2014, and cut in from the right-hand side to unleash a 30-yard shot on his favoured left foot. The ball flew inside the post and ended high into the net. It was a dream start for Celtic, who looked to be fulfilling former Polish Celt, Maciej Zurawiski's prophecy that "The Hoops would have nothing to worry about against Legia Warsaw." The dream became a nightmare two minutes later though, as the Pole's drew level and then took charge of proceedings. Celtic were embarrassed by a 4-1 defeat and failed to make amends at Murrayfield in the second leg. This time the Bhoys fell to another defeat by two goals to nil.

Celtic had bowed out of the Champions League before the end of August for the second time in three years. Yet just as three years previous, the club was offered a lifeline when it emerged that 86th minute substitute in the second leg, Bartosz Bereszynski, was in fact ineligible to play in the match as he should have been serving a suspension.

Bereszynski had been sent off for clashing with Apollon Limassol's Gaston Sangoy during Legia's final Europa League match of the previous season and was suspended for three games in European competition. He did not feature in the opening round of Champions League qualification against St Patrick's Athletic, nor did he play in the first leg of the next round against Celtic. However, the player wasn't included in Legia Warsaw's squad registration for the 5-0 victory or 1-1 draw over St Patrick's, which meant that his omission from the games did not count towards serving his suspension.

The administration error meant that UEFA awarded Celtic a 3-0 victory in the second leg, which resulted in a 4-4 aggregate scoreline, as opposed 6-1 in Legia Warsaw's favour. Callum McGregor's goal in the Polish capital then became crucial as it handed the Glasgow side victory in the tie by virtue of the away goals rule!

UEFA released a statement regarding the sanction on Friday 8th August 2014:

Legia have been sanctioned for fielding an ineligible player (article 18 of the UEFA Champions League regulations and article 21 of the disciplinary regulations). The match has been declared as forfeit meaning Legia Warsaw have lost the match 3-0. As a consequence, Celtic have qualified for the Champions League play-offs on away goals (agg: 4-4) and Legia will compete in the Europa League play-offs.

In addition, the player Bartosz Bereszynski, has been suspended for one additional UEFA competition match for which he would be otherwise eligible. This suspension shall be added to the remaining two match suspension which the player still has to serve in accordance with the control and disciplinary body decision of 13 February 2014.

Whilst the Scottish champions were drawn against NK Maribor on 8th August 2014, Legia Warsaw were plotting an appeal to present to European football's governing body. In the intervening period, on 10th August, under-fire Legia Chairman, Dariusz Mioduski, held a press conference in which he issued an open letter urging Celtic officials to meet with him and "Do the honourable thing." The Warsaw boss said: "We sent letters to Celtic asking for a meeting and their co-operation. Unfortunately, these have not been answered. I'm disgusted with Celtic's position and how they have acted. I've been a big fan of Celtic before. Now I am disappointed. I'm surprised the board of Celtic has behaved this way. I will send an open letter to Celtic's board today. We beat them and we're proud of it. There is an Article 34 Paragraph 5 in the UEFA regulations that allows a fair play in such circumstances. I appeal to the men who have helped to establish the best traditions of honour and integrity over the last 126 years, that have been characterised by your great club. Do not destroy the beautiful heritage that you have been left from previous generations. We challenge you, in the spirit of the game and principles of fair play and on the basis of sport, to meet in Warsaw or in Glasgow, and let's settle this matter with honour."

Celtic responded to criticism from Legia Warsaw and the Polish FA with a succinct statement:

We are disappointed by Legia Warsaw's comments. This is entirely a matter for UEFA and its processes. Accordingly, we will reserve further comment for the appropriate time.

Understandably, Legia supporters were disappointed at what had gone on, yet a minority undoubtedly overstepped the mark when it was reported that club administrator, Marta Ostrowska, had received death threats a day before UEFA's hearing on the matter. Ostrowska and her family had to flee Warsaw, on the advice of police, until the matter had either been resolved or blown over. There was no respite for the Legia official on 14th August, when UEFA announced the outcome of their investigations regarding the Polish club's appeal:

The UEFA Appeals Body met yesterday following an appeal by Legia Warszawa against the decision taken by the UEFA Control, Ethics and Disciplinary Body on Aug. 8.

The appeal lodged by the Polish club was rejected and, therefore, the original decision of the UEFA Control, Ethics and Disciplinary Body is confirmed.

The Control, Ethics and Disciplinary Body had sanctioned Legia for fielding a suspended player (Article 18 of the Regulations of the UEFA Champions League, 2014-15 competition, and Article 21 of the UEFA Disciplinary Regulations, 2014 edition) in the 2014-15 UEFA Champions League third qualifying round return leg against Celtic FC in Edinburgh on Aug. 6. That match has been declared as a forfeit, meaning Legia lost 3-0.

After learning their fate, Legia announced that they would take the matter to the Court of Arbitration for Sport (CAS) that afternoon. A tweet by the outspoken Dariusz Mioduski at 2.01pm on 14th August 2014 read: 'Unfortunately for now football is not winning... we are going to CAS.'

Although Celtic didn't have complete confirmation of their place in the Champions League until the ruling from CAS had been made, the club had to prepare for the trip to Slovenia and attempt to make the most of their second bite at the cherry. Ronny Deila was interviewed in the lead up to the match and when asked about the saga, the Celtic Manager said: "It is a tough decision and I really feel sorry for Legia but we have to go into the game and prepare for Maribor. The players want to play in the Champions League. It looks like we have been given another chance and I think it will be no problem to get the players up for the game."

Confirmation did come through from CAS, on 18th August, that they had ruled against Legia Warsaw and that Celtic would indeed be playing against Maribor in Slovenia on the 20th. It was a decision that rankled with Dariusz Mioduski, who had the final word on the topic: "We know we will be playing in the Europa League. We accept that, but we will not give up on our pursuit on what we believe is justice for football." Nevertheless, Legia professionally prepared to take on Khazakstani outfit, FC Aktobe, who they brushed aside with a 3-0 aggregate win. In the meantime, Celtic earned a relatively pleasing 1-1 draw in Stadion Ljudski vrt. Callum McGregor again put the Hoops ahead with an early goal when he smashed home Jo Inge Berget's rebounded shot from close range. Yet the fragility at the heart of the Celtic defence was exposed as Zeljko Filipovic slid a pass between Virgil van Dijk and Jason Denayer for Bohar to tuck past the hitherto untroubled Craig Gordon. The Bhoys squandered second half chances but could return to Glasgow relatively pleased with a draw, an away goal and avoiding Legia-esque drama, for the Hoops had travelled to Slovenia without Efe Ambrose, believing him to be suspended. However, an uncanny administrative error was highlighted when it was confirmed that the Nigerian defender had fulfilled his ban and could join his teammates once special travel arrangements were put in place!

The return leg at Celtic Park, on the 26th August, epitomised the club's diabolical qualification campaign. Celtic, helped in no way by the absence of the boycotting Green Brigade Ultras, suffered a shock 1-0 defeat to exit the competition for a second time. All eyes were now fixed on the Europa League draw and the question on everyone's lips... will Celtic be paired with Legia Warsaw? Thankfully the clubs weren't pitted against each other. Instead, Celtic faced Red Bull Salzburg, Dynamo Zagreb and Astra Giurgiu; a group from which Deila's team successfully qualified in second place, after amassing a total of eight points. As for Legia, the Polish club topped their group with an impressive five wins from six games against Trabzonspor, K.S.C. Lokeren Oost-Vlaanderen and FC Metalist Kharkiv. It was none too surprising when the draw for the knockout stages threw up the question of Celtic and Legia colliding once more. Again though, it wasn't to be as the Celts were presented with a mouth-watering clash against Inter Milan; whilst Legia were drawn against opponents of equal European stature in the form of Ajax.

Finally, Ronny Deila got to experience the magic of a European night at Celtic Park when his Celtic team played superbly well to earn a 3-3 draw against the Italians. The match ebbed and flowed with Inter bursting into a 2-0 lead, before a quick-fire Stuart Armstrong double raised the roof and put Celtic level before the break. Inter restored the advantage early in the second half, but in typical Celtic fashion, John Guidetti thundered a volley into the top corner in the final minute of the match. Paradise reached a decibel level that hadn't been heard for some time and it was hoped that this could be the springboard for Ronny Deila to propel his Celtic career forward. Guidetti summed up the evening with the following post-match comments: "The myths I have heard about Celtic Park on a European night are true."

In the return leg at the San Siro, Virgyl Van Djik got himself sent off early in the game which presented Celtic with a mountainous task. Nevertheless, the Bhoys played manfully and only befell a 1-0 loss through a stunning long-range strike by Guarin in the 88th minute. Celtic had bowed out of a European competition for the third time that season, but they could do so with their heads held aloft on this occasion.

Legia Warsaw were dumped out of the Europa League, 4-0 on aggregate, against Ajax. The result brought any potential drama between Celtic and Legia to an end for that season.

Legia Warsaw fans hit out at UEFA

ADDITIONAL INFORMATION

(RENTON V HIBERNIAN - LINKS TO BROTHER WALFRID'S CONFIRMATION)

Renton's triumph was astonishing as Hibs were a good side in those days. The Edinburgh club became world champions a week later, on 13th August 1887, when they beat Preston North End 2-1 at Hibernian Park. Preston was among the foremost names in English football, eventually going on to become the first 'Invincibles' in the sport's history, during the English League's debut season of 1888/89. The Lancashire club were touring Scotland and many in the media didn't deem the game as anything more than a friendly, whilst the associations of English and Scottish football both billed the match as an 'Association Football Championship of the World' decider. After losing to the Hibees, Preston played and beat Dundee, Strathmore, Arbroath and Rangers.

Hibs could claim to be the best team in Scotland with some credence, having won the national cup (this being the days when league football did not yet exist). Whereas Preston had crashed out of the English national cup competition at the Semi-Final stage, when the 'Lily whites' fell to a shock 3-1 defeat against West Bromwich Albion. It was Aston Villa who lifted the trophy that year, having beaten Rangers by the same score line in the Semi-Final, before dispatching of West Brom, 2-0 at the Kennington Oval in London.

One may wonder what Rangers were doing in the Semi-Final of the English FA Cup, however, teams could dual compete in national competitions throughout the UK at the time. The FA Cup of 1886/87 included the following teams from outside of England: Hearts, Queen's Park, Partick Thistle, Third Lanark, Renton, Rangers, Cliftonville (Ireland), Druids (now Acrefair United FC – Wales), Chirk AAA (Wales), Davenham (located in Cheshire but now play in Welsh league system).

Ironically, Renton became World Club Champions themselves the following year. On 19th May 1888, at Cathkin Park, the exhibition match encountered two teams who had both won their national competition. Renton prevailed 4-1 against West Brom in the inaugural Football World Championship tie.

By the next season, the English Football League was established and so the competition was revamped to bring together the English League champions and Scottish Cup winners. The contest was again edited in 1890 when the Scottish League was founded. Games simply involved the league winners of both countries as of then. The final match of this kind was held in 1902, which reverted to its original format with English and Scottish Cup holders, Spurs and Hearts, on a collision course for the title of 'World Club Champions'. There was one exception - this final football World Championship would be a two-legged affair. Hearts won 3-1 in both matches to emphatically earn the accolade by way of a 6-2 aggregate margin.

Matches of this kind were soon dropped. Instead, they were replaced by The British League Cup a few months later (see page 73), which relinquished the 'World Championship' billing, as other leagues were formed around the world.

(BRAKE CLUBS - LINKS TO QUILLANITE QUISLINGS)

The first example of the Celtic support organising themselves was with the creation of Brake Clubs. Brake Clubs were mostly restricted to Glasgow and initially consisted of up to 25 supporters travelling by horse drawn carriage. They would carry a distinct banner, which depicted the club name and a painting of a Celtic player from the period. The first of its kind was formed in 1889 in St Mary's parish of the Calton. The original Brake Club's banner proudly bore the name and image of Tom Maley, with the title 'St Mary's League' at the top. The reference to the 'League' is due to the organisation from which birth was given to the club – the established branch of the League of the Cross.

The League was actually a temperance society, committed to alcohol abstinence, set up by the Catholic Church. Every parish in Glasgow had a branch of its own. As with St Mary's, the vast majority of Brake Clubs were also formed in this way. Though, it is quite an oxymoron that within a matter of months, there are references to 'Celtic carriages' being accredited as 'mobile drinking parlours!'

Despite their disobedient charisma, an entire federation of Brake Clubs could soon be boasted. They changed the whole face of football support. In that era, early football fans only tended to attend home matches. However, the wider reach, tendered by horse powered transport, meant that Celtic fans began to pitch up at away fixtures within Glasgow and neighbouring areas. A host of fellowships in the Scottish game followed suit, and the country started to develop a number of active away followings.

As the Brakes became better organised, distant travel became possible and a proper structure was incumbent to have in place. Membership worked in such a way that subscribers would pay a weekly fee, sometimes as high as 5 shillings. By necessity, payees were viewed as an appendage to the overall continuation of Brake Clubs. Therefore, value for money was not always at the forefront in leadership psyche. Payment of a stipulated fee entitled a member to travel anywhere. Of course, meaning that home games were much less value for money than distant away trips.

Traditionally, the clubs would congregate in Celtic strongholds. They would then travel together in a large convoy. It must have been quite something to hear the unmistakeable pounding of horse shoes on the cobbled streets and see the array of banners – always positioned behind the driver so that they were on display. However, as greater numbers could be accommodated, the tradition of collective club travel fell by the wayside. Only an annual jamboree of the 'United Celtic Brake Clubs' remained.

Members carried a sense of identity dear. Many were working class, Catholic, Irishmen. Inevitably, the social context that such an aggregation of men found themselves in made them somewhat politically charged. Trade Unionist and Irish Nationalist banners were the norm when on their travels and reported favourites from the songbook were patriotic ballads. 'Wearing of the Green', 'Hail Glorious Saint Patrick' and 'God Save Ireland' were the three widely revered songs that carriage occupants sang. It is also fascinating that after a clash, in which a vehicle was blemished, the perpetrating Rangers Brake Club sent £4 for the damage and said that they would stop singing 'Boyne

Water' if their counterparts promised to refrain from singing 'Hail Glorious Saint Patrick'.

Given the Catholic roots of the Brakes, faith played a considerable part in their activity. Some, in 1897, called upon Celtic to field an exclusively Catholic team. Most fans were, nonetheless, pleased that this notion was not taken seriously by the football club. The Catholic and Celtic ethos of charity was a key motivation for the movement's fundraising efforts. They did a lot of work to raise money on their travels, serving the communities that they represented, beyond reproach.

Yet, for all the culture and commitment, the 1920s saw Brake Clubs enter a fatal decline. The advent of motorised transport and the enhancement of railway lines caused a large loss of membership. People began to travel independently, and masses of Celtic supporters enjoyed a match like experience on trains and buses. Ironically, drunken trouble did little to further the movement's cause as well. Newspaper articles around the time also allude to complaints of rowdiness, when clubs travelled through the night. There was, in fact, strong condemnation from the League of the Cross over the behaviours of some Celtic Brake Clubs, particularly when they collided with fans of Rangers in Edinburgh. On said occasion, Celtic visited Easter Road, whilst Rangers visited Tynecastle. The inevitable happened when the two sets of supporters crossed paths. A man (it is undisclosed which team he supported) was thrown from his carriage and struck his head on the neck of one of the horses. The scene was bloody. The clash cemented the erosion of a wonderful tradition, though in reality, the motorised vehicle had signalled the end of the road for horse drawn carriage anyway.

(BELFAST CELTIC – LINKS TO SOLITUDE AGAINST CLIFTONVILLE)

Celtic's very earliest, closest and most important friendship would have to be that with Belfast Celtic. Celtic had toured Belfast in 1889 and drew crowds of over 8,000 for victories against Distillery and United Belfast. It was the club's first tour and full season, so the crowds for that era were quite staggering.

The Belfast Celts were formed in 1891 and were established in the image of Celtic Football Club. The moulding of the new club, in its design, extending to include its association with charity, the attractive style of football and an indiscriminate signing policy. The club Chairman, James Keenan, suggested the name 'Celtic' and Secretary, Bob Hayes, wrote to the Glasgow namesake for their blessing in using the title. Not only did he receive as much, but a sizeable financial donation was also offered in response.

By 1901, the club became a limited company and had to register as 'Belfast Celtic Ltd' because 'Celtic Football Club Ltd' had already been taken. Their football was played on Donegal Road in West Belfast at a multi-purpose facility named Celtic Park: 'Paradise' to the Belfast Celtic fans. The stadium actually became the first in Ireland to host greyhound racing (in April 1927) and continued to be used a greyhound track right up until the 1980s.

Belfast Celtic enjoyed very early success, winning the Irish League title in 1899/1900. Their ascendancy and wider symbolism generated big support and they soon became the beacon for the Nationalist community. The Celts had phenomenal ability to draw fans from across the 32 counties of Ireland, so much so that special train services were provided for supporters from Dundalk and smaller towns in County Louth. However, most match goers came from Ulster.

Many people throughout Ireland would follow Belfast Celtic but also the results of their larger namesake in Glasgow. This was reciprocated in Scotland, where an affinity to their County Antrim counterparts was certainly felt. In terms of actual attendance, of course, in that era financial limitation would restrict the ability to travel across the sea on a regular basis.

Savoured it was when the two teams met. On all but one occasion, the match was held at Celtic Park (Belfast), giving the Irish fans a great opportunity to see their beloved teams. Celtic of Glasgow shared the field with the Belfast outfit on no fewer than 16 occasions, the latter winning just twice. Naturally, huge crowds were lured, and gate receipts were often donated to charity.

> 1897 Belfast Celtic 0-4 Celtic
> 1902 Belfast Celtic 0-1 Celtic
> 1904 Belfast Celtic 1-0 Celtic
> 1910 Belfast Celtic 0-1 Celtic
> 1911 Belfast Celtic 0-1 Celtic
> 1915 Celtic 4-0 Belfast Celtic
> 1925 Belfast Celtic 0-3 Celtic
> 1926 Belfast Celtic 2-3 Celtic
> 1927 Belfast Celtic 4-2 Celtic
> 1928 Belfast Celtic 0-1 Celtic
> 1929 Belfast Celtic 4-7 Celtic
> 1930 Belfast Celtic 1-2 Celtic
> 1932 Belfast Celtic 0-3 Celtic
> 1936 Belfast Celtic 1-2 Celtic

1947 Belfast Celtic 4-4 Celtic
1952 Belfast Celtic 2-3 Celtic

One of the key components of the friendship was Charles Patrick Tully – Ireland's original superstar. He was quite a character and a wonderful entertainer. Not only is Tully a legendary link between the clubs but he was, as mentioned earlier in the book, the centrepiece behind Glen Daly's Celtic Song (see page 164). The bulk of the words to Glen Daly's tone are documented in a 1927 Belfast Celtic match programme, further proof that they owned the song first. Tully was a fanatic and brought with him, to Glasgow, the famous anthem.

Tully didn't just bring a song with him – he also brought a wealth of talent and trickery. That talent was nurtured in a typically mischievous manner at St Kevin's School in Belfast. He regularly found himself in trouble for playing what was regarded as a foreign game (soccer) on the premises. Tully skippered the school Gaelic football team and also played hurling. In spite of his prowess in the Gaelic codes, it was always association football that he really wanted to play.

Whilst still young, Tully was called up to fill in for a local soccer team at Falls Park. He impressed so much that the legendary Jack Myles came to hear of his ability. Myles was a famous former athlete and then school teacher at Millford Street School. It was renowned for producing footballers. Incredibly, Myles arranged for Tully to be transferred to his institute and sorted him employment as a ball boy at Belfast Celtic. Charlie found himself in an environment where he could freely play soccer but still enjoy the Gaelic games. He won a junior medal in Gaelic football, but his soccer really started to shine.

Belfast Celtic's coach, Willie MacDonald, had begun to take note of Tully's performances. MacDonald elected to play him against Glentoran in 1942. For once in his life, Tully fell speechless. Jack Vernon, a club legend, had to put Charlie's shirt on and insert shin guards such was his shock. Equally shocking was the fact that the occasion marked the first time that he wore shin guards as opposed to stuffing newspaper down his socks. He had much more to say on the park and so did the press the next day when they claimed: 'This schoolboy is an outstanding discovery of the future.'

Belfast Celtic sent Tully out on loan to Ballyclare Comrades and Cliftonville to gain experience. He built on his slender physique and by the mid-1940s he had coveted a regular starting place in the team. It was during this period that his magical playing style and charisma earned him the nickname of 'Cheeky Charlie'.

Tully's finest moment in Irish football probably arrived on April 27th 1947, when he scored the winning goal against Glentoran to hand his beloved Celts the Irish Cup. Robert Kelly had spotted Tully during a friendly against Glasgow Celtic a few years prior. He famously said: "Tully would do well here. Our support would appreciate him because he plays the Celtic way." He finally made the move after he had helped the Belfast boys to win the Irish League title in 1948. By contrast, the Scottish outfit had escaped relegation by the skin of their teeth. Some view the desperate situation of Glasgow Celtic as a catalyst for the signing.

The deal was sewn up very quickly and Tully said upon signing: "It took me three hours to decide on the Timalloys as opposed to the English glamour clubs, it had always been an ambition of mine to play for the great Scottish club." An admired magician on Irish shores, he would cement his place in Glasgow folklore by producing several magic moments throughout a wonderful 11 years at the club. In 1953 Tully took a corner kick against Falkirk at Brockville. He curled the ball straight into the net, only for the referee to disallow it. Charlie simply retook it and did the exact same again! He had in fact scored direct from a corner on another occasion for Northern Ireland against England. Cheeky Charlie was involved in the memorable Coronation Cup winning side and played in the demolition of Rangers in the 7-1 Scottish League Cup Final of 1957.

If he was loved back home then he was adored in Glasgow. Before long 'Tully cocktails' and 'Tully ice-cream scoops' had arisen in Scottish cafes. Such was the stardom he gained that he actually began writing a weekly column for The Evening Citizen newspaper, called 'Tullyvision'.

Ironically, Tully scored against Belfast Celtic in the last meeting between the two Celtic clubs. That particular fixture featured a certain Jock Stein, who was colossal at the heart of the Celtic defence. Tully was an icon, synonymous with both Celtic editions.

For all Celtic's visits and the Tully connection, one of the most influential aspects of the relationship was actually the demise of Belfast Celtic. The club had shattered most Irish records by the outbreak of World War II and looked set to continue in similarly dominant fashion. However, a partitioned Ireland and a changing society would play a key role in post war football.

Belfast Celtic faced Linfield at Windsor Park in December 1948, before a crowd of 27,000. Linfield largely represented the Unionist community of the North of Ireland. Contests as these were often fiery and this occasion was no different. Linfield finished the match with eight men on the field, Belfast Celtic with ten. However, it was the brutal actions of the Linfield support that would steal the headlines and forever change the future of Irish football.

Belfast Celtic's Jimmy Jones had collided with Jimmy Bryson in the Linfield defence. Bryson sadly broke his ankle on impact. The stadium announcer relayed information to the crowd that Bryson's leg had been broken, further inflaming the local support. The home side actually had another player taken to hospital for severe bruising, which only made the crowd vent more poison. Amongst mayhem, the Celts were awarded a penalty. Harry Walker scored and the Nationalist's looked set to take the points. The atmosphere turned so sour that many Belfast Celtic fans left early to avoid the predictable trouble. There was no segregation, just a small band of Royal Ulster Constabulary officers.

With only four minutes left, Linfield equalised. Hatred and jubilation combined as the fans spilled on to the pitch. Order was quickly restored, and play was petered out. Sadly, that was not the case at the full-time whistle as thousands of Linfield fans ran onto the park and attacked Belfast Celtic players. Jones was isolated. Given that he had injured Bryson and was a Protestant playing for the 'wrong side', he was made a target. He made way for the running track in a desperate attempt to get up the terracing and shake off his attackers, but they dragged him back down the stairs, laying into him with kicks and punches by the dozen. His life was now in perilous danger. Linfield supporters jumped and stamped on Jones' leg repeatedly. The police had no control and it was only Sean McCann, Jimmy's close friend and Ballymena goalkeeper, who came to his aide. But the damage had been done and the leg was badly broken. He was rushed to Musgrave Park Hospital, where they managed to save it, though it is now an inch and a half shorter than the other. As a result of the attack, the Irish Football Association ordered Linfield to play two matches away from Windsor Park stadium.

Belfast Celtic officials called an urgent meeting to discuss the repulsive attack. It is believed that an outcome was agreed here but nothing was publicly announced. After fulfilling the rest of the season's league commitments, the club embarked upon a tour of the USA in 1949. It was extremely successful and saw the Scottish national side (then British champions) famously defeated. The Scotland squad refused to speak to their Belfast opponents and ignorantly dismissed them, confident of certain victory. Belfast Celtic returned the serve by winning 2-0 with goals from Derry men Alec Moore and Johnny Campbell. Scotland promptly swore never to play a club side again lest they suffer a similar crushing humiliation as the one levied at Triborough Stadium in New York.

Soon after returning from the glamour excursion, it was announced that Belfast Celtic would withdraw from the Irish League. There was time for one last meeting with Glasgow Celtic in 1952 and a handful of friendly matches;

the last being an emotional farewell against Coleraine. After which, the club completely disbanded.

The significance of Belfast Celtic's disbandment from a Glasgow Celtic point of view was that the overwhelming majority of fans now pledged their sole allegiance to the Scottish club. Glasgow Celtic was an already established worldwide institution, having won exalted competitions like the Empire Exhibition Cup and had distinguished tours of Europe and the USA themselves. Supporters clubs were formed the length and breadth of Ireland, the first in St Mary's (Belfast) in 1952. It was formerly a Belfast Celtic Supporters Club. This transformation made travel to Scotland a touch easier.

As The Troubles kicked off, the Irish based contingent brought with them a hardened Republican mindset into an already politically minded diaspora. The Troubles were very emotive and certainly would have stimulated the political nature of the support and their songbook regardless. Though, the fact that many travelling over were directly affected, intensified and shaped Celtic's identity to some degree.

In 2003, the Belfast Celtic Society was formed to resurrect the memory of the club. In 2010 they immortalised it by opening a museum on the site of the old stadium. Sadly, the Celts' former home is now a shopping centre but nevertheless, the museum brings everything to life with a stack full of memorabilia and historical information. Whilst launching that project, the Society has also created the Belfast Celtic Trail. The route takes you on a journey to pivotal sites in the club's history. It is largely entwined with Irish politics, the social conditions and Celtic Football

Club alike. The trail proves popular for many Celtic supporters and is a wonderful way of exploring the connection.

A smaller version of their inspirers, but a huge club by Irish standards. A grand auld team indeed.

ACKNOWLEDGEMENTS

With thanks to Celtic supporters across the world, whose continued enthusiasm for the club and its history inspires me to keep writing. The help that I have received from those behind The Shamrock fanzine and The Celtic Graves Society epitomise this passion and I am very grateful for their assistance.

Special thanks must go to Ritchie Feeney for performing the superb graphic design work on the front and back covers, whilst my gratitude is also extended to Vagelis Georgariou for taking the picture of Celtic Park to meet our needs for the front cover of the book.

As well as using personal sources and the assistance of friends, I must also mention the following sources, which I have used in my research and to quote articles for the enhancement of the book:

Irish: The Remarkable Saga of a Nation and a City - By John Burrowes

The Shamrock website

Celtic: The Early Years - by Brendan Sweeney

Scottish property records/census records

Scottish Athletic Journal

Celtic Underground Podcast

Scottishsporthistory.com

Inflation Calculator

The Scotsman newspaper

The Scottish Umpire newspaper

London Hearts

Celtic Graves Society – Peter Dowds Commemoration

Celtic Football Club Official Handbook

The Story of Celtic - by James Handley

Dublin: Irish National Federation by University of Illinois Urbana-Champaign

A National Tragedy: Ibrox Disaster 1902 – The Herald newspaper

The History of Sunderland - by Bob Graham

Dundee Evening Post newspaper

Sunderland Daily Echo newspaper

The Evening Telegraph newspaper

Not The View fanzine

The Celtic Wiki

Hungarian News newspaper

First World War Glasgow - by Glasgow City Council

BBC Programmes

BBC – Celebrity Antiques Roadtrip Series 7 Episode 16

The Glasgow Observer newspaper

The Greenock Telegraph newspaper

The Glasgow Herald newspaper

Speedway Researcher website

John Thomson Committee

Daily Record newspaper

The Telegraph newspaper

Celtic: A Biography in Nine Lives - by Kevin McCarra

The Shamrock – Political Football Series

Irish Times newspaper

The Irish Post newspaper

Hibernian Historical Trust

The Evening Times newspaper

Celtic & Ireland In Song and Story – by Derek Warfield and Raymond Daly

The Evening Citizen newspaper

The Daily Mail newspaper

Belfast Celtic Society

Italian Libretto

The Derry Journal newspaper

When Saturday Comes magazine

The Quality Street Gang - by Paul John Dykes

Celtic TV World Club Championship documentary

Universal International News

Celtic View magazine

The Sunday Mail newspaper

Celtic In Europe - by Graham McColl

Celtic TV

Charlie And The Bhoys website

Heroes Are Forever: The Life and Times of Celtic Legend Jimmy McGrory – by John Cairney

The Meteorological Office Monthly Report

BBC Coverage

Boxrec.com

Boxinghistory.org/records

Celtic Graves Society

The Shamrock Magazine – The Five Ages Of Celtic

The New York Times newspaper

BBC Sport Scotland

Scottish Sun newspaper

The Herald newspaper

Celtic Mad website

Sunday Times newspaper

The Celtic Star podcast

Clash of the Titans documentary

Videocelts.com

Sporting-heroes.net

Jungle Tales – by John Quinn

STV Archives

Eurocupshistory.com

Anyone But Celtic documentary – by Paul Larkin

The Independent newspaper

Worldfootball.net

FIFA.com

Football50.co.uk – by Jim Craig

Sky Sports

The Guardian newspaper

Celticunderground.net

Sky Sports On Demand

The Sun newspaper

BBC Sport football

Youtube

Uefa.com

Court of Arbitration for Sport

Sportsmole.co.uk

ESPN.co.uk

Express.co.uk

Legia Warsaw Official Twitter

Celtic History Podcast

Lancaster Evening Post

Nottingham Evening Post

Scotland on Sunday newspaper

Printed in Great Britain
by Amazon

23773981R00212